TASTE OF THE EAST

TASTE OF THE EAST

With over 200 recipes and 1000 photographs

Deh-Ta Hsiung • Rafi Fernandez • Steven Wheeler

Photography by Edward Allwright

ACROPOLIS BOOKS

This edition first published by
Acropolis Books
Desford Road, Enderby
Leicestershire, LE9 5AD

Boundary Row Studios
1 Boundary Row
London SE1 8HP

ISBN 1 873762 11 9

Distributed in Australia by
Treasure Press

Editorial Director: Joanna Lorenz
Project Editor: Lindsay Porter
Photography: Edward Allwright
Styling: Maria Kelly
Design: David Rowley Design

Printed and bound in Hong Kong

CONTENTS

TASTE OF CHINA

DEH-TA HSIUNG

China is a vast country – about the same size as Western Europe or the United States – and its climate and food products are similarly varied. Consequently, each region has a very distinctive style of cooking, resulting in the world's most diverse cuisine. Yet the fundamental character of Chinese cooking remains the same throughout the land. From Peking in the north to Canton in the south and Shanghai in the east to Sichuan in the west, different ingredients are all prepared, cooked and served in accordance with the same centuries-old principles.

THE PRINCIPLES OF CHINESE COOKING

Chinese cooking is distinguished from all other food cultures in its emphasis on the harmonious blending of colour, aroma, flavour and texture both in a single dish and in a course of dishes for a meal.

Balance and contrast are the key words, based on the ancient Taoist philosophy of yin and yang. Consciously or unconsciously, any Chinese cook, from the housewife to the professional chef, will work to this yin-yang principle, and will vary ingredients, shapes, seasonings and cooking methods accordingly.

In order to achieve this, two important factors should be observed: the degree of heat and duration of cooking, which in turn means applying the right cooking method to the right food. The size and shape of a particular ingredient must be appropriate to the chosen method of cooking. Ingredients for quick stir-frying, for instance, should be cut into small, thin slices or shreds of uniform size, instead of large, thick chunks. This is not just for the sake of appearance, but because ingredients of the same size and shape will retain their natural colour, aroma and flavour and achieve the required texture if they are cooked for the same amount of time.

EQUIPMENT AND UTENSILS

There are only a few basic implements essential to Chinese cooking and equivalent equipment is always available in a Western kitchen. However, authentic Chinese cooking utensils are of an ancient design, are usually made of inexpensive materials, and have been in continuous use for several thousand years. They do serve a special function, which is not always fulfilled by their more sophisticated and expensive Western counterparts.

Chinese cleaver (1) This is an all-purpose cook's knife used for slicing, shredding, peeling, crushing and chopping. Different sizes and weights are available.

Ladle and spatula (2) Some wok sets consist of a pair of stirrers in the form of a ladle and spatula. Of the two, the flat ladle or scooper (as it is sometimes called) is more versatile. It is used by Chinese cooks for adding ingredients and seasonings to the wok as well as for stirring.

Sand-pot (casserole) (3) Made of earthenware, casseroles are always used for braising and slow cooking on the stove top as they retain an even heat.

Steamer (4) The traditional Chinese steamer is made of bamboo, and the modern version is made of aluminium. The wok can also be used as a steamer with a rack or trivet and the dome-shaped wok lid.

Strainer (5) There are two basic types of strainer. One is made of copper or steel wire with a long bamboo handle, the other of perforated iron or stainless steel. Several different sizes are available.

Wok (6) The round-bottomed iron wok conducts and retains heat evenly. Because of its shape, the ingredients always return to the centre where the heat is most intense. The wok has many functions. It is ideal for deep-frying because its shape requires far less oil than the flat-bottomed deep-fryer. It also has more depth, which means more heat is generated, and a larger cooking surface, which means more food can be cooked at one time. Besides being a frying pan, the wok is also used for braising, steaming, boiling and poaching – in fact, the whole spectrum of Chinese cooking methods can be executed in one single utensil.

INGREDIENTS

Agar-agar (1) Also known as isinglass (*Kanten* in Japanese), agar-agar is a product of seaweed and is sold dried in paper-thin strands or powdered form. Gelatine may be substituted.

Baby corn cobs (2) Baby corn cobs have a wonderfully sweet fragrance and flavour, and an irresistible texture. They are available both fresh and canned.

Bamboo shoots (3) Bamboo shoots are available in cans only. Once opened, the contents may be kept in fresh water in a covered jar for up to a week in the refrigerator. Try to get winter bamboo shoots, which have a firmer texture. Ready sliced bamboo shoots are also available.

Bean curd (tofu) (4) This custard-like preparation of puréed and pressed soya beans is exceptionally high in protein. It is usually sold in cakes about 7.5cm/3in square and 2.5cm/1in thick and can be found in Oriental and health food stores. It will keep for a few days if submerged in water in a container and placed in the refrigerator.

Bean sprouts (5) Fresh bean sprouts, from mung or soya beans, are widely available from Oriental stores and all supermarkets. They can be kept in the refrigerator for two to three days.

Black bean sauce (6) Black bean sauce is made up of salted black beans crushed and mixed with flour and spices (such as ginger, garlic or chilli) to make a thickish paste. Sold in jars or cans; once opened, it should be kept in the refrigerator.

Chilli bean sauce (7) Chilli bean sauce is made from fermented bean paste mixed with hot chilli and other seasonings. Sold in jars, some chilli bean sauces are quite mild, but some are very hot. You will have to try out the various brands yourself to see which one is to your taste.

Chilli oil (8) Chilli oil is made from dried red chillies, garlic, onions, salt and vegetable oil. It is used more as a dip than as a cooking ingredient.

Chilli sauce (9) This is a very hot sauce made from chillies, vinegar, sugar and salt. Usually sold in bottles, it should be used sparingly in cooking or as a dip. Tabasco sauce can be a substitute.

Chinese leaves (10) There are two widely available varieties of Chinese leaves (also known as Chinese cabbage) found in supermarkets and greengrocers. The most commonly seen variety has a pale green colour and tightly-wrapped elongated head, and about two-thirds of the cabbage is stem which has a crunchy texture. The other variety found has a shorter and fatter head with curlier, pale yellow or green leaves, and white stems.

Coriander (11) Fresh coriander leaves, also known as Chinese parsley or *cilantro*, are widely used in Chinese cooking as a garnish.

Dried Chinese mushrooms (shiitake) (12) These highly fragrant dried mushrooms are sold in plastic bags. They are not cheap, but a small amount will go a long way, and they will keep indefinitely in an airtight jar. Soak them in warm water for 20–30 minutes (or in cold water for several hours), squeeze dry and discard the hard stalks before use.

Egg noodles (13) There are many varieties of noodles in China – ranging from flat, broad ribbons to long and narrow strands. Both dried and fresh noodles are available.

Five-spice powder (14) A mixture of star anise, fennel seeds, cloves, cinnamon bark and Sichuan pepper make up five-spice powder. It is highly piquant, so should be used very sparingly, and will keep indefinitely in an airtight container.

Ginger root (15) Fresh ginger, sold by weight, should be peeled and sliced and finely chopped or shredded before use. It will keep for weeks in a dry, cool place. Dried ginger powder is no substitute.

Hoi Sin sauce (16) This tasty sauce is also known as barbecue sauce, and is made from soy beans, sugar, flour, vinegar, salt, garlic, chilli and sesame seed oil. Sold in cans or jars, it will keep in the refrigerator for several months.

Oyster sauce (17) This soya based, thickish sauce is used as a flavouring in Cantonese cooking. Sold in bottles, it will keep in the refrigerator for months.

Plum sauce (18) Plum sauce has a unique fruity flavour – a sweet and sour sauce with a difference.

Red bean paste (19) This reddish-brown paste is made from puréed red beans and crystallized sugar. Sold in cans, the left-over contents should be transferred to a covered container and will keep in the refrigerator for several months.

Rice vinegar (20) There are two basic types of rice vinegar – red vinegar is made from fermented rice and has a distinctive dark colour and depth of flavour; white vinegar is stronger in flavour as it is distilled from rice.

Rice wine (21) Chinese rice wine, made from glutinous rice, is also known as 'Yellow wine' (*Huang Jiu* or *Chiew* in Chinese), because of its golden amber colour. The best variety is called Shao Hsing or Shaoxing from the southeast of China. A good dry or medium sherry can be an acceptable substitute.

Rock sugar (22) Rock sugar is made with a combination of cane sugar and honey. It adds a special sheen to foods that have been stewed with it.

Salted black beans (23) Salted black beans are very salty and pungent. They are sold in plastic bags, jars or cans and should be crushed with water or wine before use. The beans will keep almost indefinitely in a covered jar.

Sesame oil (24) Sesame oil is sold in bottles and widely used in China as a garnish rather than for cooking. The refined yellow sesame oil sold in Middle Eastern stores is not so aromatic .

a very satisfactory substitute

Sichuan peppercorns (25) Also known as *farchiew*, these are wild red peppers from Sichuan. More aromatic but less hot than either white or black peppers, they do give quite a unique flavour to the food.

Soy sauce (26) Sold in bottles or cans, this most popular Chinese sauce is used both for cooking and at the table. Light soy sauce has more flavour than the sweeter dark soy sauce, which gives the food a rich, reddish colour.

Straw mushrooms (*Volvariella volvacea*) (27) Grown on beds of rice straw, hence the name, straw mushrooms have a pleasant slippery texture and a subtle taste. Canned straw mushrooms should be rinsed and drained.

Water chestnuts (28) Water chestnuts are not nuts as they are the roots of a plant (*Heleocharis tuberosa*). They are also known as horse's hooves in China,

on account of their appearance before the skin is peeled off and are available fresh or in cans. Canned water chestnuts retain only part of the texture, and even less of the flavour, of fresh ones. They will keep for about a month in the refrigerator in a covered jar, if the water is changed every two days.

Wonton skins (29) Made from wheat flour, egg and water, these wafer-thin wonton wrappers are sold in 7.5cm/3in squares from Oriental stores. They can be frozen, and will keep for up to six months.

Wood-ears (30) Also known as cloud-ears, these are dried black fungus (*Auricularia polytricha*). Sold in plastic bags in Oriental stores, wood-ears should be soaked in cold or warm water for 20 minutes, then rinsed in fresh water before use. They have a crunchy texture and a mild but subtle flavour.

Yellow bean sauce (31) Yellow bean sauce is a thick paste made from salted, fermented yellow soya beans, crushed with flour and sugar. It will keep in the refrigerator for months if stored in a screw-top jar.

Crispy Spring Rolls

Zha Chu Kuen

These small and dainty vegetarian spring rolls are ideal served as appetizers, or as cocktail snacks. For a non-vegetarian version, just replace the mushrooms with chicken or pork, and the carrots with shrimp.

MAKES 40 ROLLS

Ingredients

225g/8oz fresh bean sprouts
115g/4oz tender leeks or spring onions (scallions)
115g/4oz carrots
115g/4oz bamboo shoots, sliced
115g/4oz white mushrooms
3–4 tbsp vegetable oil
1 tsp salt
1 tsp light brown sugar
1 tbsp light soy sauce
1 tbsp Chinese rice wine or dry sherry
20 frozen spring roll skins, defrosted
1 tbsp cornflour (cornstarch) paste
flour, for dusting
oil, for deep-frying

Cornflour (cornstarch) paste

To make cornflour (cornstarch) paste, mix 4 parts dry cornflour (cornstarch) with about 5 parts cold water until smooth.

1 Cut all the vegetables into thin shreds, roughly the same size and shape as the bean sprouts.

2 Heat the oil in a wok and stir-fry the vegetables for about 1 minute. Add the salt, sugar, soy sauce and wine or sherry and continue stirring for 1½–2 minutes. Remove and drain the excess liquid, then leave to cool.

3 To make the spring rolls, cut each spring roll skin in half diagonally, then place about 1 tbsp of the vegetable mixture one-third of the way down on the skin, with the triangle pointing away from you.

4 Lift the lower flap over the filling and roll once.

5 Fold in both ends and roll once more, then brush the upper edge with a little cornflour (cornstarch) paste, and roll into a neat package. Lightly dust a tray with flour and place the spring rolls on the tray with the flap-side down.

6 To cook, heat the oil in a wok or deep-fryer until hot, then reduce the heat to low. Deep-fry the spring rolls in batches (about 8–10 at a time) for 2–3 minutes or until golden and crispy, then remove and drain. Serve the spring rolls hot with a dip sauce such as soy sauce or Spicy Salt and Pepper.

Deep-fried Spareribs with Spicy Salt and Pepper

Zha Pai Ku

Ideally, each sparerib should be chopped into 3–4 bite-sized pieces before or after cooking. If this is not possible, then serve the ribs whole.

SERVES 4–6

Ingredients

10–12 finger ribs, weighing in total about 675g/1½lb, with excess fat and gristle trimmed
about 2–3 tbsp flour
vegetable oil, for deep-frying

Marinade

1 clove garlic, crushed and finely chopped
1 tbsp light brown sugar
1 tbsp light soy sauce
1 tbsp dark soy sauce
2 tbsp Chinese rice wine or dry sherry
½ tsp chilli sauce
few drops sesame oil

Spicy Salt and Pepper

To make Spicy Salt and Pepper, mix 1 tbsp salt with 2 tsp ground Sichuan peppercorns and 1 tsp five-spice powder. Heat together in a preheated dry pan for about 2 minutes over low heat, stirring constantly. This quantity is sufficient for at least six servings.

1 Chop each rib into 3–4 pieces, then mix with all the marinade ingredients, and marinate for at least 2–3 hours.

2 Coat the ribs with flour and deep-fry in medium-hot oil for 4–5 minutes, stirring to separate. Remove and drain.

3 Heat the oil to high and deep-fry the ribs once more for about 1 minute, or until the colour is an even dark brown. Remove and drain, then serve with Spicy Salt and Pepper.

Deep-fried Squid with Spicy Salt and Pepper

Jiao Yan You Yu

This recipe is from the Cantonese school of cuisine, where seafood is one of their specialities.

SERVES 4

Ingredients
450g/1lb squid
1 tsp ginger juice
1 tbsp Chinese rice wine or dry sherry
about 575ml/1 pint/2½ cups boiling water
vegetable oil, for deep-frying
Spicy Salt and Pepper
fresh coriander leaves, to garnish

Ginger juice

To make ginger juice, mix finely-chopped or grated fresh ginger with an equal quantity of cold water and place in damp muslin (cheesecloth). Twist tightly to extract the juice. Alternatively, crush the ginger in a garlic press.

1 Clean the squid by discarding the head and the transparent backbone as well as the ink bag; peel off and discard the thin skin, then wash the squid and dry well. Open up the squid and, using a sharp knife, score the inside of the flesh in a criss-cross pattern.

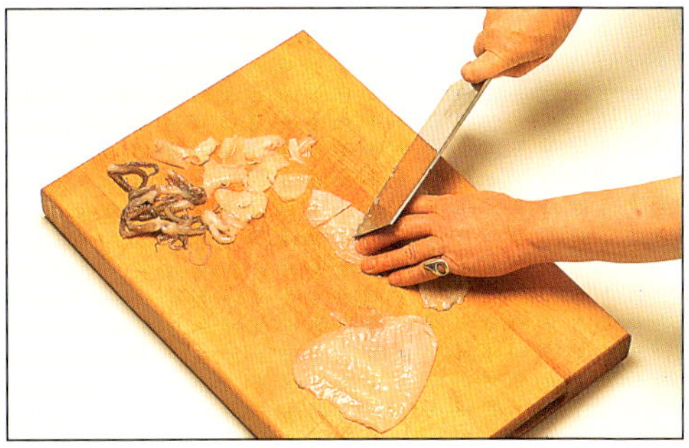

2 Cut the squid into pieces each about the size of an oblong postage stamp. Marinate in a bowl with the ginger juice and wine or sherry for 25–30 minutes.

3 Blanch the squid in boiling water for a few seconds – each piece will curl up and the criss-cross pattern will open out to resemble ears of corn. Remove and drain. Dry well.

4 Deep-fry the squid in hot oil for 15–20 seconds only, remove quickly and drain. Sprinkle with the Spicy Salt and Pepper and serve garnished with fresh coriander leaves.

Bon-bon Chicken with Sesame Sauce

Bon Bon Ji

The chicken meat is tenderized by being beaten with a stick (called a *bon* in Chinese), hence the name for this very popular Sichuan dish.

SERVES 6–8

Ingredients
1 whole chicken weighing about 1kg/2¼lb
1.1 litre/2 pints/5 cups water
1 tbsp sesame oil
shredded cucumber, to garnish

Sauce
2 tbsp light soy sauce
1 tsp sugar
1 tbsp finely-chopped spring onions (scallions)
1 tsp red chilli oil
½ tsp ground Sichuan peppercorns
1 tsp white sesame seeds
2 tbsp sesame paste, or 2 tbsp peanut butter creamed with a little sesame oil

1 Clean the chicken well. In a wok or saucepan bring the water to a rolling boil, add the chicken, reduce the heat and cook under cover for 40–45 minutes. Remove the chicken and immerse in cold water to cool.

2 After at least 1 hour, remove the chicken and drain; dry well with kitchen paper and brush on a coating of sesame oil. Carve the meat off the legs, wings and breast and pull the meat off the rest of the bones.

3 On a flat surface, pound the meat with a rolling pin, then tear the meat into shreds with your fingers.

4 Place the meat in a dish with the shredded cucumber around the edge. In a bowl, mix together all the sauce ingredients, keeping a few spring onions (scallions) to garnish. Pour over the chicken and serve.

Deep-fried Wonton Skins with Sweet and Sour Sauce

Cha Won Tun

Ready-made fresh or frozen wonton skins are available from Oriental stores.

SERVES 4–6

Ingredients
16–20 ready-made wonton skins
vegetable oil, for deep-frying

Sauce
1 tbsp vegetable oil
2 tbsp light brown sugar
3 tbsp rice vinegar
1 tbsp light soy sauce
1 tbsp tomato sauce (ketchup)
3–4 tbsp Basic Stock or water
1 tbsp cornflour (cornstarch) paste

1 Pinch the centre of each wonton skin and twist it around to form a floral shape.

2 Deep-fry the floral wonton skins in hot oil for 1–2 minutes, or until crispy. Remove and drain.

3 Heat the oil in a wok or saucepan, add the sugar, vinegar, soy sauce, tomato sauce (ketchup) and stock or water.

4 Thicken the sauce with the cornflour (cornstarch) paste, stirring until smooth, and pour it over the wonton skins. Serve immediately.

Crispy 'Seaweed'

Cai Sung

Surprisingly, the very popular 'seaweed' served in Chinese restaurants is, in fact, ordinary spring greens (collard)!

SERVES 4–6

Ingredients
450g/1lb spring greens (collard)
vegetable oil, for deep-frying
½ tsp salt
1 tsp caster (superfine) sugar
1 tbsp ground fried fish, to garnish (optional)

1 Cut off the hard stalks in the centre of each spring green (collard) leaf. Pile the leaves on top of each other, and roll into a tight 'sausage'. Thinly cut the leaves into fine shreds. Spread them out to dry.

2 Heat the oil in a wok or deep-fryer until hot. Deep-fry the shredded greens in batches, stirring to separate them.

3 Remove the greens with a slotted spoon as soon as they are crispy, but before they turn brown. Drain. Sprinkle the salt and sugar evenly all over the 'seaweed'; mix well, garnish with ground fish and serve.

Sesame Seed Prawn (Shrimp) Toasts

Hsia Jen Tu Ssu

Use uncooked prawns (shrimp) for this dish, as ready-cooked ones will separate from the bread during cooking.

SERVES 6–8

Ingredients
225g/8oz prawns (shrimp), peeled
25g/1oz/¼ stick lard (shortening)
salt and pepper, to taste
1 egg white, lightly beaten
1 tsp finely-chopped spring onions (scallions)
½ tsp finely-chopped fresh ginger
1 tbsp Chinese rice wine or dry sherry
1 tbsp cornflour (cornstarch) paste
115–140g/4–5oz/1 cup white sesame seeds
6 large slices white bread
vegetable oil, for deep-frying

1 Chop together the prawns with the lard (shortening) to form a smooth paste. In a bowl, mix with all the other ingredients except the sesame seeds and bread.

2 Spread the sesame seeds evenly on a large plate or tray; spread the prawn paste thickly on one side of each slice of bread, then press, spread-side down, onto the seeds.

3 Heat the oil in a wok until medium-hot; fry 2–3 slices at a time, spread-side down, for 2–3 minutes. Remove and drain. Cut into 6–8 fingers (without crusts).

Pickled Sweet and Sour Cucumber

Tan Chu Huang Gua

The 'pickling' can be done in hours rather than days – but the more time you have, the better the result.

SERVES 6–8

Ingredients
1 slender cucumber, about 30cm/12in long
1 tsp salt
2 tsp caster (superfine) sugar
1 tsp rice vinegar
½ tsp red chilli oil (optional)
few drops sesame oil

1 Halve the unpeeled cucumber lengthways. Scrape out the seeds and cut across the cucumber into thick chunks.

2 In a bowl, sprinkle the cucumber chunks with the salt and mix well. Leave for at least 20–30 minutes – longer if possible – then pour the juice away.

3 Mix the cucumber with the sugar, vinegar and chilli oil, if using. Sprinkle with the sesame oil just before serving.

Hot and Sour Cabbage

Suan La Pai Cai

Another popular recipe from Sichuan – this dish can be served hot or cold.

SERVES 6–8

Ingredients
450g/1lb pale green or white cabbage
3–4 tbsp vegetable oil
10–12 red Sichuan peppercorns
few whole dried red chillies
1 tsp salt
1 tbsp light brown sugar
1 tbsp light soy sauce
2 tbsp rice vinegar
few drops sesame oil

1 Cut the cabbage leaves into small pieces each roughly 2.5 × 1.25cm (1 × ½ in).

2 Heat the oil in a preheated wok until smoking, then add the peppercorns and chillies.

3 Add the cabbage to the wok and stir-fry for about 1–2 minutes. Add the salt and sugar, continue stirring for another minute, then add the soy sauce, vinegar and sesame oil. Blend well and serve.

Butterfly Prawns (Shrimp)

Feng Wei Xia

For best results, use uncooked giant or king prawns (shrimp) in their shells. Sold headless, they are about 8–10cm/3–4in long, and you should get 18–20 prawns (shrimp) per 450g/1lb.

SERVES 6–8

Ingredients

450g/1lb uncooked prawns (shrimp) in their shells, headless
1 tsp ground Sichuan peppercorns
1 tbsp light soy sauce
1 tbsp Chinese rice wine or dry sherry
2 tsp cornflour (cornstarch)
vegetable oil, for deep-frying
2 eggs, lightly beaten
4–5 tbsp breadcrumbs
lettuce leaves or Crispy 'Seaweed', to serve
2–3 spring onions (scallions), to garnish

1 Peel the prawns (shrimp) but leave the tails on. Split the prawns (shrimp) in half from the underbelly, about three-quarters of the way through, leaving the tails still firmly attached.

2 In a bowl, marinate with the pepper, soy sauce, wine or sherry and cornflour (cornstarch) for 10–15 minutes.

3 Heat the oil in a wok or deep-fryer until medium-hot. Pick up one prawn (shrimp) at a time by the tail, and dip it in the egg.

4 Roll the egg-covered prawns (shrimp) in breadcrumbs.

5 Heat the oil in the wok until medium-hot. Gently lower the prawns (shrimp) into the oil.

6 Deep-fry the prawns (shrimp) in batches until golden brown. Remove and drain. To serve, arrange the prawns (shrimp) neatly on a bed of lettuce leaves or Crispy 'Seaweed', and garnish with spring onions (scallions), which are either raw or have been soaked for about 30 seconds in hot oil.

Basic Stock

Qing Tang

The basic stock is used not only as the basis for soup making, but also for general use in cooking whenever liquid is required instead of plain water.

MAKES 2.25L/4 PINTS/10½ CUPS

Ingredients
675g/1½lb chicken pieces
675g/1½lb pork spareribs
3.25 litres/6 pints/15 cups cold water
3–4 pieces fresh ginger, unpeeled and crushed
3–4 spring onions (scallions), each tied into a knot
3–4 tbsp Chinese rice wine or dry sherry

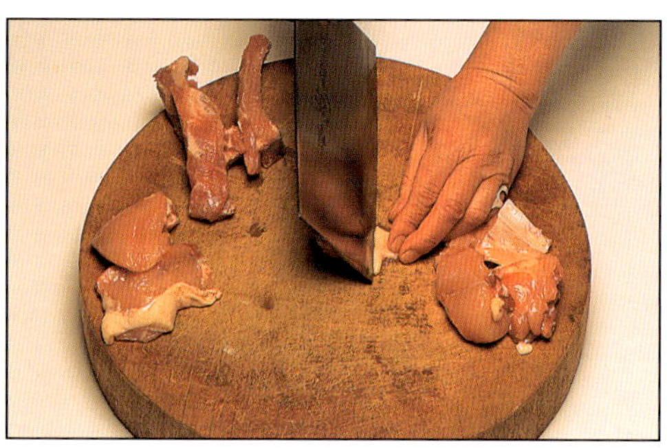

1 Trim off any excess fat from the chicken and spareribs and chop them into large pieces.

2 Place the chicken and spareribs into a large pot or pan with the water. Add the ginger and spring onion (scallion) knots.

3 Bring to the boil and, using a sieve (strainer), skim off the froth. Reduce the heat and simmer, uncovered, for 2–3 hours.

4 Strain the stock, discarding the chicken, pork, ginger and spring onions (scallions); add the wine or sherry and return to the boil. Simmer for 2–3 minutes. Refrigerate the stock when cool. It will keep for up to 4–5 days. Alternatively, it can be frozen in small containers and defrosted when required.

Hot and Sour Soup

Suan La Tang

This surely must be the all-time favourite soup in Chinese restaurants and take-aways throughout the world. It is fairly simple to make once you have got all the necessary ingredients together.

SERVES 4

Ingredients
4–6 dried Chinese mushrooms (shiitake), soaked
115g/4oz pork or chicken
1 cake bean curd (tofu)
50g/2oz sliced bamboo shoots, drained
575ml/1 pint/2½ cups Basic Stock
1 tbsp Chinese rice wine or dry sherry
1 tbsp light soy sauce
1 tbsp rice vinegar
salt, to taste
½ tsp ground white pepper
1 tbsp cornflour (cornstarch) paste

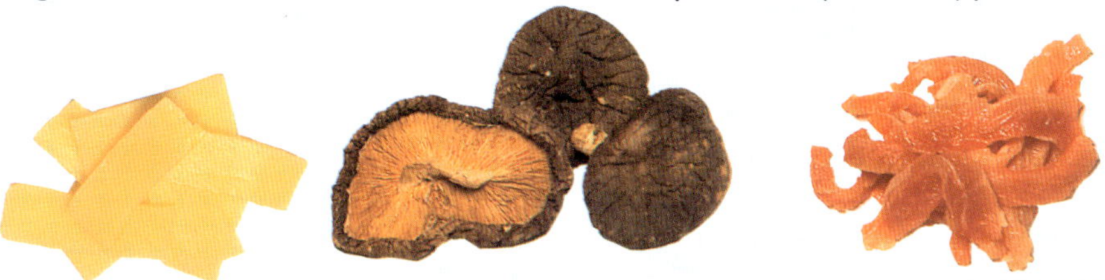

1 Squeeze the soaked mushrooms dry, then discard the hard stalks. Thinly shred the mushrooms, meat, bean curd (tofu) and bamboo shoots.

2 In a wok or saucepan, bring the stock to a rolling boil and add the shredded ingredients. Bring back to the boil and simmer for about 1 minute.

3 Add the seasonings and bring back to the boil once more. Now add the cornflour (cornstarch) paste and stir until thickened. Serve hot.

Corn and Crabmeat/Chicken Soup

Xie Rou Yumi Tang

This soup originated in the USA but it has since been introduced into China. You must use creamed corn in the recipe to achieve the right consistency.

SERVES 4

Ingredients
115g/4oz crabmeat or chicken breast fillet
½ tsp finely-chopped fresh ginger
2 egg whites
2 tbsp milk
1 tbsp cornflour (cornstarch) paste
575ml/1 pint/2½ cups Basic Stock
225g/8oz can creamed corn
salt and pepper, to taste
finely-chopped spring onions (scallions), to garnish

1 Flake the crabmeat (or coarsely chop the chicken breast) and mix with the ginger.

2 Beat the egg whites until frothy, add the milk and cornflour (cornstarch) paste and beat again until smooth. Blend with the crabmeat or chicken breast.

3 In a wok or saucepan, bring the stock to the boil, add the creamed sweetcorn and bring back to the boil once more.

4 Stir in the crabmeat or chicken breast and egg-white mixture, adjust the seasonings and stir gently until well blended. Serve garnished with finely-chopped spring onions (scallions).

Chicken and Asparagus Soup

Lusun Ji Rou Tang

This is a very delicate and delicious soup. When fresh asparagus is not in season, canned white asparagus is an acceptable substitute.

SERVES 4

Ingredients
140g/5oz chicken breast fillet
pinch of salt
1 tsp egg white
1 tsp cornflour (cornstarch) paste
115g/4oz asparagus
700ml/1 ¼ pints/3 cups Basic Stock
salt and pepper, to taste
fresh coriander leaves, to garnish

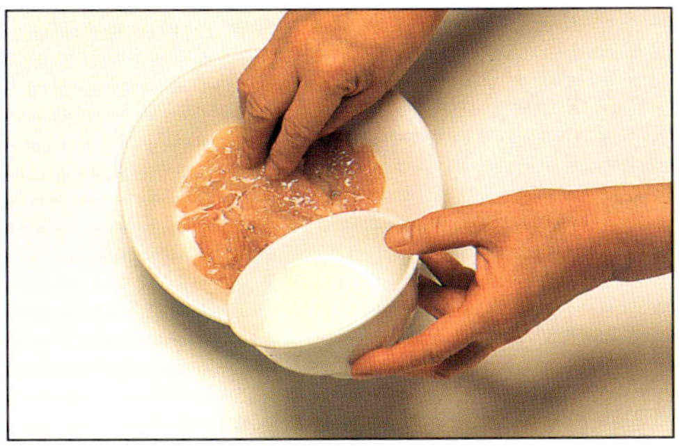

1 Cut the chicken meat into thin slices each about the size of a postage stamp. Mix with a pinch of salt, then add the egg white, and finally the cornflour (cornstarch) paste.

2 Discard the tough stems of the asparagus, and diagonally cut the tender spears into short lengths.

3 In a wok or saucepan, bring the stock to a rolling boil, add the asparagus and bring back to the boil, cooking for 2 minutes. (This is not necessary if using canned asparagus.)

4 Add the chicken, stir to separate and bring back to the boil once more. Adjust the seasonings. Serve hot, garnished with fresh coriander leaves.

Spinach and Bean Curd (Tofu) Soup

Pao Cai Dao Fu Tang

This soup is delicious. If fresh spinach is not in season, watercress or lettuce can be used instead.

SERVES 4

Ingredients

- 1 cake bean curd (tofu)
- 115g/4oz spinach leaves (weight exclusive of stems)
- 700ml/1 ¼ pints/3 cups Basic Stock
- 1 tbsp light soy sauce
- salt and pepper, to taste

1 Cut the bean curd (tofu) into 12 small pieces, each about 0.5cm/¼in thick. Wash the spinach leaves and cut them into small pieces.

2 In a wok or saucepan, bring the stock to a rolling boil. Add the bean curd (tofu) and soy sauce, bring back to the boil and simmer for about 2 minutes.

3 Add the spinach and simmer for a further minute. Skim the surface to make it clear, then adjust the seasoning and serve.

Sliced Fish and Coriander Soup

Yu Pian Yen Hsee Tang

It is not necessary to remove the skin from the fish, as it helps to keep the flesh together when cooked.

SERVES 4

Ingredients

- 225g/8oz white fish fillet such as lemon sole or plaice
- 1 tsp egg white
- 2 tsp cornflour (cornstarch) paste
- 700ml/1 ¼ pints/3 cups Basic Stock
- 1 tbsp light soy sauce
- about 50g/2oz fresh coriander leaves, chopped
- salt and pepper, to taste

1 Cut the fish into large slices each about the size of a matchbox. Mix with the egg white and cornflour (cornstarch) paste.

2 In a wok or saucepan, bring the stock to a rolling boil and poach the fish slices for about 1 minute.

3 Add the soy sauce and coriander leaves, adjust the seasonings and serve.

Three-delicacy Soup

San Xian Tang

This delicious soup combines the three ingredients of chicken, ham and prawns (shrimp).

SERVES 4

Ingredients
115g/4oz chicken breast fillet
115g/4oz honey-roast ham
115g/4oz peeled prawns (shrimp)
700ml/1 ¼ pints/3 cups Basic Stock
salt, to taste

Cook's tip

Fresh, uncooked prawns impart the best flavour. If these are not available you can use ready-cooked prawns. They must be added at the last stage to prevent over-cooking.

1 Thinly slice the chicken and ham into small pieces. If the prawns (shrimp) are large, cut each in half lengthways.

2 In a wok or saucepan, bring the stock to a rolling boil, add the chicken, ham and prawns (shrimp). Bring back to the boil, add the salt and simmer for 1 minute. Serve hot.

Lamb and Cucumber Soup

Yang Rou Huang Gua Tang

This is a variation on Hot and Sour Soup, but is much simpler to prepare.

SERVES 4

Ingredients
225g/8oz lamb steak
1 tbsp light soy sauce
2 tsp Chinese rice wine or dry sherry
½ tsp sesame oil
1 piece cucumber, 7.5cm/3in long
700ml/1 ¼ pints/3 cups Basic Stock
1 tbsp rice vinegar
salt and ground white pepper, to taste

1 Trim off any excess fat from the lamb and discard. Thinly slice the lamb into small pieces. Marinate with the soy sauce, wine or sherry and sesame oil for 25–30 minutes. Discard the marinade.

2 Halve the cucumber piece lengthways (do not peel), then cut into thin slices diagonally.

3 In a wok or saucepan, bring the stock to a rolling boil, add the lamb and stir to separate. Return to the boil, then add the cucumber slices, vinegar and seasonings. Bring to the boil once more, and serve at once.

Fried Seafood with Vegetables

Chao San Xian

Another colourful and delicious dish from south-east China, combining prawns (shrimp), squid and scallops. The squid can be replaced by another fish, or omitted altogether.

SERVES 4

Ingredients

- 115g/4oz squid, cleaned
- 4–6 fresh scallops
- 115g/4oz uncooked prawns (shrimp)
- ½ egg white
- 1 tbsp cornflour (cornstarch) paste
- 2–3 stalks of celery
- 1 small red (bell) pepper, cored and seeded
- 2 small carrots
- about 300ml/½ pint/1¼ cups oil
- ½ tsp finely-chopped fresh ginger
- 1 spring onion (scallion), cut into short sections
- 1 tsp salt
- ½ tsp light brown sugar
- 1 tbsp Chinese rice wine or dry sherry
- 1 tbsp light soy sauce
- 1 tsp chilli bean sauce
- 2 tbsp Basic Stock
- few drops sesame oil

1 Open up the squid and, using a sharp knife, score the inside in a criss-cross pattern. Cut the squid into pieces each about the size of an oblong stamp. Soak the squid in a bowl of boiling water until all the pieces curl up; rinse in cold water and drain.

2 Cut each scallop into 3–4 slices. Peel the prawns (shrimp) and cut each in half lengthways. Mix the scallops and prawns (shrimp) with the egg white and cornflour (cornstarch) paste.

3 Cut the celery, red (bell) pepper and carrots into thin slices, each about the size of a postage stamp.

4 Heat the oil in a preheated wok until medium-hot and stir-fry the seafood for about 30–40 seconds. Remove with a strainer and drain.

5 Pour off the excess oil, leaving about 2 tbsp in the wok, and add the vegetables with the ginger and spring onions (scallions). Stir-fry for about 1 minute.

6 Add the seafood to the wok, stir for another 30–40 seconds, then add the salt, sugar, wine or sherry, soy sauce and chilli bean sauce. Blend well, add the stock and continue stirring for another minute. Then serve garnished with sesame oil.

Braised Fish Fillet with Mushrooms

Chin Chao Yu Tiao

This is the Chinese version of the French *filets de sole bonne femme* (sole with mushrooms and wine sauce).

SERVES 4

Ingredients
450g/1lb fillet of lemon sole or plaice
1 tsp salt
½ egg white
2 tbsp cornflour (cornstarch) paste
about 575ml/1 pint/2½ cups vegetable oil
1 tbsp finely-chopped spring onions (scallions)
½ tsp finely-chopped fresh ginger
115g/4oz white mushrooms, thinly sliced
1 tsp light brown sugar
1 tbsp light soy sauce
2 tbsp Chinese rice wine or dry sherry
1 tbsp brandy
about 100ml/4fl oz/½ cup Basic Stock
few drops sesame oil, to garnish

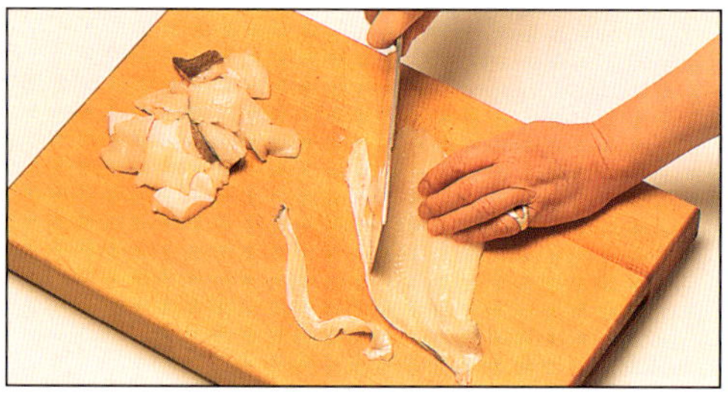

1 Trim off the soft bones along the edge of the fish, but leave the skin on. Cut each fillet into bite-sized pieces. Mix the fish with a little salt, the egg white and about half of the cornflour (cornstarch) paste.

2 Heat the oil until medium-hot, add the fish slice by slice and stir gently so the pieces do not stick. Remove after about 1 minute and drain. Pour off the excess oil, leaving about 2 tbsp in the wok.

3 Stir-fry the onions (scallions), ginger and mushrooms for 1 minute. Add the other ingredients except the cornflour (cornstarch) paste. Bring to the boil. Braise the fish for 1 minute. Thicken with the paste, and garnish.

Prawn (Shrimp) Fu-yung

Fu Ron Xia

This is a very colourful dish that is simple to make. Most of the preparation can be done well in advance.

SERVES 4

Ingredients
3 eggs, beaten, reserving 1 tsp of egg white
1 tsp salt
225g/8oz uncooked prawns (shrimp), peeled
2 tsp cornflour (cornstarch) paste
1 tbsp finely-chopped spring onions (scallions)
3–4 tbsp vegetable oil
175g/6oz green peas
1 tbsp Chinese rice wine or dry sherry

1 Beat the eggs with a pinch of the salt and a few bits of the spring onions (scallions). In a wok, scramble the eggs in a little oil over moderate heat. Remove and reserve.

2 Mix the prawns (shrimp) with a little salt, 1 tsp of egg white, and the cornflour (cornstarch) paste. Stir-fry the peas in hot oil for 30 seconds. Add the prawns (shrimp).

3 Add the spring onions (scallions). Stir-fry for another minute. Then stir the mixture into the scrambled egg with a little salt and the wine or sherry. Blend well and serve.

Sweet and Sour Prawns (Shrimp)

Tang Cu Xia

It is best to use uncooked prawns (shrimp) if available. If using ready-cooked ones, they can be added to the sauce without the initial deep frying.

SERVES 4–6

Ingredients
450g/1lb king prawns (shrimp) in their shells
vegetable oil, for deep-frying
lettuce leaves, to serve

Sauce
1 tbsp vegetable oil
1 tbsp finely-chopped spring onions (scallions)
2 tsp finely-chopped fresh ginger
2 tbsp light soy sauce
2 tbsp light brown sugar
3 tbsp rice vinegar
1 tbsp Chinese rice wine or dry sherry
about 100ml/4fl oz/½ cup Basic Stock
1 tbsp cornflour (cornstarch) paste
few drops sesame oil

1 Pull the soft legs off the prawns (shrimp) without removing the shells. Dry well with kitchen paper.

2 Deep-fry the prawns (shrimp) in hot oil for 35–40 seconds, or until their colour changes from grey to bright orange. Remove and drain.

3 To make the sauce, heat the oil in a preheated wok, add the spring onions (scallions) and ginger, followed by the seasonings and stock, and bring to the boil.

4 Add the prawns (shrimp) to the sauce, blend well, then thicken the sauce with the cornflour (cornstarch) paste, stirring until smooth. Sprinkle with the sesame oil. Serve on a bed of lettuce leaves.

Stir-fried Prawns (Shrimp) with Broccoli

Xi Lan Chao Xia Ren

This is a very colourful dish, highly nutritious and at the same time extremely delicious; furthermore, it is not time-consuming or difficult to prepare.

SERVES 4

Ingredients

175–225g/6–8oz prawns (shrimp), shelled and deveined
1 tsp salt
1 tbsp Chinese rice wine or dry sherry
1 tbsp cornflour (cornstarch) paste
½ egg white
225g/8oz broccoli
about 300ml/½ pint/1¼ cups vegetable oil
1 spring onion (scallion), cut into short sections
1 tsp light brown sugar
about 2 tbsp Basic Stock or water
1 tsp light soy sauce
few drops sesame oil

1 Cut each prawn (shrimp) in half lengthways. Mix with a pinch of salt, and about 1 tsp of the wine, egg white and cornflour (cornstarch) paste.

2 Cut the broccoli heads into florets; remove the rough skin from the stalks, then diagonally slice the florets into diamond-shaped chunks.

3 Heat the oil in a preheated wok and stir-fry the prawns (shrimp) for about 30 seconds. Remove with a strainer and drain.

4 Pour off the excess oil, leaving 2 tbsp in the wok. Add the broccoli and spring onion (scallion), stir-fry for about 2 minutes, then add the remaining salt, and the sugar, followed by the prawns (shrimp) and stock or water. Add the soy sauce and remaining wine or sherry. Blend well, then finally add the sesame oil and serve.

Squid with Green (Bell) Pepper and Black Bean Sauce

Si Jiao You Yu

This dish is a product of the Cantonese school, and makes an attractive meal that is as delicious as it looks.

SERVES 4

Ingredients
350–400g/12–14oz squid
1 medium green (bell) pepper, cored and seeded
3–4 tbsp vegetable oil
1 clove garlic, finely chopped
½ tsp finely-chopped fresh ginger
1 tbsp finely-chopped spring onions (scallions)
1 tsp salt
1 tbsp black bean sauce
1 tbsp Chinese rice wine or dry sherry
few drops sesame oil

1 To clean the squid, discard the head, the transparent backbone and the ink bag. Peel off and discard the skin, then wash the squid and dry well. Open up the squid and, with a sharp knife, score the inside of the flesh in a criss-cross pattern.

2 Cut the squid into pieces each about the size of an oblong postage stamp. Blanch the squid in a pan of boiling water for a few seconds. Remove and drain; dry well.

3 Cut the green (bell) pepper into small triangular pieces. Heat the oil in a wok and stir-fry the green (bell) pepper for about 1 minute.

4 Add the garlic, ginger, spring onion (scallion), salt and squid, then continue stirring for another minute. Finally add the black bean sauce and wine or sherry, and blend well. Sprinkle with sesame oil and serve.

Fish with Sweet and Sour Sauce

Wu Liu Yu

Another name for this dish is Five-Willow Fish, after the five shredded ingredients in the dressing.

SERVES 4–6

Ingredients

- 1 carp, bream, sea bass, trout, grouper or grey mullet, weighing about 675g/1½lb, gutted
- 1 tsp salt
- about 2 tbsp plain (all-purpose) flour
- vegetable oil, for deep-frying
- fresh coriander leaves, to garnish

Sauce

- 1 tbsp vegetable oil
- 50g/2oz carrot, thinly shredded
- 50g/2oz sliced bamboo shoots, drained and shredded
- 25g/1oz green (bell) pepper, thinly shredded
- 25g/1oz red (bell) pepper, thinly shredded
- 2–3 spring onions (scallions), finely shredded
- 1 tbsp thinly-shredded fresh ginger
- 1 tbsp light soy sauce
- 2 tbsp light brown sugar
- 2–3 tbsp rice vinegar
- about 100ml/4fl oz/½ cup Basic Stock
- 1 tbsp cornflour (cornstarch) paste

1 Clean and dry the fish well. Using a sharp knife, score both sides of the fish as far in as the bone with diagonal cuts at intervals of about 2.5cm/1in.

2 Rub the whole fish with salt both inside and out, then coat it from head to tail with flour.

3 Deep-fry the fish in the hot oil for about 3–4 minutes on both sides, or until golden brown. Remove the fish and drain, then place on a heated platter.

4 For the sauce, heat the oil and stir-fry all the vegetables for about 1 minute, then add the seasoning. Blend well, add the stock and bring to the boil. Add the cornflour (cornstarch) paste, stirring well until the sauce thickens and is smooth. Pour the sauce over the fish and garnish with fresh coriander leaves.

Braised Whole Fish in Chilli and Garlic Sauce

Gan Shao Yu

This is a classic Sichuan recipe. When served in a restaurant, the fish's head and tail are usually discarded before cooking, and used in other dishes. A whole fish may be used, however, and always looks impressive, especially for formal occasions and dinner parties.

SERVES 4–6

Ingredients

- 1 carp, bream, sea bass, trout, grouper or grey mullet, weighing about 675g/1½lb, gutted
- 1 tbsp light soy sauce
- 1 tbsp Chinese rice wine or dry sherry
- vegetable oil, for deep-frying

Sauce

- 2 cloves garlic, finely chopped
- 2–3 spring onions (scallions), finely chopped with the white and green parts separated
- 1 tsp finely-chopped fresh ginger
- 2 tbsp chilli bean sauce
- 1 tbsp tomato purée (paste)
- 2 tsp light brown sugar
- 1 tbsp rice vinegar
- about 100ml/4fl oz/½ cup Basic Stock
- 1 tbsp cornflour (cornstarch) paste
- few drops sesame oil

1 Rinse and dry the fish well. Using a sharp knife, score both sides of the fish as far down as the bone with diagonal cuts about 2.5cm/1in apart. Rub the whole fish with soy sauce and wine or sherry on both sides, then leave to marinate for 10–15 minutes.

2 In a wok, deep-fry the fish in hot oil for about 3–4 minutes on both sides or until golden brown.

3 Pour off the excess oil, leaving about 1 tbsp in the wok. Push the fish to one side of the wok and add the garlic, the white part of the spring onions (scallions), ginger, chilli bean sauce, tomato purée (paste), sugar, vinegar and stock. Bring to the boil and braise the fish in the sauce for 4–5 minutes, turning it over once. Add the green part of the spring onions (scallions). Thicken the sauce with the cornflour (cornstarch) paste, sprinkle with the sesame oil and serve.

Steamed Fish with Ginger and Spring Onions (Scallions)

Qing Zheng Yu

Any firm and delicate fish steaks, such as salmon or turbot, can be cooked by this same method.

SERVES 4–6

Ingredients

- 1 sea bass, trout or grey mullet, weighing about 675g/1½lb, gutted
- ½ tsp salt
- 1 tbsp sesame oil
- 2–3 spring onions (scallions), cut in half lengthways
- 2 tbsp light soy sauce
- 2 tbsp Chinese rice wine or dry sherry
- 1 tbsp finely-shredded fresh ginger
- 2 tbsp vegetable oil
- finely-shredded spring onions (scallions), to garnish

1 Using a sharp knife, score both sides of the fish as far down as the bone with diagonal cuts about 2.5cm/1in apart. Rub the fish all over, inside and out, with salt and sesame oil.

2 Sprinkle the spring onions (scallions) on a heatproof platter and place the fish on top. Blend together the soy sauce and wine or sherry with the ginger shreds and pour evenly all over the fish.

3 Place the platter in a very hot steamer (or inside a wok on a rack), and steam vigorously, under cover, for 12–15 minutes.

4 Heat the oil until hot; remove the platter from the steamer, place the shredded spring onions (scallions) on top of the fish, then pour the hot oil along the whole length of the fish. Serve immediately.

Red and White Prawns (Shrimp) with Green Vegetables

Yuan Yang Xia

The Chinese name for this dish is Yuan Yang Prawns (Shrimp). Pairs of mandarin ducks are also known as *yuan yang*, or love birds, because they are always seen together. They often symbolize affection and happiness.

SERVES 4–6

Ingredients
450g/1lb uncooked prawns (shrimp)
pinch of salt
½ egg white
1 tbsp cornflour (cornstarch) paste
175g/6oz mange-tout (snow peas)
about 575ml/1 pint/2½ cups vegetable oil
½ tsp salt
1 tsp light brown sugar
1 tbsp finely-chopped spring onions (scallions)
1 tsp finely-chopped fresh ginger
1 tbsp light soy sauce
1 tbsp Chinese rice wine or dry sherry
1 tsp chilli bean sauce
1 tbsp tomato purée (paste)

1 Peel and de-vein the prawns (shrimp), and mix with the pinch of salt, the egg white and the cornflour (cornstarch) paste. Top and tail the mange-tout (snow peas).

2 Heat about 2–3 tbsp of the oil in a preheated wok and stir-fry the mange-tout (snow peas) for about 1 minute, then add the salt and sugar and continue stirring for another minute. Remove and place in the centre of a serving platter.

3 Heat the remaining oil, par-cook the prawns (shrimp) for 1 minute, remove and drain.

4 Pour off the excess oil, leaving about 1 tbsp in the wok, and add the spring onions (scallions) and ginger to flavour the oil.

5 Add the prawns (shrimp) and stir-fry for about 1 minute, then add the soy sauce and wine or sherry. Blend well and place about half of the prawns (shrimp) at one end of the platter.

6 Add the chilli bean sauce and tomato purée (paste) to the remaining prawns (shrimp) in the wok, blend well and place the 'red' prawns (shrimp) at the other end of the platter. Serve.

Baked Lobster with Black Beans

Jiang Cong Guo Long Xia

The term 'baked', as described on most Chinese restaurant menus, is not strictly correct – 'pot-roasted' or 'pan-baked' is more accurate. Ideally, buy live lobsters and cook them yourself. Ready-cooked ones have usually been boiled for far too long and have lost much of their delicate flavour and texture.

SERVES 4–6

Ingredients

- 1 large or 2 medium lobsters, weighing about 800g/1¾lb in total,
- vegetable oil, for deep-frying
- 1 clove garlic, finely chopped
- 1 tsp finely-chopped fresh ginger
- 2–3 spring onions (scallions), cut into short sections
- 2 tbsp black bean sauce
- 2 tbsp Chinese rice wine or dry sherry
- 100ml/4fl oz/½ cup Basic Stock
- fresh coriander leaves, to garnish

1 Starting from the head, cut the lobster in half lengthways. Discard the legs, remove the claws and crack them with the back of a cleaver. Discard the feathery lungs and intestine. Cut each half into 4–5 pieces.

2 In a wok, deep-fry the lobster pieces in hot oil for about 2 minutes, or until the shells turn bright orange; remove and drain.

3 Pour off the excess oil leaving about 1 tbsp in the wok. Add the garlic, ginger, spring onions (scallions) and black bean sauce.

4 Add the lobster pieces to the sauce and blend well. Add the wine or sherry and stock, bring to the boil and cook for 2–3 minutes under cover. Serve garnished with coriander leaves.

Baked Crab with Spring Onions (Scallions) and Ginger

Zha Xie

This recipe is far less complicated to make than it looks. Again, use live crabs if you can for the best flavour and texture.

SERVES 4

Ingredients

1 large or 2 medium crabs, weighing about 675g/1½lb in total
2 tbsp Chinese rice wine or dry sherry
1 egg, lightly beaten
1 tbsp cornflour (cornstarch) paste
3–4 tbsp vegetable oil
1 tbsp finely-chopped fresh ginger
3–4 spring onions (scallions), cut into short sections
2 tbsp light soy sauce
1 tsp light brown sugar
about 5 tbsp Basic Stock
few drops sesame oil

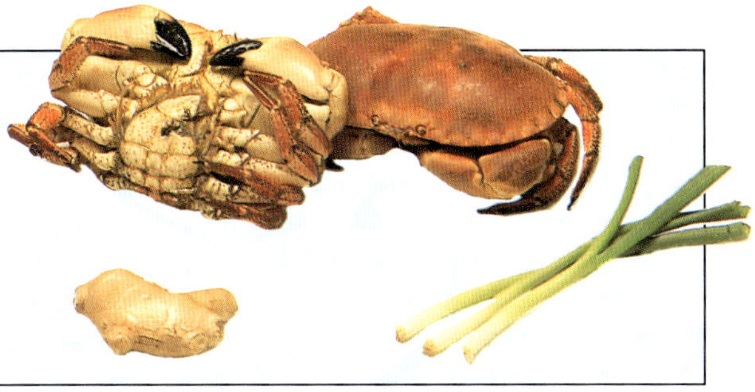

1 Cut the crab in half from the underbelly. Break off the claws and crack them with the back of a cleaver. Discard the legs and crack the shell, breaking it into several pieces. Discard the feathery gills and the sac.

2 Marinate with the wine or sherry, egg and cornflour (cornstarch) for 10–15 minutes.

3 Heat the oil in a preheated wok and stir-fry the crab pieces with the ginger and spring onions (scallions) for about 2–3 minutes.

4 Add the soy sauce, sugar and stock, blend well and bring to the boil; braise under cover for 3–4 minutes. Sprinkle with sesame oil and serve.

Crispy and Aromatic Duck

Xiang Cui Ya

Because this dish is often served with pancakes, spring onions (scallions), cucumber and duck sauce (a sweet bean paste), many people mistakenly think this is the Peking Duck. This recipe however, uses quite a different cooking method. The result is just as crispy but the delightful aroma makes this dish particularly distinctive. Plum sauce may be substituted for the duck sauce.

SERVES 6–8

Ingredients

- 1 oven-ready duckling, weighing about 2–2.3kg/4½–5lb
- 2 tsp salt
- 5–6 whole star anise
- 1 tbsp Sichuan peppercorns
- 1 tsp cloves
- 2–3 cinnamon sticks
- 3–4 spring onions (scallions)
- 3–4 slices fresh ginger, unpeeled
- 5–6 tbsp Chinese rice wine or dry sherry
- vegetable oil, for deep-frying
- lettuce leaves, to garnish

1 Remove the wings from the duck. Split the body in half down the backbone.

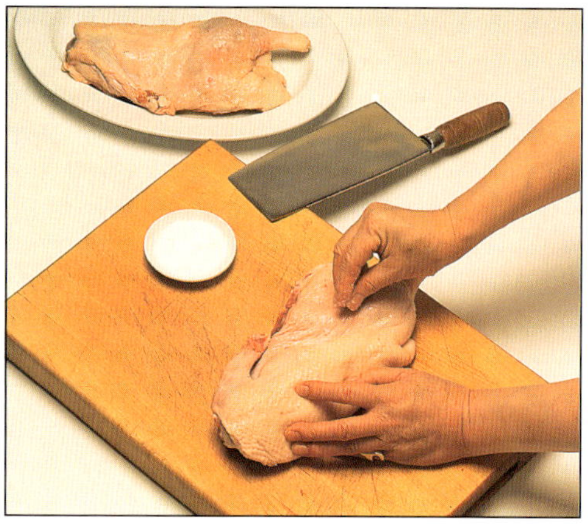

2 Rub salt all over the two duck halves taking care to rub it well in.

3 Marinate in a dish with the spices, spring onions (scallions), ginger and wine or sherry for at least 4–6 hours.

4 Vigorously steam the duck with the marinade for 3–4 hours (longer if possible), then remove from the cooking liquid and leave to cool for at least 5–6 hours. The duck must be completely cold and dry or the skin will not be crispy.

5 Heat the oil in a wok until smoking, place the duck pieces in the oil, skin-side down, and deep-fry for 5–6 minutes or until crisp and brown, turning just once at the very last moment.

6 Remove, drain and place on a bed of lettuce leaves. To serve, scrape the meat off the bone and wrap a portion in each pancake with a little sauce, shredded spring onion (scallion) and cucumber. Eat with your fingers.

Fu-yung Chicken

Fu Ron Ji

Because the egg whites (*Fu-yung* in Chinese) mixed with milk are deep-fried, they have prompted some imaginative cooks to refer to this dish as 'Deep-fried Milk'!

SERVES 4

Ingredients

175g/6oz chicken breast fillet
1 tsp salt
4 egg whites, lightly beaten
1 tbsp cornflour (cornstarch) paste
2 tbsp milk
vegetable oil, for deep-frying
1 lettuce heart, separated into leaves
about 100ml/4fl oz/½ cup Basic Stock
1 tbsp Chinese rice wine or dry sherry
1 tbsp green peas
few drops sesame oil
1 tsp minced (ground) ham, to garnish

1 Finely mince (grind) the chicken meat, then mix with a pinch of the salt, the egg whites, cornflour (cornstarch) paste and milk. Blend well until smooth.

2 Heat the oil in a very hot wok, but before the oil gets too hot, gently spoon the chicken and egg-white mixture into the oil in batches. Do not stir, otherwise it will scatter. Stir the oil from the bottom of the wok so that the *Fu-yung* will rise to the surface. Remove as soon as the colour turns bright white. Drain.

3 Pour off the excess oil, leaving about 1 tbsp in the wok. Stir-fry the lettuce leaves with the remaining salt for 1 minute, add the stock and bring to the boil.

4 Add the chicken to the wok with the wine and peas, and blend well. Sprinkle with the sesame oil and garnish with the ham.

'Kung Po' Chicken – Sichuan Style

Kung Po Ji Ding

Kung Po was the name of a court official in Sichuan; his cook created this dish.

SERVES 4

Ingredients
350g/12oz chicken thigh, boned and skinned
¼ tsp salt
½ egg white, lightly beaten
2 tsp cornflour (cornstarch) paste
1 medium green (bell) pepper, cored and seeded
4 tbsp vegetable oil
3–4 whole dried red chillies, soaked in water for 10 minutes
1 spring onion (scallion), cut into short sections
few small pieces of fresh ginger, peeled
1 tbsp sweet bean paste or Hoi Sin sauce
1 tsp chilli bean paste
1 tbsp Chinese rice wine or dry sherry
115g/4oz/1 cup roasted cashew nuts
few drops sesame oil

1 Cut the chicken meat into small cubes each about the size of a sugar lump. In a bowl mix together with the salt, egg white and the cornflour (cornstarch) paste.

2 Cut the green (bell) pepper into cubes about the same size as the chicken.

3 Heat the oil in a preheated wok. Stir-fry the chicken cubes for about 1 minute, or until the colour changes, remove with a perforated spoon and keep warm.

4 Add the green (bell) pepper, dried red chillies, spring onion (scallion) and ginger and stir-fry for about 1 minute; then add the chicken with the bean pastes or sauce and wine or sherry. Blend well and cook for another minute. Finally add the cashew nuts and sesame oil. Serve hot.

Peking Duck

Bei Jing Ya

This has to be the *pièce de résistance* of any Chinese banquet. It is not too difficult to prepare and cook at home – the secret is to use duckling with a low fat content. Also, make sure that the skin of the duck is absolutely dry before cooking – the drier the skin, the crispier the duck.

SERVES 6–8

Ingredients

1 oven-ready duckling, weighing about 2.3–2.5kg/5–5½lb

2 tbsp maltose or honey, dissolved in 150ml/¼ pint/⅔ cup warm water

For serving

20–24 Thin Pancakes

100ml/4fl oz/½ cup Duck Sauce (see below) or plum sauce

6–8 spring onions (scallions), thinly shredded

½ cucumber, thinly shredded

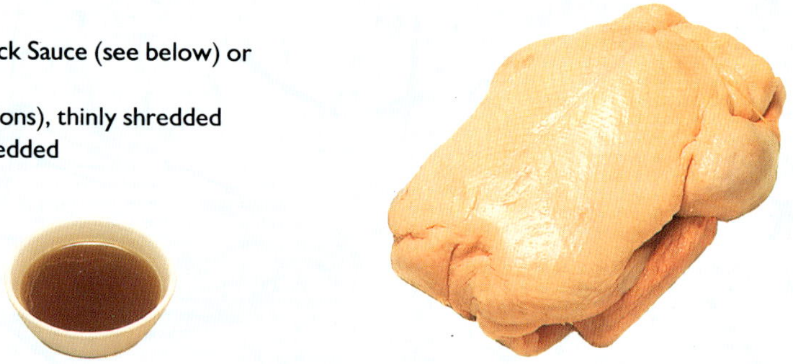

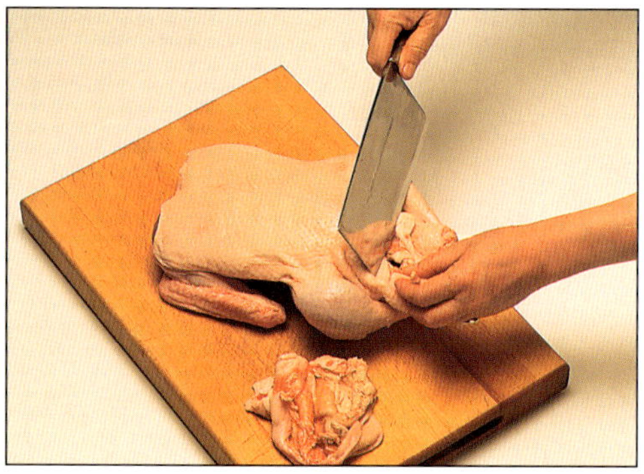

1 Remove any feather studs and any lumps of fat from inside the vent of the duck. Plunge the duck into a pot of boiling water for 2–3 minutes to seal the pores. This will make the skin air-tight, thus preventing the fat from escaping during cooking. Remove and drain well, then dry thoroughly.

2 Brush the duck all over with the dissolved maltose or honey, then hang the duck up in a cool place for at least 4–5 hours.

3 Place the duck, breast side up, on a rack in a roasting pan, and cook in a preheated oven (200°C/400°F/Gas Mark 6) for 1½–1¾ hours without basting or turning.

4 To serve, peel off the crispy duck skin in small slices using a sharp carving knife or cleaver, then carve the juicy meat in thin strips. Arrange the skin and meat on separate serving plates.

5 Open a pancake on each plate, spread about 1 tsp of sauce in the middle, with a few strips of shredded spring onions (scallions) and cucumber. Top with 2–3 slices each of duck skin and meat.

Duck Sauce

To make Duck Sauce, heat 2 tbsp sesame oil in a small saucepan. Add 6–8 tbsp crushed yellow bean sauce and 2–3 tbsp light brown sugar. Stir until smooth and allow to cool. Serve cold.

Shredded Chicken with Celery

Qing Cai Chao Ji Si

The tender chicken breast contrasts with the crunchy texture of the celery, and the red chillies add colour and flavour.

SERVES 4

Ingredients
285g/10oz chicken breast fillet
1 tsp salt
½ egg white, lightly beaten
2 tsp cornflour (cornstarch) paste
about 500ml/16 fl oz/2 cups vegetable oil
1 celery heart, thinly shredded
1–2 fresh red chillies, seeded and thinly shredded
1 spring onion (scallion), thinly shredded
few strips fresh ginger, thinly shredded
1 tsp light brown sugar
1 tbsp Chinese rice wine or dry sherry
few drops sesame oil

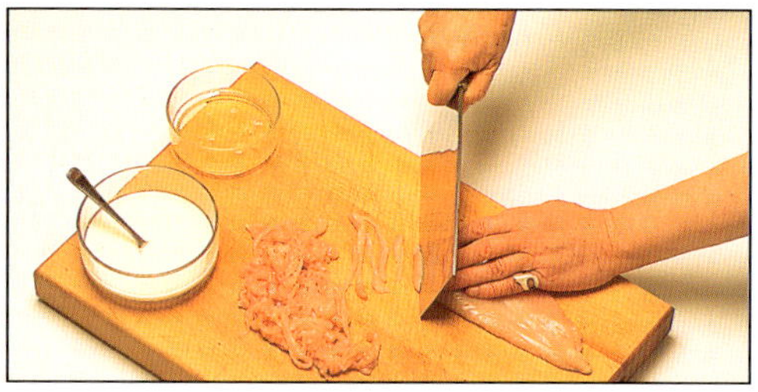

1 Using a sharp knife, thinly shred the chicken. In a bowl, mix together with a pinch of the salt, the egg white, and the cornflour (cornstarch) paste.

2 Heat the oil in a wok until warm, add the chicken and stir to separate the shreds. When the chicken turns white, remove with a strainer and drain. Keep warm.

3 In 2 tbsp of oil, stir-fry the celery, chillies, spring onion (scallion) and ginger for 1 minute. Add the chicken, salt, sugar and wine. Cook for 1 minute and add the sesame oil. Serve hot.

Chicken with Chinese Vegetables

Ji Pian Chao Shi Cai

The chicken can be replaced by almost any other meat, such as pork, beef, liver or prawns (shrimp).

SERVES 4

Ingredients
225–285g/8–10oz chicken, boned and skinned
1 tsp salt
½ egg white, lightly beaten
2 tsp cornflour (cornstarch) paste
4 tbsp vegetable oil
6–8 small dried Chinese mushrooms (shiitake), soaked
115g/4oz sliced bamboo shoots, drained
115g/4oz mange-tout (snow peas), trimmed
1 spring onion (scallion), cut into short sections
few small pieces fresh ginger, peeled
1 tsp light brown sugar
1 tbsp light soy sauce
1 tbsp Chinese rice wine or dry sherry
few drops sesame oil

1 Cut the chicken into thin slices each about the size of an oblong postage stamp. In a bowl, mix with a pinch of the salt, the egg white and the cornflour (cornstarch) paste.

2 Heat the oil in a preheated wok, stir-fry the chicken over medium heat for about 30 seconds, then remove with a perforated spoon and keep warm.

3 Stir-fry the vegetables over high heat for about 1 minute. Add the salt, sugar and chicken. Blend, then add the soy sauce and wine or sherry. Stir a few more times. Sprinkle with the sesame oil and serve.

Soy-braised Chicken

Jiang You Ji

This dish can be served hot or cold as part of a buffet-style meal.

SERVES 6–8

Ingredients

- 1 whole chicken, weighing about 1.35–1.5kg/ 3–3½lb
- 1 tbsp ground Sichuan peppercorns
- 2 tbsp minced (ground) fresh ginger
- 3 tbsp light soy sauce
- 2 tbsp dark soy sauce
- 3 tbsp Chinese rice wine or dry sherry
- 1 tbsp light brown sugar
- vegetable oil, for deep-frying
- about 575ml/1 pint/2½ cups Basic Stock or water
- 2 tsp salt
- 25g/1oz rock (crystal) sugar
- lettuce leaves, to garnish

1 Rub the chicken both inside and out with the ground pepper and fresh ginger. Marinate the bird with the soy sauces, wine or sherry and sugar for at least 3 hours, turning it several times.

2 Heat the oil in a preheated wok, remove the chicken from the marinade and deep-fry for 5–6 minutes, or until brown all over. Remove and drain.

3 Pour off the excess oil, add the marinade with the stock or water, salt and rock (crystal) sugar and bring to the boil. Braise the chicken in the sauce for 35–40 minutes under cover, turning once or twice.

4 Remove the chicken from the wok and let it cool down a little before chopping it into approximately 30 bite-sized pieces. Arrange the pieces on a bed of lettuce leaves, then pour some of the sauce over the chicken and serve. The remains of the sauce can be stored in the refrigerator to be re-used again and again.

Chicken and Ham with Green Vegetables

Jin Hua Yi Shu Ji

The Chinese name for this colourful dish means 'Golden Flower and Jade Tree Chicken'. It makes a marvellous buffet-style dish for all occasions.

SERVES 6–8

Ingredients

- 1 whole chicken weighing about 1–1.35kg/ 2¼–3lb
- 2 spring onions (scallions)
- 2–3 pieces fresh ginger
- 1 tbsp salt
- 225g/8oz honey-roast ham
- 285g/10oz broccoli
- 3 tbsp vegetable oil
- 1 tsp light brown sugar
- 2 tsp cornflour (cornstarch)

1 Place the chicken in a large pan and cover it with cold water. Add the spring onions (scallions), ginger and about 2 tsp of the salt. Bring to the boil, then reduce the heat and simmer for 10–15 minutes under a tightly-fitting cover. Turn off the heat and let the chicken cook itself in the hot water for at least 4–5 hours – you must not lift up the cover, as this will let out the residual heat.

2 Remove the chicken from the pan, reserving the liquid, and carefully cut the meat away from the bones, keeping the skin on. Slice both the chicken and ham into pieces, each the size of a matchbox, and arrange the meats in alternating layers on a plate.

3 Cut the broccoli into small florets and stir-fry in the hot oil with the remaining salt and the sugar for about 2–3 minutes. Arrange the vegetables between the rows of chicken and ham and around the edge of the plate, making a border for the meat.

4 Heat a small amount of the chicken stock and thicken with the cornflour (cornstarch). Stir until smooth, then pour it evenly all over the chicken and ham so that it forms a thin coat of transparent jelly resembling 'jade'. Allow to cool before serving.

Mu Shu Pork with Eggs and Wood-ears

Mu Shu Rou

Mu Shu is the Chinese name for a bright yellow flower. Traditionally, this dish is served as a filling wrapped in thin pancakes, but it can also be served on its own with plain rice.

SERVES 4

Ingredients
15g/½oz dried black fungus (wood-ears)
175–225g/6–8oz pork fillet
225g/8oz Chinese leaves
115g/4oz bamboo shoots, drained
2 spring onions (scallions)
3 eggs
1 tsp salt
4 tbsp vegetable oil
1 tbsp light soy sauce
1 tbsp Chinese rice wine or dry sherry
few drops sesame oil

1 Soak the fungus in cold water for 25–30 minutes, rinse and discard the hard stalks, if any. Drain, then thinly shred.

2 Cut the pork into matchstick-size shreds. Thinly shred the Chinese leaves, bamboo shoots and spring onions (scallions).

3 Beat the eggs with a pinch of the salt and lightly scramble in a little of the warm oil until set, but not too dry. Remove.

4 Heat the remaining oil in the wok and stir-fry the pork for about 1 minute, or until the colour changes.

5 Add the vegetables to the wok, stir-fry for another minute, then add the remaining salt, the soy sauce and wine or sherry.

6 Stir for 1 more minute before adding the scrambled eggs. Break up the scrambled eggs and blend well. Sprinkle with sesame oil and serve.

Stuffed Green (Bell) Peppers

Niang Qing Chaio.

Ideally, use small, thin-skinned green (bell) peppers for this recipe.

SERVES 4

Ingredients

225–285g/8–10oz minced (ground) pork
4–6 water chestnuts, finely chopped
2 spring onions (scallions), finely chopped
½ tsp finely-chopped fresh ginger
1 tbsp light soy sauce
1 tbsp Chinese rice wine or dry sherry
3–4 green (bell) peppers, cored and seeded
1 tbsp cornflour (cornstarch)
vegetable oil, for deep-frying

Sauce

2 tsp light soy sauce
1 tsp light brown sugar
1–2 fresh hot chillies, finely chopped (optional)
about 5 tbsp Basic Stock or water

1 In a bowl, mix the minced (ground) pork with the water chestnuts, spring onions (scallions), ginger, soy sauce and wine or sherry.

2 Halve or quarter the green (bell) peppers. Stuff the sections with the pork mixture and sprinkle with a little cornflour (cornstarch).

3 Heat the oil in a preheated wok and deep-fry the stuffed (bell) peppers, with the meat-side down, for 2–3 minutes, then remove and drain.

4 Pour off the excess oil, then return the stuffed green (bell) peppers to the wok with the meat-side up. Add the sauce ingredients, shaking the wok gently to make sure they do not stick to the bottom, and braise for 2–3 minutes. Carefully lift the stuffed peppers onto a serving dish, meat-side up, and pour the sauce over them. Serve.

TWICE-COOKED PORK – SICHUAN STYLE

Hui Guo Rou

Any left-overs from a roast joint of pork can be used for this dish.

SERVES 4

Ingredients

225g/8oz shoulder or knuckle of pork
1 small green (bell) pepper, cored and seeded
115g/4oz sliced bamboo shoots, rinsed and drained
1 spring onion (scallion)
3 tbsp vegetable oil
1 tsp salt
½ tsp light brown sugar
1 tbsp yellow bean sauce
1 tsp chilli bean sauce
1 tbsp Chinese rice wine or dry sherry

1 Immerse the whole piece of pork into a pot of boiling water, return to the boil and skim the surface. Reduce the heat and simmer, covered, for 25–30 minutes. Turn off the heat and leave the pork in the water, covered, to cool, for at least 3–4 hours before removing.

2 Trim off and remove any excess fat from the pork and cut the meat into thin slices, each about the size of a large postage stamp. Cut the green (bell) peppers into pieces the size of the bamboo shoots and cut the spring onion (scallion) into short sections.

3 Heat the oil in a preheated wok, add the green (bell) pepper, the spring onion (scallion) and bamboo shoots, and stir-fry for about 1 minute.

4 Add the pork followed by the salt, sugar, yellow bean sauce, chilli bean sauce and wine or sherry. Continue stirring for a further 1–2 minutes. Serve.

Sweet and Sour Pork

Tang Cu Gu Luo Rou

Sweet and Sour Pork must be one of the most popular dishes served in Chinese restaurants and take-aways in the Western world. Unfortunately, it is too often spoiled by cooks who use too much tomato ketchup in the sauce. Here is a classic recipe from Canton, the city of its origin.

SERVES 4

Ingredients
350g/12oz lean pork
¼ tsp salt
½ tsp ground Sichuan peppercorns
1 tbsp Chinese rice wine or dry sherry
115g/4oz bamboo shoots
2 tbsp plain (all-purpose) flour
1 egg, lightly beaten
vegetable oil, for deep-frying

Sauce
1 tbsp vegetable oil
1 clove garlic, finely chopped
1 spring onion (scallion), cut into short sections
1 small green (bell) pepper, cut into small cubes
1 fresh red chilli, seeded and thinly shredded
1 tbsp light soy sauce
2 tbsp light brown sugar
2–3 tbsp rice vinegar
1 tbsp tomato purée (paste)
about 100ml/4fl oz/½ cup Basic Stock or water

1 Cut the pork into small bite-sized cubes. Marinate with the salt, pepper and wine or sherry for 15–20 minutes.

2 Cut the bamboo shoots into small cubes the same size as the pork.

3 Dust the pork with flour, dip in the beaten egg, and coat with more flour. Deep-fry in moderately hot oil for 3–4 minutes, stirring to separate the pieces. Remove.

4 Reheat the oil to hot, add the pork and bamboo shoots and fry for about 1 minute or until golden. Remove and drain.

5 Heat the oil and add the garlic, spring onion (scallion), green (bell) pepper and red chilli. Stir-fry for 30–40 seconds, then add the seasoning with the stock. Bring to the boil, then add the pork and bamboo shoots.

STIR-FRIED PORK WITH VEGETABLES I

Rou Pian Chao Shucai

This is a basic recipe for cooking any meat with any vegetables, according to seasonal availability.

SERVES 4

Ingredients
225g/8oz pork fillet
1 tbsp light soy sauce
1 tsp light brown sugar
1 tsp Chinese rice wine or dry sherry
2 tsp cornflour (cornstarch) paste
115g/4oz mange-tout (snow peas)
115g/4oz white mushrooms
1 medium or 2 small carrots
1 spring onion (scallion)
4 tbsp vegetable oil
1 tsp salt
Basic Stock or water, if necessary
few drops sesame oil

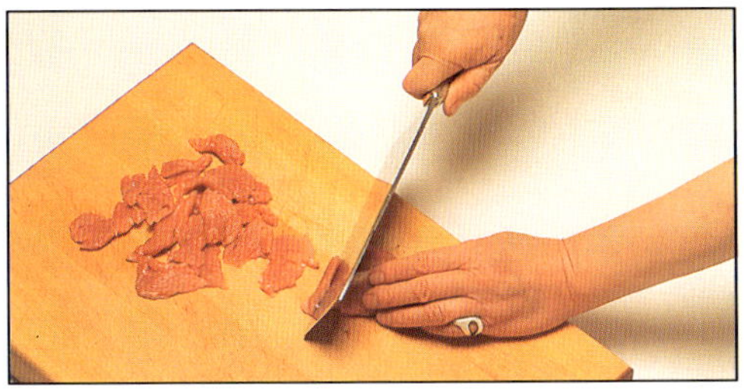

1 Cut the pork into thin slices each about the size of an oblong postage stamp. Marinate with about 1 tsp of the soy sauce, sugar, wine or sherry and cornflour (cornstarch) paste.

2 Top and tail the mange-tout (snow peas); thinly slice the mushrooms; cut the carrots into pieces roughly the same size as the pork, and cut the spring onion (scallion) into short sections.

3 Heat the oil in a preheated wok and stir-fry the pork for about 1 minute or until its colour changes. Remove with a perforated spoon and keep warm.

4 Stir-fry the vegetables for about 2 minutes, add the salt and the partly-cooked pork, and a little stock or water only if necessary. Continue stirring for another minute or so, then add the remaining soy sauce and blend well. Sprinkle with the sesame oil and serve.

LION'S HEAD CASSEROLE

Shi Zi Tou

The meatballs are supposed to resemble a lion's head, and the Chinese leaves its mane, hence the dish's name.

SERVES 4–6

Ingredients
450g/1lb minced (ground) pork
2 tsp finely-chopped spring onions (scallions)
1 tsp finely-chopped fresh ginger
50g/2oz white mushrooms, finely chopped
50g/2oz peeled prawns (shrimp) or crabmeat, finely chopped
1 tbsp light soy sauce
1 tsp light brown sugar
1 tbsp Chinese rice wine or dry sherry
1 tbsp cornflour (cornstarch)
675g/1½lb Chinese leaves
3–4 tbsp vegetable oil
1 tsp salt
about 300ml/½ pint/1¼ cups Basic Stock or water

1 Mix the pork with the spring onions (scallions), ginger, mushrooms, prawns (shrimp), soy sauce, sugar, wine and cornflour (cornstarch). Shape into 4–6 meatballs.

2 Cut the Chinese leaves into large pieces, all roughly the same size.

3 Heat the oil and stir-fry the Chinese leaves with the salt for 2–3 minutes. Add the meatballs and the stock, bring to the boil, cover and simmer gently for 30–45 minutes.

STIR-FRIED PORK WITH VEGETABLES II

Rou Pian Chao Shucai

In this simple, colourful dish, the courgettes (zucchini) can be replaced by cucumber or green (bell) peppers.

SERVES 4

Ingredients
225g/8oz pork fillet, thinly sliced
1 tbsp light soy sauce
1 tsp light brown sugar
1 tsp Chinese rice wine or dry sherry
2 tsp cornflour (cornstarch) paste
115g/4oz firm tomatoes, peeled
175g/6oz courgettes (zucchini)
1 spring onion (scallion)
4 tbsp vegetable oil
1 tsp salt (optional)
Basic Stock or water, if necessary

1 In a bowl, marinate the pork with about 1 tsp of the soy sauce, the sugar, wine and cornflour (cornstarch) paste. Cut the tomatoes and courgettes (zucchini) into wedges and the spring onion (scallion) into sections.

2 Heat the oil in a preheated wok and stir-fry the pork for about 1 minute or until the colour changes. Remove with a perforated spoon and keep warm.

3 Stir-fry the vegetables for about 2 minutes, add the salt if using, the pork and a little stock or water. Stir for another minute or so, then add the remaining soy sauce and blend well. Serve.

Sweet and Sour Lamb

Tang Cu Yang Rou

This recipe from the Imperial kitchens of the Manchu Dynasty is perhaps a forerunner of Sweet and Sour Pork.

SERVES 4

Ingredients

350–400g/12–14oz leg of lamb fillet
1 tbsp yellow bean sauce
vegetable oil, for deep-frying
½ tsp finely-chopped fresh ginger
1 tbsp light soy sauce
1 tbsp Chinese rice wine or dry sherry
2 tbsp rice vinegar
2 tbsp light brown sugar
3–4 tbsp Basic Stock or water
1 tbsp cornflour (cornstarch) paste
½ tsp sesame oil

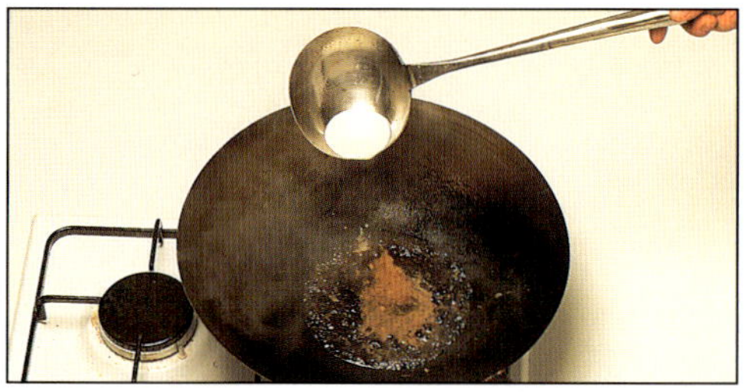

1 Cut the lamb into thin slices each about the size of an oblong postage stamp. In a bowl, marinate the lamb with the yellow bean sauce for 35–40 minutes.

2 In a wok, deep-fry the lamb in the hot oil for about 30–40 seconds or until the colour changes. Remove with a perforated spoon and drain.

3 Pour off the excess oil, leaving about ½ tbsp in the wok. Add the ginger and the remaining ingredients and stir until smooth. Add the lamb, blend well and serve.

Stir-fried Lamb with Spring Onions (Scallions)

Cong Bao Yang Rou

This is a classic Beijing 'meat and veg' recipe, in which the lamb can be replaced with either beef or pork, and the spring onions (scallions) by other strongly-flavoured vegetables, such as leeks or onions.

SERVES 4

Ingredients

350–400g/12–14 oz leg of lamb fillet
1 tsp light brown sugar
1 tbsp light soy sauce
1 tbsp Chinese rice wine or dry sherry
2 tsp cornflour (cornstarch) paste
15g/½oz dried black fungus (wood-ears)
6–8 spring onions (scallions)
about 300ml/½ pint/1¼ cups vegetable oil
few small pieces fresh ginger
2 tbsp yellow bean sauce
few drops sesame oil

1 Slice the lamb thinly. Marinate with the sugar, soy sauce, wine and cornflour (cornstarch) paste for 30–45 minutes. Soak the fungus for 25–30 minutes, then cut into small pieces with the spring onions (scallions).

2 Heat the oil in a preheated wok until hot and stir-fry the meat for about 1 minute, or until the colour changes. Remove with a perforated spoon and drain.

3 Keep about 1 tbsp of oil in the wok, then add the spring onions (scallions), ginger, fungus and yellow bean sauce. Blend well, then add the meat and stir for about 1 minute. Sprinkle with the sesame oil.

Dry-fried Shredded Beef

Gan Shao Niu Rou

Dry-frying is a unique Sichuan cooking method, in which the main ingredient is firstly stir-fried slowly over a low heat until dry, then finished off quickly with other ingredients over a high heat.

SERVES 4

Ingredients
350–400g/12–14oz beef steak
1 large or 2 small carrots
2–3 stalks celery
2 tbsp sesame oil
1 tbsp Chinese rice wine or dry sherry
1 tbsp chilli bean sauce
1 tbsp light soy sauce
1 clove garlic, finely chopped
1 tsp light brown sugar
2–3 spring onions (scallions), finely chopped
½ tsp finely-chopped fresh ginger
ground Sichuan peppercorns, to taste

1 Cut the beef into matchstick-size strips. Thinly shred the carrots and celery.

2 Heat the sesame oil in a preheated wok (it will smoke very quickly). Reduce the heat and stir-fry the beef shreds with the wine or sherry until the colour changes.

3 Pour off the excess liquid and reserve. Continue stirring until the meat is absolutely dry.

4 Add the chilli bean sauce, soy sauce, garlic and sugar; blend well, then add the carrot and celery shreds. Increase the heat to high and add the spring onions (scallions), ginger and the reserved liquid. Continue stirring, and when all the juice has evaporated, season with Sichuan pepper and serve.

Beef with Cantonese Oyster Sauce

Hao You Niu Rou

This is a classic Cantonese recipe in which any combination of vegetables can be used. Broccoli may be used instead of mange-tout (snow peas), bamboo shoots instead of baby corn cobs, and white or black mushrooms instead of straw mushrooms, for example.

SERVES 4

Ingredients

285–350g/10–12oz beef steak
1 tsp light brown sugar
1 tbsp light soy sauce
2 tsp Chinese rice wine or dry sherry
2 tsp cornflour (cornstarch) paste
115g/4oz mange-tout (snow peas)
115g/4oz baby corn cobs
115g/4oz canned straw mushrooms, drained
1 spring onion (scallion)
300ml/½ pint/1¼ cups vegetable oil
few small pieces fresh ginger
½ tsp salt
2 tbsp oyster sauce

1 Cut the beef into thin slices each about the size of an oblong postage stamp. In a bowl, marinate the beef with the sugar, soy sauce, wine or sherry and cornflour (cornstarch) paste for 25–30 minutes.

2 Top and tail the mange-tout (snow peas); cut the baby corn cobs in half and also the straw mushrooms if large, but leave whole if small. Cut the spring onion (scallion) into short sections.

3 Heat the oil in a preheated wok and stir-fry the beef until the colour changes. Remove with a perforated spoon and drain.

4 Pour off the excess oil, leaving about 2 tbsp in the wok, then add the spring onion (scallion), ginger and the vegetables. Stir-fry for about 2 minutes with the salt, then add the beef and the oyster sauce. Blend well and serve.

STIR-FRIED MIXED VEGETABLES I

Su Shi Jin

Black or oyster mushrooms may be used in place of the white mushrooms in this dish.

SERVES 4

Ingredients
115g/4oz mange-tout (snow peas)
115g/4oz courgettes (zucchini)
115g/4oz white mushrooms
1 medium red (bell) pepper, cored and seeded
4 tbsp vegetable oil
1 tsp salt
1 tsp light brown sugar
Basic Stock or water, if necessary
1 tbsp light soy sauce
few drops sesame oil (optional)

1 Cut the vegetables into roughly similar shapes and sizes. Top and tail the mange-tout (snow peas) and leave whole if small, otherwise cut in half.

2 Heat the oil in a wok and stir-fry the vegetables for about 2 minutes.

3 Add the salt and sugar, and a little stock or water *only* if necessary, and stir for 1 minute. Finally add the soy sauce and sesame oil, if using. Blend well and serve.

STIR-FRIED MIXED VEGETABLES II

Su Shi Jin

When selecting different items for a dish, never mix ingredients indiscriminately. The idea is to achieve a harmonious balance of colour and texture.

SERVES 4

Ingredients
225g/8oz Chinese leaves
115g/4oz baby corn cobs
115g/4oz broccoli
1 medium or 2 small carrots
4 tbsp vegetable oil
1 tsp salt
1 tsp light brown sugar
Basic Stock or water, if necessary
1 tbsp light soy sauce
few drops sesame oil (optional)

1 Cut the vegetables into roughly similar shapes and sizes.

2 Heat the oil in a wok and stir-fry the vegetables for about 2 minutes.

3 Add the salt and sugar, and a little stock or water *only* if necessary, and continue stirring for another minute. Add the soy sauce and sesame oil, if using. Blend well and serve.

Sichuan Spicy Bean Curd (Tofu)

Ma Po Dao Fu

This universally popular dish originated in Sichuan in the nineteenth century. The meat used in the recipe can be omitted to create a purely vegetarian dish.

SERVES 4

Ingredients

3 cakes bean curd (tofu)
1 leek
115g/4oz minced (ground) beef
3 tbsp vegetable oil
1 tbsp black bean sauce
1 tbsp light soy sauce
1 tsp chilli bean sauce
1 tbsp Chinese rice wine or dry sherry
about 3–4 tbsp Basic Stock or water
2 tsp cornflour (cornstarch) paste
ground Sichuan peppercorns, to taste
few drops sesame oil

1 Cut the bean curd (tofu) into 1cm/½in square cubes; blanch the cubes in a pan of boiling water for 2–3 minutes to harden. Remove and drain. Cut the leek into short sections.

2 Stir-fry the minced (ground) beef in oil until the colour changes, then add the leek and black bean sauce. Add the bean curd (tofu) with the soy sauce, chilli bean sauce and wine or sherry. Stir gently for 1 minute.

3 Add the stock or water, bring to the boil and braise for 2–3 minutes.

4 Thicken the sauce with the cornflour (cornstarch) paste, season with the ground Sichuan pepper and sprinkle with the sesame oil. Serve.

YU HSIANG AUBERGINE (EGGPLANT) IN SPICY SAUCE

Yu Hsiang Gai

Yu Hsiang, which literally means 'fish fragrance', is a Sichuan cookery term indicating that the dish is cooked with seasonings originally used in fish dishes.

SERVES 4

Ingredients

450g/1lb aubergines (eggplant)
3–4 whole dried red chillies, soaked in water for 10 minutes
vegetable oil, for deep-frying
1 clove garlic, finely chopped
1 tsp finely-chopped fresh ginger
1 tsp finely-chopped spring onion (scallion), white part only
115g/4oz lean pork, thinly shredded (optional)
1 tbsp light soy sauce
1 tsp light brown sugar
1 tbsp chilli bean sauce
1 tbsp Chinese rice wine or dry sherry
1 tbsp rice vinegar
2 tsp cornflour (cornstarch) paste
1 tsp finely-chopped spring onions (scallions), green part only, to garnish
few drops sesame oil

1 Cut the aubergines (eggplant) into short strips the size of chips (French fries) – the skin can either be peeled or left on, whichever you prefer. Cut the soaked red chillies into 2–3 small pieces and discard the seeds.

2 In a wok, heat the oil and deep-fry the aubergine (eggplant) 'chips' for about 3–4 minutes or until limp. Remove and drain.

3 Pour off the excess oil, leaving about 1 tbsp in the wok. Add the garlic, ginger, white spring onions (scallions) and chillies, stir a few times then add the pork, if using. Stir-fry the meat for about 1 minute or until the colour changes to pale white. Add all the seasonings, then bring to the boil.

4 Add the aubergines (eggplant) to the wok, blend well and braise for 30–40 seconds, then thicken the sauce with the cornflour (cornstarch) paste, stirring until smooth. Garnish with the green spring onions (scallions) and sprinkle with the sesame oil.

Cook's tip

Soaking dried chillies in water will reduce their spicy flavour. If you prefer a milder chilli taste, soak for longer than the recommended 10 minutes.

Broccoli in Oyster Sauce

Hao You Xi Lan

Vegetarians may prefer to replace oyster sauce with soy sauce.

SERVES 4

Ingredients
450g/1lb broccoli
3–4 tbsp vegetable oil
½ tsp salt
½ tsp light brown sugar
2–3 tbsp Basic Stock or water
2 tbsp oyster sauce

1 Cut the broccoli heads into florets; remove the rough skin from the stalks, and diagonally slice the florets into diamond-shaped chunks.

2 Heat the oil in a preheated wok and add the salt, then stir-fry the broccoli for about 2 minutes. Add the sugar and stock or water, and continue stirring for another minute. Finally add the oyster sauce, blend well and serve.

Stir-fried Chinese Leaves with Mushrooms

Pia Cai Cao Gu

You can also use fresh button mushrooms for this recipe.

SERVES 4

Ingredients
225g/8oz fresh straw mushrooms or 1 350g/12oz can straw mushrooms, drained
4 tbsp vegetable oil
400g/14oz Chinese leaves, cut in strips
1 tsp salt
1 tsp light brown sugar
1 tbsp cornflour (cornstarch) paste
100ml/4fl oz/½ cup milk

1 Cut the mushrooms in half lengthways. Heat half the oil, stir-fry the Chinese leaves for 2 minutes, then add half the salt and half the sugar. Stir for 1 minute, then place on a dish.

2 Stir-fry the mushrooms for 1 minute. Add salt and sugar, cook for 1 minute, then thicken with the cornflour (cornstarch) paste and milk. Serve with the greens.

Stir-fried Bean Sprouts

Chao Dao Ya

It is not necessary to top and tail the bean sprouts for this quick and simple recipe. Simply rinse in a bowl of cold water, and discard any husks that float to the surface.

SERVES 4

Ingredients
2–3 spring onions (scallions)
225g/8oz fresh bean sprouts
3 tbsp vegetable oil
1 tsp salt
½ tsp light brown sugar
few drops sesame oil (optional)

1 Cut the spring onions (scallions) into short sections about the same length as the bean sprouts.

2 Heat the oil in a wok and stir-fry the bean sprouts and spring onions (scallions) for about 1 minute. Add the salt and sugar and continue stirring for another minute. Sprinkle with the sesame oil, if using, and serve. Do not over-cook, or the sprouts will go soggy.

Braised Chinese Vegetables

Lo Han Zhai

The original recipe calls for no less than 18 different ingredients to represent the 18 Buddhas (*Lo Han*). Later, this was reduced to eight, but nowadays anything between four and six items is regarded as quite sufficient.

SERVES 4

Ingredients

7g/¼oz dried black fungus (wood-ears)
85g/3oz straw mushrooms, drained
85g/3oz sliced bamboo shoots, drained
50g/2oz mange-tout (snow peas)
1 cake bean curd (tofu)
175g/6oz Chinese leaves
3–4 tbsp vegetable oil
1 tsp salt
½ tsp light brown sugar
1 tbsp light soy sauce
few drops sesame oil (optional)

1 Soak the black fungus in cold water for 20–25 minutes, then rinse and discard the hard stalks, if any. Cut the straw mushrooms in half lengthways, if large – keep them whole, if small. Rinse and drain the bamboo shoot slices. Top and tail the mange-tout (snow peas). Cut the bean curd (tofu) into about 12 small pieces. Cut the Chinese leaves into small pieces about the same size as the mange-tout (snow peas).

2 Harden the bean curd (tofu) pieces by placing them in a pan of boiling water for about 2 minutes. Remove and drain.

3 Heat the oil in a flameproof casserole or saucepan and lightly brown the bean curd (tofu) pieces on both sides. Remove with a slotted spoon and keep warm.

4 Stir-fry all the vegetables in the casserole or saucepan for about 1½ minutes, then add the bean curd (tofu) pieces, salt, sugar and soy sauce. Continue stirring for another minute, then cover and braise for 2–3 minutes. Sprinkle with sesame oil (if using) and serve.

Bamboo Shoots and Chinese Mushrooms

Chao Shang Dong

Another name for this dish is 'Twin Winter Vegetables', because both bamboo shoots and mushrooms are at their best during the winter season. For that reason, try using canned winter bamboo shoots and extra 'fat' mushrooms.

SERVES 4

Ingredients
50g/2oz dried Chinese mushrooms (shiitake)
285g/10oz winter bamboo shoots
3 tbsp vegetable oil
1 spring onion (scallion), cut into short sections
2 tbsp light soy sauce or oyster sauce
1 tbsp Chinese rice wine or dry sherry
½ tsp light brown sugar
2 tsp cornflour (cornstarch) paste
few drops sesame oil

1 Soak the mushrooms in cold water for at least 3 hours, then squeeze dry and discard any hard stalks, reserving the water. Cut the mushrooms in half, or quarters if they are large – keep them whole if small.

2 Rinse and drain the bamboo shoots, then cut them into small, wedge-shaped pieces.

3 Heat the oil in a preheated wok and stir-fry the mushrooms and bamboo shoots for about 1 minute. Add the spring onion (scallion) and seasonings with about 2–3 tbsp of the mushroom water. Bring to the boil and braise for another minute or so, then thicken the gravy with the cornflour (cornstarch) paste and sprinkle with the sesame oil.

Stir-fried Tomatoes, Cucumber and Eggs

Chao San Wei

The cucumber can be replaced by a green (bell) pepper or courgette (zucchini) if preferred.

SERVES 4

Ingredients
175g/6oz firm tomatoes, peeled
⅓ cucumber, unpeeled
4 eggs
1 tsp salt
1 spring onion (scallion), finely chopped
4 tbsp vegetable oil
2 tsp Chinese rice wine or dry sherry (optional)

1 Halve the tomatoes and cucumber, then cut across into small wedges. In a bowl, beat the eggs with a pinch of the salt and a few pieces of the spring onion (scallion).

2 Heat about half of the oil in a preheated wok, then lightly scramble the eggs over a moderate heat until set, but not too dry. Remove and keep warm.

3 Heat the remaining oil over a high heat, add the vegetables and stir-fry for 1 minute. Add the remaining salt, then the scrambled eggs and wine or sherry, if using.

Noodles in Soup

Tang Mein

In China, noodles in soup (*Tang Mein*) are far more popular than Fried Noodles (*Chow Mein*). This is a basic recipe which you can adapt by using different ingredients for the 'dressing'.

SERVES 4

Ingredients

225g/8oz chicken breast fillet, pork fillet, or ready-cooked meat
3–4 Chinese dried mushrooms (shiitake), soaked
115g/4oz sliced bamboo shoots, drained
115g/4oz spinach leaves, lettuce hearts, or Chinese leaves
2 spring onions (scallions)
350g/12oz dried egg noodles
575ml/1 pint/2½ cups Basic Stock
2 tbsp vegetable oil
1 tsp salt
½ tsp light brown sugar
1 tbsp light soy sauce
2 tsp Chinese rice wine or dry sherry
few drops sesame oil

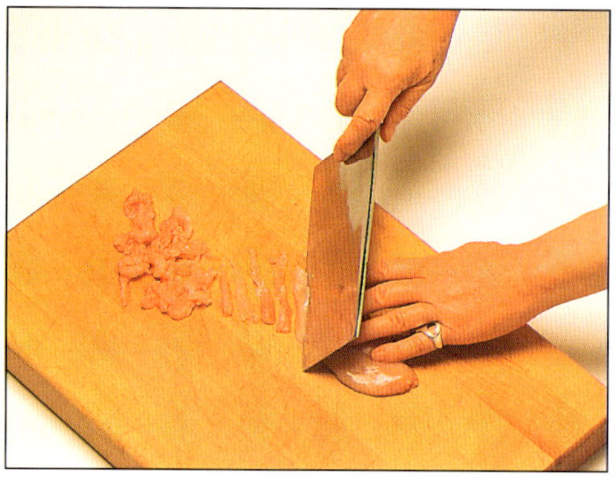

1 Thinly shred the meat. Squeeze dry the mushrooms and discard any hard stalks. Thinly shred the mushrooms, bamboo shoots, greens and spring onions (scallions).

2 Cook the noodles in boiling water according to the instructions on the packet, then drain and rinse under cold water. Place in a serving bowl.

3 Bring the stock to the boil and pour over the noodles; keep warm.

4 Heat the oil in a preheated wok, add about half of the spring onions (scallions) and the meat, and stir-fry for about 1 minute.

5 Add the mushrooms, bamboo shoots and greens and stir-fry for 1 minute. Add all the seasonings and blend well.

6 Pour the 'dressing' over the noodles, garnish with the remaining spring onions (scallions) and serve.

Plain Rice

Pai Fan

Use long grain or patna rice, or fragrant rice from Thailand. Allow 50–55g/2oz/⅓ cup raw rice per person.

SERVES 4

Ingredients
225g/8oz/1⅓ cups rice
about 250ml/8fl oz/1 cup cold water
pinch of salt
½ tsp vegetable oil

1 Wash and rinse the rice. Place the rice in a saucepan and add the water. There should be no more than 2cm/⅔in of water above the surface of the rice.

2 Bring to the boil, add the salt and oil, then stir to prevent the rice sticking to the bottom of the pan. Reduce the heat to very, very low and cook for 15–20 minutes, covered.

3 Remove from the heat and leave to stand for 10 minutes. Fluff up the rice with a fork or spoon just before serving.

Egg Fried Rice

Dan Chao Fan

Use rice with a fairly firm texture. Ideally, the raw rice should be soaked in water for a short time before cooking.

SERVES 4

Ingredients
3 eggs
1 tsp salt
2 spring onions (scallions), finely chopped
2–3 tbsp vegetable oil
450g/1lb cooked rice
115g/4oz green peas

1 In a bowl, lightly beat the eggs with a pinch of the salt and a few pieces of the spring onions (scallions).

2 Heat the oil in a preheated wok, and lightly scramble the eggs.

3 Add the rice and stir to make sure that each grain of rice is separated. Add the remaining salt, spring onions (scallions) and the peas. Blend well and serve.

Pork Dumplings

Jiao Zi

These dumplings make a good starter to a multi-course meal when shallow-fried. They can also be served on their own as a snack, if steamed, or as a complete meal when poached in large quantities.

MAKES ABOUT 80–90 DUMPLINGS

Ingredients

450g/1lb/4 cups plain (all-purpose) flour
about 450ml/¾ pint/2 cups water
flour, for dusting

Filling

450g/1lb Chinese leaves or white cabbage
450g/1lb minced (ground) pork
1 tbsp finely-chopped spring onions (scallions)
1 tsp finely-chopped fresh ginger
2 tsp salt
1 tsp light brown sugar
2 tbsp light soy sauce
1 tbsp Chinese rice wine or dry sherry
2 tsp sesame oil

Dip Sauce

2 tbsp red chilli oil
1 tbsp light soy sauce
1 tsp finely-chopped garlic
1 tbsp finely-chopped spring onions (scallions)

Combine all the ingredients in a small bowl, and serve with Pork Dumplings.

1 Sift the flour into a bowl, then slowly pour in the water and mix to a firm dough. Knead until smooth and soft, then cover with a damp cloth and set aside for 25–30 minutes.

2 For the filling, blanch the cabbage leaves until soft. Drain and finely chop. Mix the cabbage with the remaining ingredients

3 Lightly dust a work surface with the flour. Knead and roll the dough into a long sausage about 2.5cm/1in in diameter. Cut the sausage into about 80–90 small pieces and flatten each piece with the palm of your hand.

4 Using a rolling pin, roll out each piece into a thin pancake about 6cm/2.5in in diameter.

5 Place about 1½ tbsp of the filling in the centre of each pancake and fold into a half-moon-shaped pouch.

6 Pinch the edges firmly so that the dumpling is tightly sealed.

Shallow-frying: Heat 3 tbsp of oil in a wok or frying pan. Place the dumplings in rows in the oil and fry over a medium heat for 2–3 minutes.

Steaming: Place the dumplings on a bed of lettuce leaves on the rack of a bamboo steamer and steam for 10–12 minutes on a high heat. Serve hot with a dip sauce.

Poaching: Cook the dumplings in about 150ml/¼ pint/⅔ cup salted boiling water for 2 minutes. Remove from the heat, and leave the dumplings in the water for about 15 minutes.

Special Fried Rice

Yangchow Chao Fan

Special Fried Rice is more elaborate than Egg Fried Rice, and almost a meal in itself.

SERVES 4

Ingredients
50g/2oz peeled and cooked prawns (shrimp)
50g/2oz cooked ham
115g/4oz green peas
3 eggs
1 tsp salt
2 spring onions (scallions), finely chopped
4 tbsp vegetable oil
1 tbsp light soy sauce
1 tbsp Chinese rice wine or dry sherry
450g/1lb cooked rice

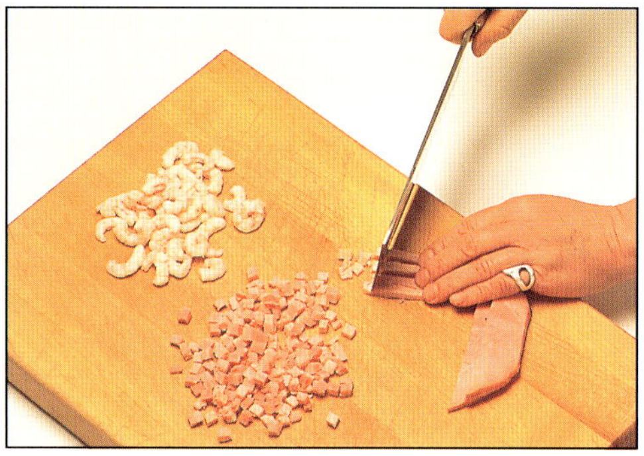

1 Pat dry the prawns (shrimp) with absorbent paper. Cut the ham into small dice about the same size as the peas.

2 In a bowl, lightly beat the eggs with a pinch of the salt and a few pieces of the spring onions (scallions).

3 Heat about half of the oil in a preheated wok, stir-fry the peas, prawns (shrimp) and ham for 1 minute, then add the soy sauce and wine or sherry. Remove and keep warm.

4 Heat the remaining oil in the wok and lightly scramble the eggs. Add the rice and stir to make sure that each grain of rice is separated. Add the remaining salt, spring onions (scallions) and the prawns (shrimp), ham and peas. Blend well and serve either hot or cold.

Wonton Soup

Wun Tun Tang

In China, wonton soup is served as a snack or Dim Sum rather than as a soup course during a large meal.

SERVES 4

Ingredients

175g/6oz pork, not too lean, coarsely chopped
50g/2oz peeled prawns (shrimp), finely minced (ground)
1 tsp light brown sugar
1 tbsp Chinese rice wine or dry sherry
1 tbsp light soy sauce
1 tsp finely-chopped spring onions (scallions)
1 tsp finely-chopped fresh ginger
24 ready-made wonton skins
about 700ml/1 ¼ pints/3 cups Basic Stock
1 tbsp light soy sauce
finely-chopped spring onions (scallions), to garnish

1 In a bowl, mix the pork and prawns (shrimp) with the sugar, wine or sherry, soy sauce, spring onions (scallions) and ginger. Blend well and leave to stand for 25–30 minutes.

2 Place about 1 tsp of the filling at the centre of each wonton skin.

3 Wet and join the edges of each wonton, pressing down with your fingers to seal, then fold each wonton over.

4 To cook, bring the stock to a rolling boil in a wok or saucepan, add the wontons and cook for 4–5 minutes. Season with the soy sauce and garnish with the spring onions (scallions). Serve.

Seafood Chow Mein

Hai Wei Chao Mein

This basic recipe can be adapted using different items for the 'dressing'.

SERVES 4

Ingredients

85g/3oz squid, cleaned
85g/3oz uncooked prawns (shrimp)
3–4 fresh scallops
½ egg white
1 tbsp cornflour (cornstarch) paste
250g/9oz egg noodles
5–6 tbsp vegetable oil
50g/2oz mange-tout (snow peas)
½ tsp salt
½ tsp light brown sugar
1 tbsp Chinese rice wine or dry sherry
2 tbsp light soy sauce
2 spring onions (scallions), finely shredded
Basic Stock, if necessary
few drops sesame oil

1 Open up the squid and, using a sharp knife, score the inside in a criss-cross pattern. Cut the squid into pieces each about the size of a postage stamp. Soak the squid in a bowl of boiling water until all the pieces curl up. Rinse in cold water and drain.

2 Peel the prawns (shrimp) and cut each in half lengthways.

3 Cut each scallop into 3–4 slices. Mix the scallops and prawns (shrimp) with the egg white and cornflour (cornstarch) paste.

4 Cook the noodles in boiling water according to the instructions on the packet, then drain and rinse under cold water. Mix with about 1 tbsp of the oil.

5 Heat about 2–3 tbsp of the oil in a wok until hot. Stir-fry the mange-tout (snow peas) and seafood for about 2 minutes then add the salt, sugar, wine or sherry, half of the soy sauce and about half of the spring onions (scallions); blend well and add a little stock, if necessary. Remove and keep warm.

6 Heat the remaining oil in the wok and stir-fry the noodles for 2–3 minutes with the remaining soy sauce. Place in a large serving dish, pour the 'dressing' on top, garnish with the remaining spring onions (scallions) and sprinkle with sesame oil. Serve hot or cold.

富
貴
福

Thin Pancakes

Bao Bing

Thin pancakes are not too difficult to make, but quite a lot of practice and patience is needed to achieve the perfect result. Nowadays, even restaurants buy frozen ready-made ones from Chinese supermarkets. If you decide to use ready-made pancakes, or are reheating home-made ones, steam them for about 5 minutes, or microwave on high (650 watts) for 1–2 minutes.

MAKES 24–30

Ingredients

450g/1lb/4 cups plain (all-purpose) flour
about 300ml/½ pint/1 ¼ cups boiling water
1 tsp vegetable oil
flour, for dusting

Cook's tip

Cooked pancakes can be stored in the refrigerator for several days.

1 Sift the flour into a mixing bowl, then pour in the boiling water very gently, stirring as you pour. Mix with the oil and knead the mixture into a firm dough. Cover with a damp towel and let stand for about 30 minutes. Lightly dust a work surface with flour.

2 Knead the dough for about 5–8 minutes or until smooth, then divide it into 3 equal portions. Roll out each portion into a long 'sausage', cut each into 8–10 pieces and roll each into a ball. Using your palm, press each piece into a flat pancake. With a rolling pin, gently roll each into a 15cm/6in circle.

3 Heat an ungreased frying pan until hot, then reduce the heat to low and place the pancakes, one at a time, in the pan. Remove the pancakes when small brown spots appear on the underside. Keep under a damp cloth until all the pancakes are cooked.

Red Bean Paste Pancakes

Hong Dao Guo Ping

If you are unable to find red bean paste, sweetened chestnut purée or mashed dates are possible substitutes.

SERVES 4

Ingredients

about 8 tbsp sweetened red bean paste
8 Thin Pancakes
2–3 tbsp vegetable oil
granulated or caster (superfine) sugar, to serve

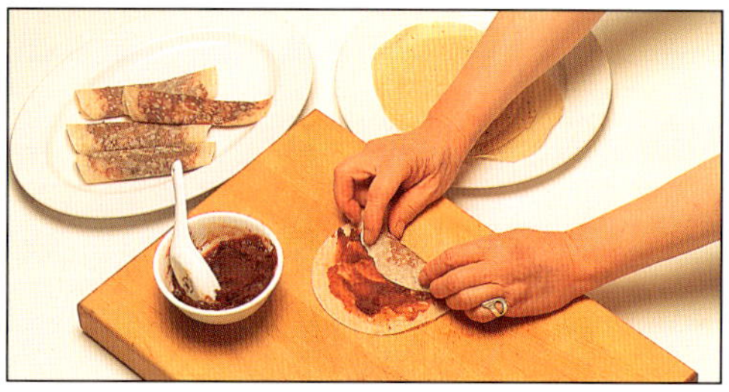

1 Spread about 1 tbsp of the red bean paste over about three-quarters of each pancake, then roll each pancake over three or four times.

2 Heat the oil in a wok or frying pan and shallow-fry the pancake rolls until golden brown, turning once.

3 Cut each pancake roll into 3–4 pieces and sprinkle with sugar to serve.

Toffee Apples

Ba Tsu Ping Guo

A variety of fruits, such as banana and pineapple, can be prepared and cooked the same way.

SERVES 4

Ingredients

4 firm eating apples, peeled and cored
115g/4oz/1 cup plain (all-purpose) flour
about 100ml/4fl oz/½ cup cold water
1 egg, beaten
vegetable oil, for deep-frying, plus 2 tbsp for the toffee
115g/4oz/½ cup granulated or caster (superfine) sugar

1 Cut each apple into 8 pieces. Dust each piece with a little of the flour.

2 Sift the remaining flour into a mixing bowl, then slowly add the cold water and stir to make a smooth batter. Add the beaten egg and blend well.

3 Heat the oil in a wok. Dip the apple pieces in the batter and deep-fry for about 3 minutes or until golden. Remove and drain.

4 Heat 2 tbsp of the oil in the wok, add the sugar and stir continuously until the sugar has caramelized. Quickly add the apple pieces and blend well so that each piece of apple is coated with the 'toffee'. Dip the apple pieces in cold water to harden before serving.

Almond Curd Junket

Xing Ren Tou Fou

Also known as Almond Float, this is usually made from agar-agar or isinglass, though gelatine can also be used.

SERVES 4–6

Ingredients

7g/¼oz agar-agar or isinglass or 25g/1oz gelatine powder
about 575ml/1 pint/2½ cups water
4 tbsp granulated or caster (superfine) sugar
300ml/½ pint/1¼ cups milk
1 tsp almond essence (extract)
fresh or canned mixed fruit salad with syrup, to serve

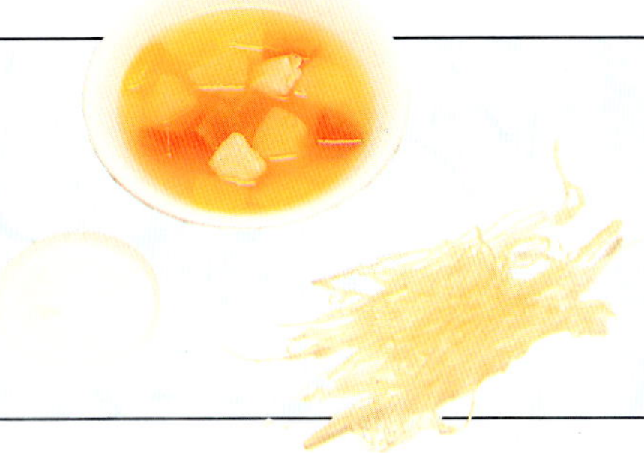

1 In a saucepan, dissolve the agar-agar or isinglass in about half of the water over a gentle heat. This will take at least 10 minutes. If using gelatine, follow the instructions.

2 In a separate saucepan, dissolve the sugar in the remaining water over a medium heat. Add the milk and the almond essence (extract), blending well, but do not boil.

3 Mix the milk and sugar with the agar-agar or isinglass mixture in a large serving bowl. When cool, place in the refrigerator for 2–3 hours to set.

4 To serve, cut the 'junket' into small cubes and spoon into a serving dish or into individual bowls. Pour the fruit salad, with the syrup, over the junket and serve.

TASTE OF ASIA

STEVEN WHEELER

The cooking of South-east Asia provides a fascinating glimpse of its people and way of life. This section includes recipes from Thailand, Vietnam, Malaysia, Singapore, Indonesia, the Philippines and Japan and the dishes reveal how each country has established its own style of eating. Characteristics vary among the three main religions – Muslim, Buddhist and Christian – but it is accepted by all that ingredients must be fresh and full of flavour. It is this commitment to perfect ingredients that puts life into much of the cooking of these regions. With such a wide variety of produce now available in Western supermarkets, there is every opportunity to explore a new side to our own cooking.

THE PRINCIPLES OF SOUTH-EAST ASIAN COOKING

The cuisines of the countries of South-east Asia vary considerably, from the Spanish-influenced dishes of the Philippines to the dietary demands of the Buddhist and Muslim faiths. One practice common to most countries is the method of serving. Mealtimes are relaxed, informal affairs, with all dishes arriving at the table at the same time. Guests help themselves, either with chopsticks or with the left hand. Dishes should offer a balance of textures and aromas, and ingredients must be fresh and flavoursome.

EQUIPMENT AND UTENSILS

Bamboo skewers (1) Bamboo skewers are widely used for barbecues and grilled (broiled) foods. They are disposed of after use.
Chopping board (2) It is worth investing in a solid chopping board. Thick boards provide the best surface and will last for many years.
Citrus zesting tool (3) The outer peel or zest of citrus fruit imparts a distinctive flavour to many South-east Asian dishes. This tool is designed to remove the zest while leaving behind the bitter white pith of the fruit.
Cleavers (4, 5) At first sight cleavers may look and feel out of place for domestic use, but they are ideally suited to fine chopping and transferring ingredients from chopping board to wok. Small cleavers are used mostly for chopping and shredding fruits and vegetables. They can also be used for the preparation of meat and fish.
Cooking chopsticks (6) Extra long chopsticks can be used to stir ingredients in the wok. Their length permits you to keep at a distance from the cooking ingredients.
Draining wire (7) Draining wires are designed to rest on the side of a wok. They are used mainly for deep-frying.
Food processor (8) The food processor is a useful alternative to the more traditional pestle and mortar, and is suitable for grinding wet spices.
Large chopping knife (9) If you are not comfortable using a cleaver, a large Western-style chopping knife can be used instead. Choose one with a deep blade to give you the best control.
Rice paddle (10) These are generally made from a large section of bamboo. Rice paddles are used to stir and fluff rice after cooking. A pair of chopsticks may also be used for fluffing rice.
Rice saucepan and lid (11) A good rice saucepan with a close-fitting lid is an essential piece of equipment for South-east Asian cooking. Stainless steel pans with a heavy base are best.
Sharpening stone (12) Sharpening stones are used for sharpening knives and cleavers. They are available from hardware stores and should be immersed in water before use.

Stainless steel skimmer (13) Stainless steel skimmers should be used when strong flavours are likely to affect bare metal utensils.
Wire skimmer (14) Wire skimmers are used to retrieve cooked food from boiling water or hot fat. Bare metal skimmers can retain strong flavours and are therefore not recommended for use with fish-based liquids.
Wok (15) The wok is used in all parts of South-east Asia. The shape of the wok allows deep-frying and stir-frying in a minimum of fat, thus retaining the freshness and flavour of ingredients.
Wok ladle (16) Wok ladles are used to stir liquid ingredients while cooking. They are also useful for transferring cooked food to serving bowls.
Wok lid (17) Wok lids have a large domed surface and are designed to retain moisture given off during cooking. The steam held beneath the lid is often used to keep ingredients from taking on too much colour when frying.
Wok scoop (18) The wok scoop is designed to make contact with the curved surface of the wok. Most scoops are made of stainless steel and will not retain strong flavours.

INGREDIENTS

Acorn squash (1) Many varieties of squash and pumpkin are grown in South-east Asia. They are used mainly as a vegetable, but may sometimes be used in desserts.
Aubergine (egg plant) (2) The dark-skinned aubergine (egg plant) is included in a variety of slow-cooking dishes and is renowned for its smooth texture. Large aubergines can be bitter and should be salted before use.
Banana leaves (3) The banana leaf is widely used for wrapping ingredients before cooking. If banana leaves are unavailable use aluminium foil.
Cardamom pods (4) Cardamom is a member of the ginger family. The sweetest flavour is contained in the seed of the olive-green pods and is usually ground with other spices. Large black pods have a bitter flavour and combine well with sweet curry ingredients.
Celophane noodles (bean thread noodles) (5) These fine noodles are usually made from mung bean flour, although some varieties contain rice, soy and pea starch. When boiled, they have a smooth texture and are an important ingredient for spring roll stuffings. Celophane noodles become crispy when deep-fried.
Chillies (6) Used in moderation, chillies provide the hot sweet glow typical of many South-east Asian curries and dipping sauces. As a rule, small chillies are the hottest and green varieties tend to be less sweet than red.
Chinese red onions (shallots) (7) The Chinese red onion has a strong flavour despite its small size. If unavailable, use golden shallots or an increased quantity of white onions.
Cinnamon (cassia) (8) Tightly-curled cinnamon has a smooth, warm flavour which is given to sweet and savoury cooking. Cassia, pictured here, has a more robust flavour and is used with other strong spices.
Coconut (9) The coconut is essential to many dishes of South-east Asia. Coconut milk is obtained from the white flesh of the nut and is both rich and smooth-tasting.
Coriander leaf (10) Fresh coriander has a strong, pungent smell that combines well with other rich flavours. The white coriander root is used when the green colouring is not required. Bunches of coriander will keep for up to five days in a jar of water. Cover with a plastic bag and store in the refrigerator.

Coriander seeds (11) Coriander is common to all styles of cooking throughout South-east Asia. The seeds are dry-fried with other spices to release the unique flavour.
Cumin seeds (12) Cumin has a similar ribbed shape to fennel seed and comes from the parsley family. It has a warm, heady flavour that combines well with coriander and is widely used in beef dishes. Cumin seeds are usually dry-fried before use.
Egg noodles (13) Egg noodles are made from wheat flour and are sold dried in single portions. When cooked, egg noodles are used in dishes such as Mee Goreng from Singapore and Pansit Guisado from the Philippines.
Enokitake mushrooms (14) These slender mushrooms have a sweet, peppery taste and are used to enhance the clear broths of Japan. Enokitake can also be eaten raw as a salad ingredient.
Fennel seeds (15) Plump green fennel seeds are similar in character to cumin, and have a sweet aniseed flavour. The seeds combine well with peanuts and the zest of citrus fruit, and are an aid to digestion.
Fermented shrimp paste (Blachan, Kapi) (16) The smell of fermented shrimp paste by itself is quite repellent, but when blended with other spices, shrimp paste loses its unpleasant flavour and provides the unique taste and character typical of many South-east Asian sauces.
Galingal (17) Galingal is a member of the ginger family and grows in a similar root shape. The fibrous root has a resinous quality similar to pine and combines well with fish dishes. Dried galingal is increasingly available. It should be soaked in boiling water before use.
Garlic (18) Garlic marries well with the strong pungent flavours of the East. Individual cloves can be finely chopped or crushed in a garlic press.
Ginger (19) Fresh ginger is well-known in the West for its warm, pungent flavour. In its native region of South-east Asia, it features in many intriguing spice combinations.
Lime leaves (20) Lime leaves are an essential part of many slow-cooking dishes. The deep, citrus flavour of the leaf combines especially well with rich coconut milk and hot chilli spices.
Limes (21) Limes are widely used to add sharpness to finished dishes. Wedges are often served at the table so that guests may season dishes to taste.
Lemon grass (22) Fresh lemon grass is common to many dishes throughout South-east Asia. Its flavour has a rich lemon quality that combines well with other wet spices. Lemon grass is also available dried.
Lychees (23) The brittle skin of this fine fruit peels away like the shell of a boiled egg. The white scented fruit has a clean fresh taste and is served at the end of a meal.
Mandarin oranges (24) The flavour obtained from the outer zest of the mandarin orange combines well with the rich spices of the East. Satsumas and clementines are also suitable.
Mango (25) The mango offers a rich scented flavour to both sweet and savoury dishes. Mangoes are ripe when the green skin is flushed with red.
Mint (26) Varieties of mint feature in the cooking of Vietnam. The fresh flavour combines particularly well with coriander leaf, peanuts and the zest of mandarin orange. Mint is also used in sweet and savoury fruit salads.
Moolie (27) The giant white radish is common to many Japanese dishes and is ideal for making flower garnishes. If unavailable, white turnip or red radish may be substituted.
Nutmeg (28) The flavour of nutmeg is obtained by grating the nut on a fine grater. The fresh oils that are released provide strength and character to many well-known spice mixtures.
Pickled ginger (29) Thinly-sliced pink pickled ginger is served as a condiment with Japanese sushi, grilled fish and beef. It has a warm, sweet flavour and is found in most oriental food stores.
Pineapple (30) Pineapple offers a clean refreshing flavour and is an aid to digestion. It may be served at the end of a meal, or as an ingredient in a main dish.
Seaweed (31) Dried seaweed is widely used in Japanese cooking to impart a salty, rich flavour of the sea. Nori is a dried, flat seaweed used for making sushi. Kelp is also dried and should be soaked in water before use.
Sesame seeds (32) White sesame seeds are widely used in Japanese cooking. The seeds should be dry-fried, to release their flavour. Toasted seeds are often ground finely to thicken and enrich sauces.

Shiitaki mushrooms (33) Fresh shiitaki mushrooms have a rich, meaty flavour that combines especially well with shellfish and poultry. Shiitake are widely available dried and yield a good flavour when soaked in boiling water.
Sichuan pepper (34) Sichuan pepper has a warm, fruity flavour without the intense heat of white or black peppercorns. To obtain the best flavour, Sichuan pepper should be dry-fried and coarsely ground before use.
Somen noodles (35) Somen noodles are made from wheat flour and are an important part of the Japanese diet. It is most common to find somen noodles in a flavoursome chicken broth.
Spring onions (scallions) (36) Spring onions (scallions) have a milder flavour than onions and are suited to dishes that are cooked quickly. Both the white and green parts are used.
Star anise (37) This attractive spice is sold in star-shaped pods and carries the soft scent of aniseed. The pods are used whole or ground to flavour sweet and savoury dishes.
Star fruit (38) Star fruit have a sweet scented flavour when ripe and can be eaten cooked or raw in fruit salads.
Sweet potato (39) The sweet richness of this red tuber marries well with the hot and sour flavours of South-east Asia. In Japan, the sweet potato is used to make delicious candies and sweetmeats.
Tomatoes (40) Both ripe and under-ripe tomatoes feature in the cooking of South-east Asia. Under-ripe fruit are used in slow-cooking meat dishes and lend a special sour taste.

THAILAND

Hot Chilli Duck with Crab Meat and Cashew Nut Sauce

Bhed Sune Khan

This dish may be served with Thai rice and a dish of Thai Dipping Sauce.

SERVES 4–6

Ingredients

2.7kg/6lb duck
1.1 litre/2 pints/5 cups water, to cover
2 lime leaves
1 tsp salt
2–3 small red chillies, seeded and finely chopped
5 tsp sugar
½ tsp salt
2 tbsp coriander seeds
1 tsp caraway seeds
115g/4oz raw cashew nuts, chopped
1 piece lemon grass, 7.5cm/3in long, shredded
1 piece galingal or fresh ginger, 2.5cm/1in long, peeled and finely chopped
2 cloves garlic, crushed
4 shallots, or 1 medium onion, finely chopped
1 piece shrimp paste, 2cm/¾in square
25g/1oz coriander white root or stem, finely chopped
175g/6oz frozen white crab meat, thawed
50g/2oz creamed coconut
1 small bunch coriander, chopped, to garnish

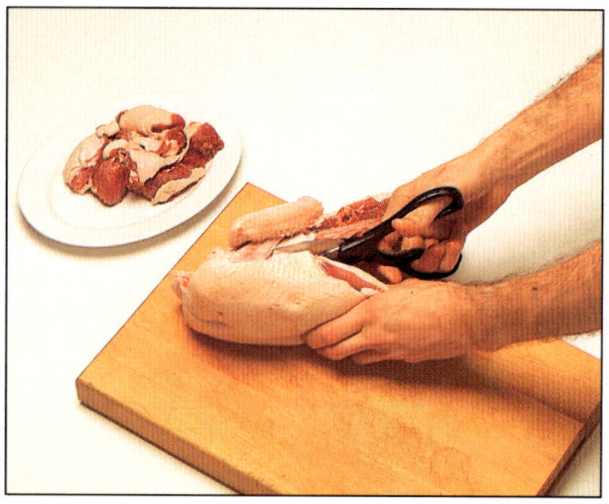

1 To portion the duck into manageable pieces, first remove the legs. Separate the thighs from the drumsticks and chop each thigh and drumstick into 2 pieces. Trim away the lower half of the duck with kitchen scissors. Cut the breast piece in half down the middle, then chop each half into 4 pieces.

2 Put the duck flesh and bones into a large saucepan and cover with the water. Add the lime leaves and salt, bring to the boil and simmer, uncovered, for 35–40 minutes, until the meat is tender. Discard the duck bones, skim off the fat from the stock and set aside.

3 To make the curry sauce, grind the red chillies together with the sugar and salt using a pestle and mortar or a food processor. Dry-fry the coriander and caraway seeds and the cashew nuts in a wok to release their flavour, about 1–2 minutes. Add the chillies, the lemon grass, galingal or ginger, garlic and shallots or onion and reduce to a smooth paste. Add the shrimp paste and coriander.

4 Add a cup of the liquid in which the duck was cooked and blend to make a thin paste.

5 Stir the curry seasoning in with the duck, bring to the boil and simmer, uncovered, for 20–25 minutes.

6 Add the crab meat and creamed coconut and simmer briefly. Turn out onto an attractive serving dish, decorate with chopped coriander.

Thai Grilled Chicken

Kai Yang

Thai grilled chicken is especially delicious when cooked on the barbecue. It should be served with a dipping sauce.

SERVES 4–6

Ingredients
900g/2lb chicken drumsticks or thighs
1 tsp whole black peppercorns
½ tsp caraway or cumin seeds
4 tsp sugar
2 tsp paprika
1 piece fresh ginger, 2cm/¾in long
3 cloves garlic, crushed
15g/½oz coriander, white root or stem, finely chopped
3 tbsp vegetable oil
salt, to season
6–8 lettuce leaves, to serve
½ cucumber, cut into strips, to garnish
4 spring onions (scallions), trimmed, to garnish
2 limes, quartered, to garnish

1 Chop through the narrow end of each drumstick with a heavy knife. Score the chicken pieces deeply to allow the marinade to penetrate. Set aside in a shallow bowl.

2 Grind the peppercorns, caraway or cumin seeds and sugar in a pestle and mortar or a food processor. Add the paprika, ginger, garlic, coriander and oil and grind.

3 Spread the marinade over the chicken and chill for 6 hours. Cook the chicken under a moderate grill for 20 minutes, turning once. Season, arrange on lettuce, and garnish.

Thai Chicken and Prawn (Shrimp) Soup

Tom Yum Gung

In Thailand a soup such as this is often served with a dry curry to help balance the texture of the curry dish.

SERVES 4–6

Ingredients
2 × 175g/6oz chicken breasts, on the bone
½ chicken stock cube
400g/14oz canned coconut milk
1 piece galingal or fresh ginger, 2cm/¾in long finely chopped
1 piece lemon grass, 7.5cm/3in long
2 cloves garlic, crushed
2 tbsp chopped coriander root, or stem
2–3 small red chillies, seeded and finely chopped
2 tbsp fish sauce
5 tsp sugar
½ tsp salt
2 lime leaves
225g/8oz fresh or cooked prawn (shrimp) tails, peeled and de-veined
juice of 1 lime
4 sprigs coriander, chopped, to garnish
2 spring onions (scallions), green part only, sliced, to garnish
4 large red chillies, sliced, to garnish

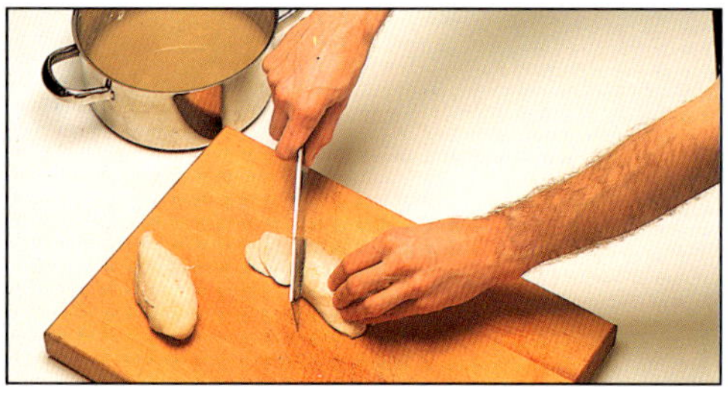

1 Cover the chicken with water, add stock cube, and simmer for 45 minutes. Slice the meat into strips (discard skin), and return to stock. Add coconut milk and simmer.

2 Blend the lemon grass, galingal or ginger, garlic, coriander and chillies. Add this to the stock with the fish sauce, sugar, salt and lime leaves. Simmer for 20 minutes.

3 Just before serving, add the prawns (shrimp) and lime juice. Simmer for 5 minutes. Decorate with the coriander, spring onions (scallions) and chillies.

Dry Beef Curry with Peanut and Lime

Nua Pad Prik

Dry curries originated from the mountainous northern regions of Thailand but are popular throughout the country. This dry beef curry is usually served with a moist dish such as Ragout of Shellfish with Sweet Scented Basil, or Thai Chicken and Prawn Soup. The curry is equally delicious made with a lean leg or shoulder of lamb.

SERVES 4–6

Ingredients
900g/2lb stewing (braising), chuck, shin or blade steak, finely chopped
400g/14oz canned coconut milk
300ml/½ pint/1¼ cups beef stock

Red curry paste
2 tbsp coriander seeds
1 tsp cumin seeds
6 green cardamom pods, seeds only
½ tsp nutmeg powder
¼ tsp clove powder
½ tsp cinnamon powder
4 tsp paprika
zest of 1 mandarin orange, finely chopped
4–5 small red chillies, seeded and finely chopped
5 tsp sugar
½ tsp salt
1 piece lemon grass, 10cm/4in long, shredded
3 cloves garlic, crushed
1 piece galingal or fresh ginger, 2cm/¾in long, peeled and finely chopped
4 red shallots or 1 medium red onion, finely chopped
1 piece shrimp paste, 2cm/¾in square
50g/2oz coriander, white root or stem, chopped
juice of 2½ limes
2 tbsp vegetable oil
2 tbsp chunky peanut butter
1 lime, sliced, to garnish
1 large red chilli, sliced, to garnish
1 small bunch coriander, shredded, to garnish

1 Place the meat in the freezer for 30–40 minutes until firm. Slice the meat thinly, cut into strips and chop finely. Strain the coconut milk into a bowl.

2 Place the thin part and half of the thick part of the milk in a large saucepan. Add the beef, and beef stock, bring to the boil, cover and simmer for 50 minutes.

3 To make the curry paste, dry-fry the coriander, cumin seeds and cardamom in a wok for 1–2 minutes. Combine with the nutmeg, clove, cinnamon, paprika and the zest of the mandarin orange. Pound the chillies with the sugar and salt. Add the chilli paste, lemon grass, garlic, galingal or ginger, shallots or onion and shrimp paste. Lastly add the coriander, juice of ½ lime and oil.

4 Place a cupful of the cooking liquid in a wok, and add 2–3 tbsp of the curry paste according to taste. Boil rapidly until the liquid has reduced completely. Add the remainder of the coconut milk, the peanut butter and the beef. Simmer, uncovered, for 15–20 minutes. Stir in the remaining lime juice. Serve decorated with the lime, chilli and coriander.

Green Curry Coconut Chicken

Kaeng Khieu Wan Gai

The recipe given here for green curry paste is a complex one and therefore takes time to make properly. Pork, prawns (shrimp) and fish can all be used instead of chicken, but cooking times must be adjusted accordingly.

SERVES 4–6

Ingredients

1.1kg/2½lb chicken, without giblets
575ml/1 pint/2½ cups canned coconut milk
425ml/¾ pint/1½ cups chicken stock
2 lime leaves

Green curry paste

2 tsp coriander seeds
½ tsp caraway or cumin seeds
3–4 medium green chillies, finely chopped
4 tsp sugar
2 tsp salt
1 piece lemon grass, 7.5cm/3in long
1 piece galingal or fresh ginger, 2cm/¾in long, peeled and finely chopped
3 cloves garlic, crushed
4 shallots or 1 medium onion, finely chopped
1 piece shrimp paste, 2cm/¾in square
3 tbsp coriander leaves, finely chopped
3 tbsp fresh mint or basil, finely chopped
½ tsp nutmeg powder
2 tbsp vegetable oil
350g/12oz sweet potatoes, peeled and roughly chopped
350g/12oz winter squash, peeled, seeded and roughly chopped
115g/4oz French beans, topped, tailed and halved
1 small bunch coriander, shredded, to garnish

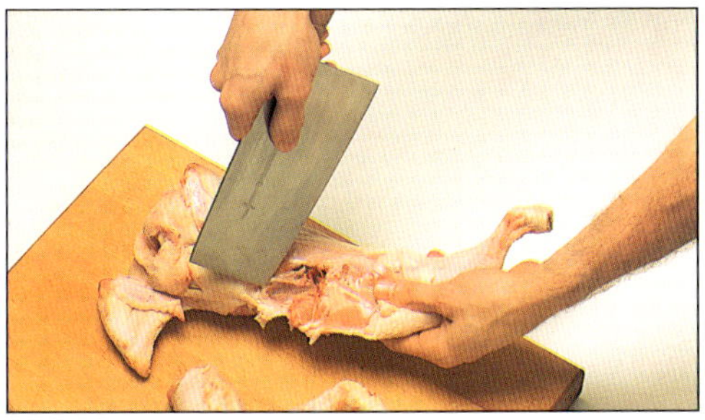

1 To prepare the chicken, remove the legs, then separate the thighs from the drumsticks. Separate the lower part of the chicken carcass by cutting through the rib section with kitchen scissors. Divide the breast part in half down the middle, then chop each half in two. Remove skin from all pieces and set aside.

2 Strain the coconut milk into a bowl, reserving the thick part. Place the chicken in a stainless steel or enamel saucepan, cover with the thin part of the coconut milk and the stock. Add the lime leaves, and simmer uncovered for 40 minutes. Remove the chicken from the bone and set aside.

3 Dry-fry the coriander and caraway or cumin seeds. Grind the chillies with the sugar and salt to make a smooth paste. Combine the seeds from the wok with the chillies, the lemon grass, galingal or ginger, garlic and shallots, then grind smoothly. Add the next 5 ingredients.

4 Place a cupful of the cooking liquid in a large wok. Add 4–5 tbsp of the curry paste to the liquid according to taste. Boil rapidly until the liquid has reduced completely. Add the chicken stock, chicken meat, sweet potatoes, squash and beans. Simmer for 10–15 minutes until potatoes are cooked. Just before serving, stir in the thick part of the coconut milk and simmer gently to thicken. Serve decorated with the shredded coriander.

Thai Steamed Fish with a Citrus Marinade

Pla Chien

Serve Thai rice or fine rice noodles as an accompaniment to this dish.

SERVES 4–6

Ingredients
- 1.3kg/3lb parrot fish, pomfret, plaice or sea bream, gutted with heads on
- 2 small red chillies, seeded and finely chopped
- 1 tbsp sugar
- 2 cloves garlic, crushed
- 3 spring onions (scallions), white part only, chopped
- 1 piece fresh galingal or fresh ginger, 2.5cm/1in long, peeled and finely chopped
- juice of 1 mandarin orange
- zest of 1 mandarin orange, finely chopped
- 1 tbsp tamarind sauce
- 1 tbsp fish sauce
- 2 tbsp light soy sauce
- juice of 1 lime
- 1 tbsp vegetable oil
- 2 limes, quartered, to garnish
- 4 spring onion (scallion) curls, to garnish

1 Wash the fish thoroughly and slash 3–4 times with a sharp knife on each side to allow the marinade to penetrate deeply. Place the fish in a shallow dish that will fit in the base of a steamer. You can also wrap the fish loosely in foil.

2 Grind the chilli and sugar together using a pestle and mortar or food processor, add the garlic, spring onion (scallion), galingal or ginger and the zest of the mandarin orange. Combine well. Lastly add the tamarind, fish and soy sauces, the lime juice and vegetable oil, then spread over the fish. Leave to marinate for at least 1 hour.

3 Cook the fish in a covered steamer for 25–30 minutes. Lift the fish onto a serving plate and decorate with wedges of lime and spring onion (scallion).

Pork and Peanut Pick-me-ups

Ma Hor

With a Thai meal, it is not customary to have a starter. Instead, appetizers are served with drinks beforehand.

MAKES 12

Ingredients
- 1 tbsp vegetable oil
- 2 shallots, or 1 small onion, finely chopped
- 1 clove garlic, crushed
- 1 piece fresh ginger, 2cm/¾in long, peeled and finely chopped
- 1 small red chilli, seeded and finely chopped
- 150g/5oz minced (ground) pork, or the contents of 150g/5oz fresh pork sausages
- 2 tbsp peanut butter
- 1 tbsp fish sauce
- juice of ½ lime
- 4 tsp sugar
- 2 tbsp chopped coriander leaves
- 4 clementines, peeled and thickly sliced
- 6 ramboutans, or lychees, peeled and stoned (pitted)
- 1 small pineapple, peeled, cored and sliced
- 1 firm pear, peeled, cored and sliced
- 1 lime, cut into small wedges, to garnish
- 12 coriander leaves, to garnish

1 Heat the oil and fry the next 4 ingredients. Add the pork and cook for 10 minutes.

2 Add the peanut butter, fish sauce, lime juice, sugar and chopped coriander.

3 Spoon the topping onto pieces of fruit. Decorate with lime and coriander leaves.

Thai Dipping Sauce

Nam Prik

Nam Prik is the most common dipping sauce in Thailand. It has a fiery strength, so use with caution.

MAKES 120ML/4 FL OZ/½ CUP

Ingredients
1 tbsp vegetable oil
1 piece shrimp paste, 12mm/½in square, or 1 tbsp fish sauce
2 cloves garlic, finely sliced
1 piece fresh ginger, 2cm/¾in long, peeled and finely chopped
3 small red chillies, seeded and chopped
1 tbsp finely-chopped coriander root or stem
4 tsp sugar
3 tbsp dark soy sauce
juice of ½ lime

1 Heat the vegetable oil in a wok, add the shrimp paste or fish sauce, garlic, ginger and chillies and soften without colouring, for about 1–2 minutes.

2 Remove from the heat and add the coriander, sugar, soy sauce and lime juice. Nam Prik Sauce will keep in a screw-top jar for up to 10 days.

Hot Coconut Prawn (Shrimp) and Paw Paw Salad

Yam Ma-La-Kaw Prik

This dish may be served as an accompaniment to beef and chicken dishes.

SERVES 4–6

Ingredients
225g/8oz fresh or cooked prawn (shrimp) tails, peeled and de-veined
2 ripe paw paws, or papayas
225g/8oz cos, iceberg or bib lettuce leaves, Chinese leaves and young spinach
1 firm tomato, skinned, seeded and roughly chopped
3 spring onions (scallions), shredded

Dressing
1 tbsp creamed coconut
2 tbsp boiling water
6 tbsp vegetable oil
juice of 1 lime
½ tsp hot chilli sauce
2 tsp fish sauce (optional)
1 tsp sugar
1 small bunch coriander, shredded, to garnish
1 large chilli, sliced, to garnish

1 To make the dressing, place the creamed coconut in a screw-top jar and add the boiling water to soften. Add the vegetable oil, lime juice, chilli sauce, fish sauce if using and sugar. Shake well and set aside. Do not refrigerate.

2 If using fresh prawn (shrimp) tails, cover with cold water in a saucepan, bring to the boil and simmer for no longer than 2 minutes. Drain and set aside.

3 To prepare the paw paws or papayas, cut each in half from top to bottom and remove the black seeds with a teaspoon. Peel away the outer skin and cut the flesh into even-sized pieces. Wash the salad leaves and toss in a bowl. Add the other ingredients. Pour on the dressing and serve.

Red Curry Beef with Tamarind

Kang Mussaman Nuea

This red curry can also be made using diced lamb, in which case reduce the cooking time by 30 minutes.

SERVES 4–6

Ingredients
900g/2lb stewing (braising), chuck, shin or blade steak
400g/14oz canned coconut milk
300ml/½ pint/1¼ cups beef stock

Red curry paste
2 tbsp coriander seeds
1 tsp cumin seeds
6 green cardamom pods, seeds only
½ tsp nutmeg powder
¼ tsp clove powder
½ tsp cinnamon powder
4 tsp paprika
zest of 1 mandarin orange, finely chopped
4–5 small red chillies, seeded and finely chopped
5 tsp sugar
½ tsp salt
1 piece lemon grass, 10cm/4in long, shredded
3 cloves garlic, crushed
1 piece galingal or fresh ginger, 2cm/¾in long, peeled and finely chopped
4 red shallots or 1 medium red onion, finely chopped
1 piece shrimp paste, 2cm/¾in square
50g/2oz coriander, white root or stem, chopped
2 tbsp vegetable oil
350g/12oz new potatoes, peeled and roughly chopped
350g/12oz pumpkin or winter squash
200g/7oz canned bamboo shoots, sliced
2 tbsp smooth peanut butter
2 tbsp tamarind sauce
juice of 2 limes
1 small bunch coriander, to garnish

1 Cut the beef into 2.5cm/1in dice and place in a stainless steel saucepan.

2 Place the coconut milk in a fine sieve and allow the thin part of the milk to drain into a bowl. Add all the thin and half of the thick part of the coconut milk to the saucepan. Add the stock, bring to the boil and simmer uncovered for 1 hour. Strain and set aside.

3 Dry-fry the coriander, cumin seeds and cardamom in a wok for 1–2 minutes. Combine with the nutmeg, clove, cinnamon, paprika and mandarin zest, and grind. Pound the chillies with the sugar and salt. Add the chilli paste, lemon grass, garlic, galingal, shallots and shrimp paste. Add the coriander and oil and reduce.

4 Place a cupful of the cooking liquid in a large wok. Add 2–3 tbsp of the paste. Boil rapidly to reduce the liquid. Add the peanut butter and tamarind sauce. Add the beef, potatoes, pumpkin and bamboo shoots and simmer for 20–25 minutes until the potatoes are cooked. Stir in the thick part of the coconut milk and the lime juice. Return to a gentle simmer. Decorate, and serve with Thai rice.

Coconut Milk

Coconut milk is used to enrich and flavour many dishes in the Far East. Only the Japanese choose not to include it in their cooking. Coconut milk is not, as many suppose, the liquid found inside the nut. Although this thin liquid does make a refreshing drink, the coconut milk used for cooking is processed from the white flesh of the nut. If left to stand, the thick part of the milk will rise to the surface like cream. If the milk is cold the thick part of the milk will separate more easily. Choose a coconut with plenty of milk inside. Shake the nut firmly. If you cannot hear the milk sloshing around, the flesh will be difficult to remove. If you can find a coconut with its green husk and fibre attached, the flesh will almost certainly be soft and creamy white. Fresh coconut milk will keep in a cool place for up to 10 days. If kept in the refrigerator, allow to soften at room temperature before using.

MAKES 400ml/14fl oz/1¾ cups

Ingredients

2 fresh coconuts

1.1 litres/2 pints/5 cups water, off the boil

1 Hold the coconut over a bowl to collect the liquid. With the back of a large knife or cleaver, crack open the coconut by striking it cleanly.

2 Scrape out the white meat with a citrus zester or a rounded butter curler. Place the coconut meat in a food processor with half of the water.

3 Process for 1 minute, then pass through a food mill or mouli fitted with a fine disk, catching the milk in a bowl beneath. Alternatively, squeeze the coconut meat with your hands and press through a nylon strainer. Return the coconut meat to the food processor or mill with the remainder of the water, blend and press for a second time. Allow the milk to settle for 30 minutes (creamy solids will rise to the surface). Sometimes the solids should be poured off and added later as a thickener.

Cook's tip

Coconut milk can be obtained directly from coconut flesh – this gives the creamiest milk; from a can – which may be expensive; as a soluble powder and as creamed coconut which is sold in block form. Powder and creamed coconut make a poor milk, but are useful additions to sauces and dressings.

Ragout of Shellfish with Sweet Scented Basil

Po-Tak

Green curry paste can be used to accompany other dishes, such as Green Curry Coconut Chicken. Curry pastes will keep for up to 3 weeks in the refrigerator if stored in a screw-top jar.

SERVES 4–6

Ingredients
575ml/1 pint/2½ cups fresh mussels in their shells, cleaned
225g/8oz medium cuttle fish or squid
350g/12oz monkfish, hokey or red snapper, skinned
150g/5oz fresh or cooked prawn (shrimp) tails, peeled and de-veined
4 scallops, sliced (optional)
400ml/14oz canned coconut milk
300ml/½ pint/1¼ cups chicken or vegetable stock
85g/3oz French beans, trimmed and cooked
50g/2oz canned bamboo shoots, drained
1 ripe tomato, skinned, seeded and roughly chopped

Green curry paste
2 tsp coriander seeds
½ tsp caraway or cumin seeds
3–4 medium green chillies, finely chopped
4 tsp sugar
2 tsp salt
1 piece lemon grass, 7.5cm/3in long
1 piece galingal or fresh ginger, 2cm/¾in long, peeled and finely chopped
3 cloves garlic, crushed
4 shallots or 1 medium onion, finely chopped
1 piece shrimp paste, 2cm/¾in square
50g/2oz coriander leaves, finely chopped
3 tbsp fresh mint or basil, finely chopped
½ tsp nutmeg
2 tbsp vegetable oil
4 sprigs large leaf basil, torn, to garnish

1 Place the mussels in a stainless steel or enamel saucepan, add 4 tbsp of water, cover, steam open and cook for 6–8 minutes. Take ¾ of the mussels out of their shells (discard any which don't open), strain the cooking liquid and set aside.

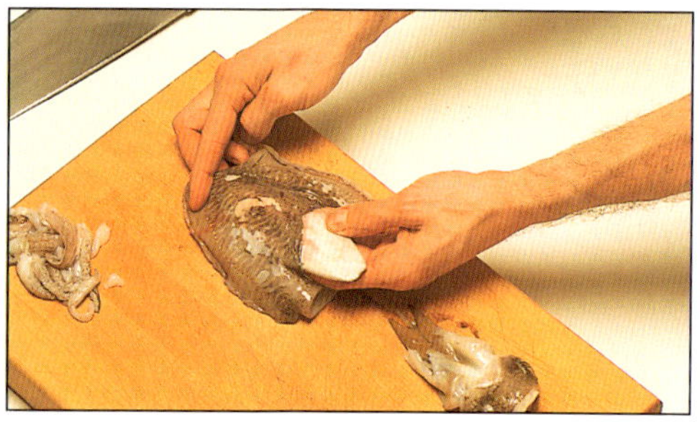

2 To prepare the cuttle fish or squid, trim off the tentacles beneath the eye. Rinse under cold running water, discarding the gut. Remove the cuttle shell from inside the body and rub off the paper-thin skin. Cut the body open and score, criss-cross, with a sharp knife. Cut into strips and set aside.

3 To make the green curry paste, dry-fry the coriander and caraway or cumin seeds in a wok to release their flavour. Grind the chillies with the sugar and salt using a pestle and mortar or food processor to make a smooth paste. Combine the seeds from the wok with the chillies, add the lemon grass, galingal or ginger, garlic and shallots or onion, then grind smoothly. Add the shrimp paste, coriander, mint or basil, nutmeg and vegetable oil. Combine well. There may seem to be a lot of coriander and mint at this stage, but their volume will reduce considerably when ground with the other spices.

4 Pour the coconut milk into a sieve. Pour the thin part of the milk together with the chicken or vegetable stock into a wok. The thick part of the coconut milk is added later. Add 4–5 tbsp of the green curry paste according to taste. You can add more paste later if you need to. Boil rapidly until the liquid has reduced completely.

5 Add the thick part of the coconut milk, then add the cuttle fish or squid and monkfish, hokey or red snapper. Simmer uncovered for 15–20 minutes. Then add the prawns (shrimp), scallops and cooked mussels with the beans, bamboo shoots and tomato. Simmer for 2–3 minutes, transfer to a bowl and decorate with the basil and chillies.

Thai Fruit and Vegetable Salad

Yam Chomphu

This fruit salad is presented with the main course and serves as a cooler to counteract the heat of the chillies.

SERVES 4–6

Ingredients
1 small pineapple
1 small mango, peeled and sliced
1 green apple, cored and sliced
6 rambutans or lychees, peeled and stoned (pitted)
115g/4oz French beans, topped, tailed and halved
1 medium red onion, sliced
1 small cucumber, cut into short fingers
115g/4oz bean sprouts
2 spring onions (scallions), sliced
1 ripe tomato, quartered
225g/8oz cos, bib or iceberg lettuce leaves

Coconut dipping sauce
6 tsp coconut cream
2 tbsp sugar
5 tbsp boiling water
¼ tsp chilli sauce
1 tbsp fish sauce
juice of 1 lime

Cook's tip

Creamed coconut is sold in 200g/7oz blocks and is available from large supermarkets and specialist food stores. In warm weather, creamed coconut should be stored in a cool place to keep it from softening.

1 To make the coconut dipping sauce, measure the coconut, sugar and boiling water into a screw-top jar. Add the chilli and fish sauces and lime juice and shake.

2 Trim both ends of the pineapple with a serrated knife, then cut away the outer skin. Remove the central core with an apple corer. Alternatively, cut the pineapple into 4 down the middle and remove the core with a knife. Roughly chop the pineapple and set aside with the other fruits.

3 Bring a small saucepan of salted water to the boil and cook the beans for 3–4 minutes. Refresh under cold running water and set aside. To serve, arrange the fruits and vegetables into small heaps on a shallow bowl. Serve the coconut sauce separately as a dip.

Sweet Cucumber Cooler

Ajad

Sweet dipping sauces such as this bring instant relief to the hot chilli flavours of Thai food.

MAKES 120ML/4 FL OZ/½ CUP

Ingredients
5 tbsp water
2 tbsp sugar
½ tsp salt
1 tbsp rice or white wine vinegar
¼ small cucumber, quartered and thinly sliced
2 shallots, or 1 small red onion, thinly sliced

1 Measure the water, sugar, salt and vinegar into a stainless steel or enamel saucepan, bring to the boil and simmer until the sugar has dissolved, for less than 1 minute.

2 Allow to cool. Add the cucumber and shallots or onion and serve at room temperature.

VIETNAM

Honey-Glazed Quail with a Five-spice Marinade

Bo Can Quay

Chinese supermarkets sell five-spice powder in packets. Provided the blend is not kept for longer than 3 months, the flavour can be good, and a useful alternative to making your own.

SERVES 4–6

Ingredients
4 quails, cleaned
2 pieces star anise
2 tsp cinnamon powder
2 tsp fennel seeds
2 tsp Sichuan, or Chinese pepper
a pinch powdered cloves
1 small onion, finely chopped
1 clove garlic, crushed
4 tbsp clear honey
2 tbsp dark soy sauce
2 roughly chopped spring onions (scallions), to garnish
mandarin orange or satsuma, to garnish
banana leaves, to serve

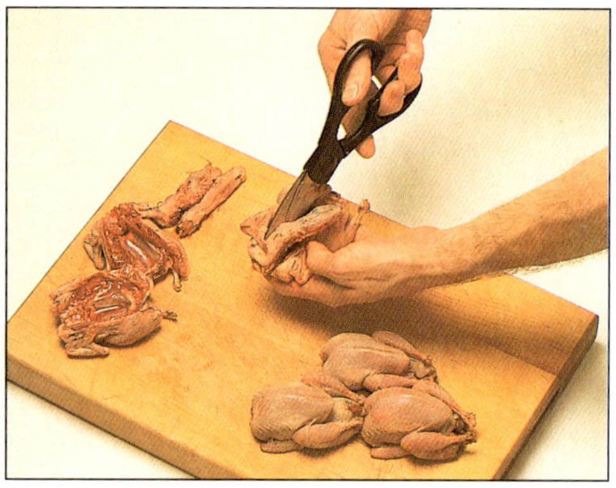

1 Remove the backbones from the quails by cutting down either side with a pair of kitchen scissors.

2 Flatten the birds with the palm of your hand and secure each bird using 2 bamboo skewers.

3 Place the five spices in a pestle and mortar or spice mill and grind into a fine powder. Add the onion, garlic, honey and soy sauce, and combine well.

4 Place the quails in a flat dish, cover with the marinade and leave for at least 8 hours for the flavours to mingle.

5 Preheat a grill or barbecue to a moderate temperature and cook the quails for 7–8 minutes on each side, basting occasionally with the marinade.

6 To garnish, remove the outer zest from the mandarin orange or satsuma with a vegetable peeler or a zesting tool. Shred the zest finely and combine with the chopped spring onions (scallions). Arrange the quails on a bed of banana leaves, garnish with the orange zest and spring onions (scallions) and serve.

HOT CHILLI CHICKEN WITH GINGER AND LEMON GRASS

Ga Xao Xa Ot

This dish can also be prepared using duck legs. Be sure to remove the jointed parts of the drumsticks and thigh bones to make the meat easier to eat with chopsticks.

SERVES 4–6

Ingredients
3 chicken legs (thighs and drumsticks)
1 tbsp vegetable oil
1 piece fresh ginger, 2cm/¾in long, peeled and finely chopped
1 clove garlic, crushed
1 small red chilli, seeded and finely chopped
1 piece lemon grass, 5cm/2in long, shredded
150ml/¼ pint/⅔ cup chicken stock
1 tbsp fish sauce (optional)
2 tsp sugar
½ tsp salt
juice of ½ lemon
50g/2oz raw peanuts
2 spring onions (scallions), shredded
1 zest of mandarin orange or satsuma, shredded
2 tbsp chopped mint
rice or rice noodles, to serve

1 With the heel of the knife, chop through the narrow end of the drumsticks. Remove the jointed parts of the drumsticks and thigh bones, then remove the skin.

2 Heat the oil in a large wok or frying pan. Add the chicken, ginger, garlic, chilli and lemon grass and cook for 3–4 minutes. Add the chicken stock, fish sauce if using, sugar, salt and lemon juice. Cover and simmer for 30–35 minutes.

3 To prepare the peanuts for the topping, the red skin must be removed. To do this, grill (broil) or roast the peanuts under a steady heat until evenly brown, for about 2–3 minutes. Turn the nuts out onto a clean cloth and rub briskly to loosen the skins.

4 Serve the chicken scattered with roasted peanuts, shredded spring onions (scallions) and the zest of the mandarin orange or satsuma. Serve with rice or rice noodles.

Crab, Pork and Mushroom Spring Rolls

Cha Gio

If you cannot obtain minced (ground) pork, use the meat from the equivalent weight of best-quality pork sausages. Filled spring rolls can be made in advance and kept in the refrigerator ready for frying.

MAKES 12 ROLLS

Ingredients

- 25g/1oz rice noodles
- 50g/2oz Chinese mushrooms (shiitake), fresh or dried
- 1 tbsp vegetable oil
- 4 spring onions (scallions), chopped
- 1 small carrot, grated
- 175g/6oz minced (ground) pork
- 100g/4oz/1 cup white crabmeat
- 1 tsp fish sauce (optional)
- salt and pepper
- 12 frozen spring roll skins, defrosted
- 2 tbsp cornflour (cornstarch) paste
- vegetable oil, for deep-frying
- 1 head iceberg or bib lettuce, to serve
- 1 bunch mint or basil, to serve
- 1 bunch coriander leaves, to serve
- ½ cucumber, sliced, to serve

1 Bring a large saucepan of salted water to the boil, and simmer the noodles for 8 minutes. Cut the noodles into finger-length pieces. If the mushrooms are dried, soak them in boiling water for 10 minutes before slicing thinly.

2 To make the filling, heat the oil in a wok or frying pan, add the spring onions (scallions), carrot and pork and cook for 8–10 minutes. Remove from the heat, then add the crabmeat, fish sauce and seasoning. Add the noodles and mushrooms, and set aside.

3 To fill the rolls, brush one spring roll skin at a time with the cornflour (cornstarch) paste, then place 1 tsp of the filling onto the skin. Fold the edges towards the middle and roll evenly to make a neat cigar shape. The paste will help seal the wrapper.

4 Heat the oil in a wok or deep-fryer until hot. Fry the spring rolls two at a time in the oil for 6–8 minutes. Make sure the fat is not too hot or the mixture inside will not heat through properly. Serve on a bed of salad leaves, mint, coriander and cucumber.

Hot and Sour Chicken Salad

Ga Nuong Ngu Vi

This salad is also delicious with prawns (shrimp). Allow 450g/1lb of fresh prawn (shrimp) tails to serve 4.

SERVES 4–6

Ingredients
2 chicken breast fillets, skinned
1 small red chilli, seeded and finely chopped
1 piece fresh ginger, 12mm/½in long, peeled and finely chopped
1 clove garlic, crushed
1 tbsp crunchy peanut butter
2 tbsp chopped coriander leaves
1 tsp sugar
½ tsp salt
1 tbsp rice or white wine vinegar
4 tbsp vegetable oil
2 tsp fish sauce (optional)
115g/4oz bean sprouts
1 head Chinese leaves, roughly shredded
2 medium carrots, cut into thin sticks
1 red onion, cut into fine rings
2 large gherkins (pickles), sliced

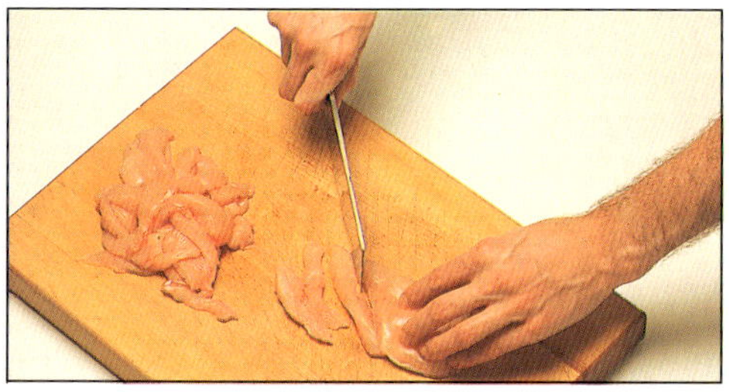

1 Slice the chicken thinly, place in a shallow bowl and set aside. Grind the chilli, ginger and garlic in a pestle and mortar. Add the peanut butter, coriander, sugar and salt.

2 Then add the vinegar, 2 tbsp of the oil and the fish sauce if using. Combine well. Cover the chicken with the spice mixture and leave to marinate for at least 2–3 hours.

3 Heat the remaining 2 tbsp of oil in a wok or frying pan. Add the chicken and cook for 10–12 minutes, tossing the meat occasionally. Serve arranged on the salad.

Alfalfa Crab Salad with Crispy Fried Noodles

Goi Gia

Alfalfa sprouts are available in many supermarkets. Alternatively, you can grow your own sprouts from seeds.

SERVES 4–6

Ingredients
vegetable oil, for deep-frying
50g/2oz Chinese rice noodles, uncooked
2 dressed crabs, or 150g/5oz frozen white crab meat, thawed
115g/4oz alfalfa sprouts
1 small iceberg or bib lettuce
4 sprigs coriander, roughly chopped
1 ripe tomato, skinned, seeded and diced
4 sprigs fresh mint, roughly chopped

Sesame lime dressing
3 tbsp vegetable oil
1 tsp sesame oil
½ small red chilli, seeded and finely chopped
1 piece stem ginger in syrup, cut into matchsticks
2 tsp stem ginger syrup
2 tsp soy sauce
juice of ½ lime

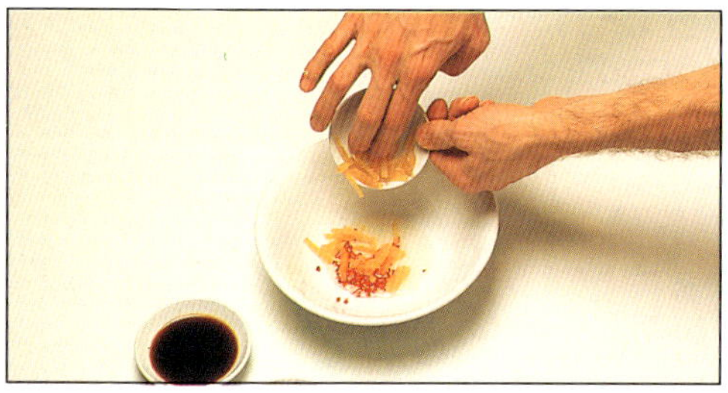

1 Combine the vegetable and sesame oils in a bowl. Add the chilli, stem ginger, stem ginger syrup and soy sauce with the lime juice.

2 Heat the oil in a deep-fryer to 196°C/385°F. Fry the noodles, one handful at a time, until crisp. Lift out and dry on paper.

3 Flake the white crab meat into a bowl and toss with the alfalfa sprouts. Serve on a nest of noodles and tossed salad ingredients.

Pork Balls with a Minted Peanut Sauce

Nem Nuong

This recipe is equally delicious made with chicken breasts.

SERVES 4–6

Ingredients
- 285g/10oz leg of pork, trimmed and diced
- 1 piece fresh ginger, 12mm/½in long, peeled and grated
- 1 clove garlic, crushed
- 2 tsp sesame oil
- 1 tbsp medium-dry sherry
- 1 tbsp soy sauce
- 1 tsp sugar
- 1 egg white
- ½ tsp salt
- a pinch of white pepper
- 350g/12oz long grain rice, washed and cooked for 15 minutes
- 50g/2oz ham, thickly sliced and diced
- 1 iceberg or bib lettuce, to serve

Minted peanut sauce
- 1 tbsp creamed coconut
- 75ml/5 tbsp/⅓ cup boiling water
- 2 tbsp smooth peanut butter
- juice of 1 lime
- 1 red chilli, seeded and finely chopped
- 1 clove garlic, crushed
- 1 tbsp freshly-chopped mint
- 1 tbsp freshly-chopped coriander
- 1 tbsp fish sauce (optional)

1 To make the pork balls, place the diced pork, ginger and garlic in a food processor and blend together smoothly for about 2–3 minutes. Add the sesame oil, sherry, soy sauce and sugar and blend. Lastly add the egg white.

2 Spread the cooked rice and ham on a shallow dish. Using wet hands, shape the pork mixture into thumb-sized balls. Roll in the rice to cover and pierce each ball with a bamboo skewer.

3 To make the sauce, put the creamed coconut in a measuring jug and cover with the boiling water. Place the peanut butter in another bowl with the lime juice, chilli, garlic, mint and coriander. Combine evenly, then add the creamed coconut and season with the fish sauce if using.

4 Place the pork balls in a bamboo steamer, cover and steam over a saucepan of boiling water for 8–10 minutes. Arrange all the lettuce leaves on a large serving plate. Place the pork balls on the leaves with the dipping sauce to one side.

Exotic Fruit Salad

Hoa Qua Tron

A variety of fruits can be used for this salad depending on what is available. Look out for mandarin oranges, star fruit, paw paw, Cape gooseberries and passion fruit.

SERVES 4–6

Ingredients
85g/3oz/6tbsp sugar
300ml/½ pint/1¼ cups water
2 tbsp stem ginger syrup
2 pieces star anise
1 piece cinnamon stick, 2.5cm/1in long
1 clove
juice of ½ lemon
2 sprigs mint
1 medium pineapple
1 mango, peeled and sliced
2 bananas, sliced
8 lychees, fresh or canned
225g/8oz fresh strawberries, trimmed and halved
2 pieces stem ginger, cut into sticks

1 Measure the sugar into a saucepan, and add the water, ginger syrup, spices, lemon juice and mint. Bring to the boil and simmer for 3 minutes. Strain into a large bowl and allow to cool.

2 Remove both the top and bottom from the mango and remove the outer skin. Stand the mango on one end and remove the flesh in two pieces either side of the flat stone (pit). Slice evenly and add to the syrup. Add the bananas, lychees, strawberries and ginger. Chill until ready to serve.

3 Cut the pineapple in half down the centre. Loosen the flesh with a small serrated knife and remove to form two boat shapes. Cut the flesh into large chunks and place in the cooled syrup.

4 Spoon the fruit salad into the pineapple halves and bring to the table on a large serving dish. There will be enough fruit salad left over to refill the pineapple halves.

Pork and Noodle Broth with Prawns (Shrimp)

Pho

This quick and delicious recipe can be made with 200g/7oz boneless chicken breast instead of pork fillet.

SERVES 4–6

Ingredients
350g/12oz pork chops or 200g/7oz pork fillet
225g/8oz fresh prawn (shrimp) tails or cooked prawns (shrimp)
150g/5oz thin egg noodles
1 tbsp vegetable oil
2 tsp sesame oil
4 shallots, or 1 medium onion, sliced
1 tbsp fresh ginger, finely sliced
1 clove garlic, crushed
1 tsp granulated sugar
1.4 litres/2½ pints/6¼ cups chicken stock
2 lime leaves
3 tbsp fish sauce
juice of ½ lime
4 sprigs coriander leaves, to garnish
chopped green part of 2 spring onions (scallions), to garnish

1 If using pork chops, trim away fat and bone completely. Place the meat in the freezer for 30 minutes to firm but not freeze the meat. Slice the meat thinly and set aside. Peel and de-vein the prawns (shrimp), if fresh.

2 Bring a large saucepan of salted water to the boil and simmer the noodles for the time stated on the packet. Drain and refresh under cold running water. Set aside.

3 Heat the vegetable and sesame oils in a large saucepan, add the shallots and brown evenly, for 3–4 minutes. Remove from the pan and set aside.

4 Add the ginger, garlic, sugar and chicken stock and bring to a simmer with the lime leaves. Add the fish sauce and lime juice. Add the pork, then simmer for 15 minutes. Add the prawns and noodles and simmer for 3–4 minutes. Serve in shallow soup bowls and decorate with the coriander leaves, the green part of the spring onions (scallions) and the browned shallots.

Vietnamese Dipping Sauce

Nuoc Cham

Serve this dip in a small bowl as an accompaniment to spring rolls or meat dishes.

MAKES 150ML/5 FL OZ/⅔ CUP

Ingredients

- 1–2 small red chillies, seeded and finely chopped
- 1 clove garlic, crushed
- 1 tbsp roasted peanuts
- 4 tbsp coconut milk
- 2 tbsp fish sauce
- juice of 1 lime
- 2 tsp sugar
- 1 tsp chopped coriander leaves

1 Crush the red chilli together with the garlic and peanuts using a pestle and mortar or food processor.

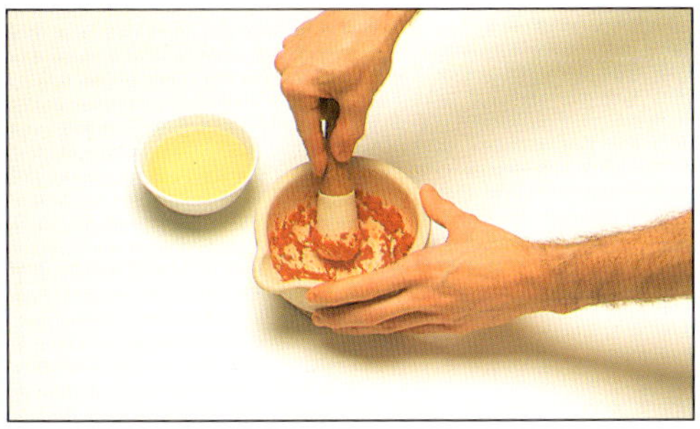

2 Add the coconut milk, fish sauce, lime juice, sugar and coriander.

Handling Chillies

Chillies are an important part of Eastern cookery and should be handled with care. The pungent oils released when chillies are cut can be harmful to sensitive parts of the skin, especially to eyes and lips. Be sure to wash your hands thoroughly with soap and water after touching cut chillies.

1 The severe heat of red and green chillies is contained in the seeds. Unless you like fiercely hot food, the seeds should be discarded before using. It is most practical to wash the seeds away under cold running water.

2 A useful chilli flavouring can be made by storing chillies in a jar of oil. Allow the hot flavours to merge for 3 weeks before using. Chilli oil is used to add a gentle heat to many Eastern dishes.

Cucumber and Carrot Garnishes

Presentation is an important part of South-east Asian cooking. These vegetable decorations are easily prepared.

MAKES 2 DECORATIVE GARNISHES

Ingredients

- ½ cucumber
- 1 large carrot

1 To make the cucumber garnish, cut the cucumber into a 7.5cm/3in strip, 2cm/¾in wide. Make 5 even cuts along the strip, 12mm/½in in from one end. Curl the second and fourth strips towards the base to form an open loop. The same cucumber strip can be spread out to form an attractive fan shape.

2 To make the carrot garnish, peel the carrot and cut into 6mm/¼in slices. Trim the slices into rectangles, 2cm/¾in × 7.5cm/3in. Make a 6mm/¼in cut along one edge of the carrot so that the strip is still joined. Make a second cut in the other direction, again so that the strip is joined. Bend the two ends together so that they cross over. This garnish can also be fashioned with giant white radish, cucumber and lemon peel.

MAIN COURSE SPICY PRAWN (SHRIMP) AND NOODLE SOUP

Laksa Lemak

This dish is served as a hot coconut broth with a separate platter of prawns (shrimp), fish and noodles. Diners are invited to add their own choice of accompaniment to the broth.

SERVES 4–6

Ingredients
25g/1oz raw cashew nuts
3 shallots, or 1 medium onion, sliced
1 piece lemon grass, 5cm/2in long, shredded
2 cloves garlic, crushed
2 tbsp vegetable oil
1 piece shrimp paste, 12mm/½in square, or 1 tbsp fish sauce
1 tbsp mild curry paste
400g/14oz canned coconut milk
½ chicken stock cube
3 curry leaves (optional)
450g/1lb white fish fillet, cod, haddock or whiting
225g/8oz prawn (shrimp) tails, fresh or cooked
1 small cos lettuce, shredded
115g/4oz bean sprouts
3 spring onions (scallions), shredded
½ cucumber, sliced and shredded
150g/5oz Laksa noodles (spaghetti-size rice noodles), soaked for 10 minutes before cooking
Prawn Crackers, to serve

1 Grind the cashew nuts using a pestle and mortar or food processor with the shallots or onion, lemon grass and garlic. Cook the noodles according to the instructions.

2 Heat the oil in a large wok or saucepan, add the contents of the mortar or food processor, and fry until the nuts begin to brown, for about 1–2 minutes.

Cook's tip

To serve, line a large serving platter with the shredded lettuce leaves. Arrange the salad ingredients in neat piles together with the cooked fish, prawns (shrimp) and noodles. Serve the salad with a bowl of Prawn Crackers and the broth in a stoneware closed-rim pot.

3 Add the shrimp paste or fish sauce and curry paste, followed by the coconut milk, stock cube and curry leaves. Simmer for 10 minutes.

4 Cut the white fish into bite-size pieces. Place the fish and prawns (shrimp) in a large frying basket, immerse into the simmering coconut stock and cook for 3–4 minutes.

Sesame Baked Fish with a Hot Ginger Marinade

Panggang Bungkus

Tropical fish are found increasingly in supermarkets, but oriental foodstores usually have a wider selection.

SERVES 4–6

Ingredients

2 red snapper, parrot fish or monkfish tails, weighing about 350g/12oz each
2 tbsp vegetable oil
2 tsp sesame oil
2 tbsp sesame seeds
1 piece fresh ginger, 2.5cm/1in long, peeled and thinly sliced
2 cloves garlic, crushed
2 small red chillies, seeded and finely chopped
4 shallots or 1 medium onion, halved and sliced
2 tbsp water
1 piece shrimp paste, 12mm/½in square, or 1 tbsp fish sauce
2 tsp sugar
½ tsp cracked black pepper
juice of 2 limes
3–4 banana leaves, or aluminium foil
1 lime, to garnish
2 red chilli flowers, to garnish

1 Clean the fish inside and out under cold running water. Pat dry with kitchen paper. Slash both sides of each fish deeply with a knife to enable the marinade to penetrate effectively. If using parrot fish, rub with fine salt and leave to stand for 15 minutes. (This will remove the chalky coral flavour often associated with the fish.)

2 To make the marinade, heat the vegetable and sesame oils in a wok, add the sesame seeds and fry until golden. Add the ginger, garlic, chillies and shallots or onion and soften over a gentle heat without burning. Add the water, shrimp paste or fish sauce, sugar, pepper and lime juice, simmer for 2–3 minutes and allow to cool.

3 If using banana leaves, remove the central stem and discard. Soften the leaves by dipping in boiling water. To keep them supple, rub all over with vegetable oil. Spread the marinade over the fish, wrap in the banana leaf and fasten with a bamboo skewer, or wrap the fish in foil. Leave the fish in a cool place to allow the flavours to mingle, for up to 3 hours.

4 Preheat the oven to 180°C/350°F/Gas Mark 4 or light a barbecue and allow the embers to settle to a steady glow. Place the wrapped fish on a wire rack or baking sheet and cook for 35–40 minutes.

Spicy Clay-pot Chicken

Ayam Golek

Clay-pot cooking stems from the practice of burying a glazed pot in the embers of an open fire. The gentle heat surrounds the base and keeps the liquid inside at a slow simmer, similar to the modern-day casserole.

SERVES 4–6

Ingredients

- 1 × 1.5kg/3½lb chicken
- 3 tbsp freshly-grated coconut
- 2 tbsp vegetable oil
- 2 shallots, or 1 small onion, finely chopped
- 2 cloves garlic, crushed
- 1 piece lemon grass, 5cm/2in long
- 1 piece galingal or fresh ginger, 2.5cm/1in long, peeled and thinly sliced
- 2 small green chillies, seeded and finely chopped
- 1 piece shrimp paste, 12mm/½in square, or 1 tbsp fish sauce
- 400g/14fl oz canned coconut milk
- 300ml/½ pint/1¼ cups chicken stock
- 2 lime leaves (optional)
- 1 tbsp sugar
- 1 tbsp rice or white wine vinegar
- 2 ripe tomatoes, to garnish
- 2 tbsp chopped coriander leaves, to garnish
- boiled rice, to serve

1 To joint the chicken, remove the legs and wings with a chopping knife. Skin the pieces and divide the drumsticks from the thighs and, using a pair of kitchen scissors, remove the lower part of the chicken leaving the breast piece. Remove as many of the bones as you can, to make the dish easier to eat. Cut the breast piece into 4 and set aside.

2 Dry-fry the coconut in a large wok until evenly brown. Add the vegetable oil, shallots or onion, garlic, lemon grass, galingal or ginger, chillies and shrimp paste or fish sauce. Fry briefly to release the flavours. Preheat the oven to 180°C/350°F/Gas Mark 4. Add the chicken joints to the wok and brown evenly with the spices for 2–3 minutes.

3 Strain the coconut milk, and add the thin part with the chicken stock, lime leaves if using, sugar and vinegar. Transfer to a glazed clay pot, cover and bake for 50–55 minutes or until the chicken is tender. Stir in the thick part of the coconut milk and return to the oven for 5–10 minutes to simmer and thicken.

4 Place the tomatoes in a bowl and cover with boiling water to loosen and remove the skins. Halve the tomatoes, remove the seeds and cut into large dice. Add the tomatoes to the finished dish, scatter with the chopped coriander and serve with a bowl of rice.

Green Vegetable Salad with Coconut Mint Dip

Syabas

This dish is served as an accompaniment to Singapore and Malaysian meat dishes.

SERVES 4–6

Ingredients
115g/4oz mange-tout (snow peas), topped and tailed and halved
114g/4oz French beans, trimmed and halved
½ cucumber, peeled, halved and sliced
115g/4oz Chinese leaves, roughly shredded
115g/4oz bean sprouts
lettuce leaves, to serve

Dipping sauce
1 clove garlic, crushed
1 small green chilli, seeded and finely chopped
2 tsp sugar
3 tbsp creamed coconut
75ml/5 tbsp/⅓ cup boiling water
2 tsp fish sauce
3 tbsp vegetable oil
juice of 1 lime
2 tbsp freshly-chopped mint

1 Bring a saucepan of salted water to the boil. Blanch the mange-tout (snow peas), beans and cucumber for 4 minutes. Refresh under cold running water. Drain and set aside.

2 To make the dressing, pound the garlic, chilli and sugar together using a pestle and mortar. Add the coconut, water, fish sauce, vegetable oil, lime juice and mint.

3 Pour the dressing into a shallow bowl and serve with the salad ingredients arranged in an open basket.

Sizzling Steak

Daging

This method of sizzling meat on a hot grill can also be applied to sliced chicken or pork.

SERVES 4–6

Ingredients
4 × 200g/7oz rump steaks
1 clove garlic, crushed
1 piece fresh ginger, 2.5cm/1in long, peeled and finely chopped
2 tsp whole black peppercorns
1 tbsp sugar
2 tbsp tamarind sauce
3 tbsp dark soy sauce
1 tbsp oyster sauce
vegetable oil, for brushing

Dipping sauce
75ml/5 tbsp/⅓ cup beef stock
2 tbsp tomato sauce (ketchup)
1 tsp chilli sauce
juice of 1 lime

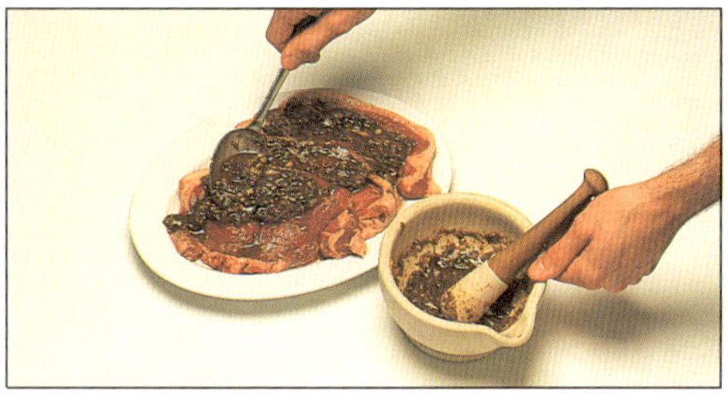

1 Pound and blend all the ingredients together. Pour the marinade over the beef and allow the flavours to mingle for up to 8 hours.

2 Heat a cast iron grilling plate over a high heat. Scrape the marinade from the meat and reserve. Brush the meat with oil and cook for 2 minutes on each side, or as you prefer.

3 Place the marinade in a pan, add the stock, sauces and lime juice and simmer briefly. Serve the steaks and the dipping sauce separately.

Chicken Sate with Peanut Sauce

Sate Ayam Saos Kacang

Both the marinated chicken and sauce can be stored in the freezer for up to 6 weeks. Allow 2 hours to thaw.

SERVES 4–6

Ingredients

4 chicken breast fillets
1 tbsp coriander seeds
2 tsp fennel seeds
2 cloves garlic, crushed
1 piece lemon grass, 5cm/2in long, shredded
½ tsp turmeric
2 tsp sugar
½ tsp salt
2 tbsp soy sauce
1 tbsp sesame oil
juice of ½ lime
lettuce leaves, to serve
1 bunch mint leaves, to garnish
1 lime, quartered, to garnish
½ cucumber, quartered, to garnish

Sauce

150g/5oz raw peanuts
1 tbsp vegetable oil
2 shallots, or 1 small onion, finely chopped
1 clove garlic, crushed
1–2 small chillies, seeded and finely chopped
1 piece shrimp paste, 12mm/½in square, or 1 tbsp fish sauce
2 tbsp tamarind sauce
100ml/4fl oz/½ cup coconut milk
1 tbsp honey

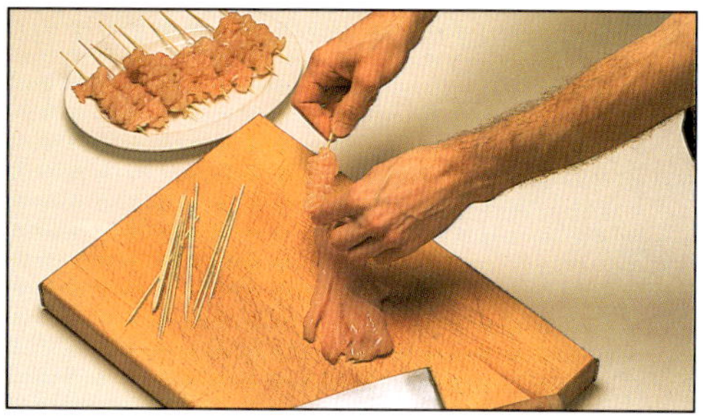

1 Cut the chicken into long thin strips and thread, zig-zag, onto 12 bamboo skewers. Arrange on a flat plate and set aside.

2 To make the marinade, dry-fry the coriander and fennel seeds in a wok. Grind smoothly using a pestle and mortar or food processor, then add to the wok with the garlic, lemon grass, turmeric, sugar, salt, soy sauce, sesame oil and lime juice. Allow the mixture to cool. Spread it over the chicken and leave in a cool place for up to 8 hours.

3 To make the peanut sauce, fry the peanuts in a wok with a little oil, or place under a moderate grill (broiler), tossing them all the time to prevent burning. Turn the peanuts out onto a clean cloth and rub vigorously with your hands to remove the papery skins. Place the peanuts in a food processor and blend for 2 minutes.

4 Heat the vegetable oil in a wok, and soften the shallots or onion, garlic and chillies. Add the shrimp paste or fish sauce together with the tamarind sauce, coconut milk and honey. Simmer briefly, add to the peanuts and process to form a thick sauce. Heat the grill (broiler) to moderately hot. If using a barbecue, let the embers settle to a white glow. Brush the chicken with a little vegetable oil and grill for 6–8 minutes. Serve on a bed of lettuce, garnished, and with a bowl of dipping sauce.

Hot Chilli Crab with Ginger and Lime

Ikan Maris

Serve this dish with a bowl of chopped cucumber and hot slices of toast.

SERVES 4–6

Ingredients
- 2 medium crabs, cooked
- 1 piece fresh ginger, 2.5cm/1in long, peeled and chopped
- 2 cloves garlic, crushed
- 1–2 small red chillies, seeded and finely chopped
- 1 tbsp sugar
- 2 tbsp vegetable oil
- 4 tbsp tomato sauce (ketchup)
- 150ml/¼ pint/⅔ cup water
- juice of 2 limes
- 2 tbsp freshly-chopped coriander leaves, to garnish

Cook's tip

Hot towels are useful towards the end of the meal to clean messy fingers. To prepare your own, moisten white flannels with cologne-scented water, wrap in a plastic bag and microwave for 2 minutes at full power. Remove from the bag and bring to the table in a covered basket.

1 To prepare the crab, twist off the legs and claws. Crack open the thickest part of the shell with a hammer or the back of a heavy knife.

2 Prise off the underside leg section with your two thumbs. From this section, remove the stomach sac and the grey gills, and discard. Cut the section into 4 with a knife. Cut the upper shell into 6 equal pieces.

3 Pound the ginger, garlic, chillies and sugar using a pestle and mortar. Heat the vegetable oil in a large wok, add the pounded spices and fry gently for about 1–2 minutes. Add the tomato sauce (ketchup), water and lime juice and simmer briefly.

4 Add the pieces of crab and heat through for 3–4 minutes. Turn out into a serving bowl and scatter with the chopped coriander.

Malaysian Fish Curry

Ikan Moolee

Hot Tomato Sambal is often served as an accompaniment to this dish.

SERVES 4–6

Ingredients

700g/1½lb monkfish, hokey or red snapper fillet
salt, to season
3 tbsp freshly-grated or desiccated (shredded) coconut
2 tbsp vegetable oil
1 piece galingal or fresh ginger, 2.5cm/1in long, peeled and thinly sliced
2 small red chillies, seeded and finely chopped
2 cloves garlic, crushed
1 piece lemon grass, 5cm/2in long, shredded
1 piece shrimp paste, 12mm/½in square, or 1 tbsp fish sauce
400g/14oz canned coconut milk
575ml/1 pint/2½ cups chicken stock
½ tsp turmeric
3 tsp sugar
juice of 1 lime, or ½ lemon

1 Cut the fish into large chunks, season with salt and set aside.

2 Dry-fry the coconut in a large wok until evenly brown. Add the vegetable oil, galingal or ginger, chillies, garlic and lemon grass and fry briefly. Stir in the shrimp paste or fish sauce. Strain the coconut milk in a sieve, then add the thin coconut milk.

3 Add the chicken stock, turmeric, sugar, a little salt and the lime or lemon juice. Simmer for 10 minutes. Add the fish and simmer for 6–8 minutes. Stir in the thick part of the coconut milk, simmer to thicken, and serve with rice.

Plain Boiled Rice

A small amount of vegetable oil added to the rice will enhance its natural flavour.

SERVES 4–6

Ingredients

400g/14oz long grain rice
1 tbsp vegetable oil
700ml/1¼ pints/3 cups boiling water
½ tsp salt

1 Wash and drain the rice several times in cold water until the water is no longer starchy. Put the rice in a heavy saucepan, add the vegetable oil, water and salt. Stir once to prevent the rice from sticking to the pan and simmer for 10–12 minutes. After this time, remove from the heat, cover and allow the rice to steam in its own heat for a further 5 minutes. Fluff the rice with a fork or chopsticks before serving.

Coconut Rice with Lemon Grass

Serve this rice dish with Sizzling Steak or other meat dishes.

SERVES 4–6

Ingredients

400g/14oz long grain rice
½ tsp salt
1 piece lemon grass, 5cm/2in long
25g/1oz creamed coconut
700ml/1¼ pints/3 cups boiling water

1 Wash and drain the rice several times in cold water until the water is no longer starchy. Put the rice, salt, lemon grass and coconut in a heavy saucepan, cover with the measured amount of boiling water. Stir once to prevent the grains from sticking to the pan, and simmer uncovered for 10–12 minutes.

2 Remove from the heat, cover and allow to steam in its own heat for a further 5 minutes. Fluff the rice with a fork or chopsticks before serving.

Singapore Sling

Singapore Sling is enjoyed in cocktail bars around the world. Recipes vary considerably, but they all use a standard measure that equates to a little less than 2 tbsp.

SERVES 1

Ingredients
ice
2 measures gin
1 measure cherry brandy
1 measure lemon juice
soda water, to taste
1 slice orange
1 slice lemon
1 Maraschino cherry, to garnish
1 sprig mint, to garnish

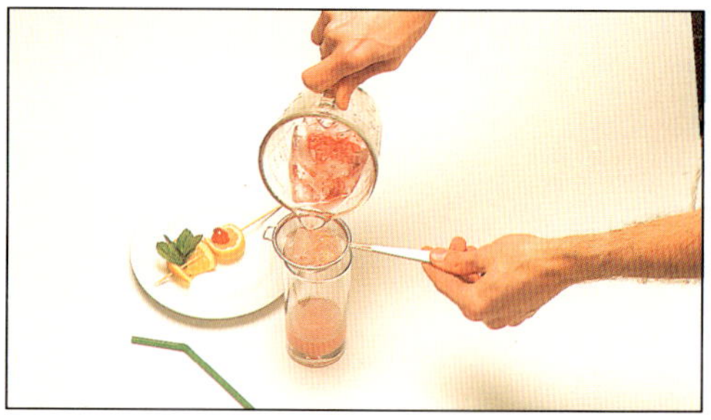

1 Wrap the ice in a clean cloth, and crush with a rolling pin or the underside of a saucepan. Half-fill a cocktail shaker with ice.

2 Add the gin, cherry brandy and lemon juice and shake.

3 Strain the mixture into a goblet or tall glass over ice cubes. Top up with soda water, to taste, and decorate with the slices of orange and lemon, and the cherry and mint.

Special Fried Noodles

Mee Goreng

Mee Goreng is perhaps the most well-known dish of Singapore. It is prepared from a wide range of ingredients.

SERVES 4–6

Ingredients
275g/10oz egg noodles
1 chicken breast fillet, skinned
115g/4oz lean pork
2 tbsp vegetable oil
175g/6oz prawn (shrimp) tails, fresh or cooked
4 shallots, or 1 medium onion, chopped
1 piece fresh ginger, 2cm/¾in long, peeled and thinly sliced
2 cloves garlic, crushed
3 tbsp light soy sauce
1–2 tsp chilli sauce
1 tbsp rice or white wine vinegar
1 tsp sugar
½ tsp salt
115g/4oz Chinese leaves, shredded
115g/4oz fresh spinach, shredded
3 spring onions (scallions), shredded

1 Bring a large saucepan of salted water to the boil and cook the noodles according to the instructions on the packet. Drain and set aside. Place the chicken breast and pork in the freezer for 30 minutes to firm but not freeze.

2 Slice the meat thinly against the grain. Heat the oil in a large wok and fry the chicken, pork and prawns (shrimp) for 2–3 minutes. Add the shallots or onion, ginger and garlic and fry without letting them colour.

3 Add the soy and chilli sauces, vinegar, sugar and salt. Bring to a simmer, add the Chinese leaves, spinach and spring onions (scallions), cover and cook for 3–4 minutes. Lastly add the noodles, heat through and serve.

Grilled (Broiled) Fish with a Cashew Ginger Marinade

Panggang Bungkus

To capture the sweet spicy flavours of this Indonesian favourite, marinated fish are wrapped in green banana leaves or foil and baked. The packets of fish are brought to the table, releasing a sweet spicy aroma.

SERVES 4

Ingredients

1.1kg/2½lb pomfret, parrot fish or sea bass, scaled and cleaned
150g/5oz raw cashew nuts
2 shallots, or 1 small onion, finely chopped
1 piece fresh ginger, 12mm/½in long, peeled and finely chopped
1 clove garlic, crushed
1 small red chilli, seeded and finely chopped
2 tbsp vegetable oil
1 tbsp shrimp paste
2 tsp sugar
½ tsp salt
2 tbsp tamarind sauce
2 tbsp tomato sauce (ketchup)
juice of 2 limes
4 young banana leaves, or aluminium foil

1 Slash the fish 3–4 times on each side with a sharp knife to help it cook through to the bone. Set aside.

2 Grind the cashew nuts, shallots or onion, ginger, garlic and chilli to a fine paste using a pestle and mortar or food processor. Add the vegetable oil, shrimp paste, sugar and salt and blend, then add the tamarind sauce, tomato sauce (ketchup) and lime juice.

3 Cover both sides of the fish with the marinade and leave for up to 8 hours to marinate.

4 To soften the banana leaves, remove the thick central stem and immerse the leaves in boiling water for 1 minute. Brush the leaves with vegetable oil. Wrap the fish in a banana leaf fastened with a bamboo skewer, or wrap in foil. Preheat the oven to 180 C/350 F/Gas Mark 4 and bake for 30–35 minutes.

Cook's tip

Banana leaves are readily available from Indian or South-east Asian food stores. However, if these are difficult to obtain, simply wrap each fish in aluminium foil.

For an authentic taste of the Far East, the fish may be barbecued. Light the barbecue and allow the embers to settle to a steady glow. Grill (broil) each fish packet for 30–35 minutes.

Beef Sate with a Hot Mango Dip

Sate Bali

Serve this dish with a green salad and a bowl of plain rice.

MAKES 12 SKEWERS

Ingredients
450g/1lb sirloin steak, 2cm/¾ in thick, trimmed
1 tbsp coriander seeds
1 tsp cumin seeds
50g/2oz raw cashew nuts
1 tbsp vegetable oil
2 shallots, or 1 small onion, finely chopped
1 piece fresh ginger, 12mm/½in long, peeled and finely chopped
1 clove garlic, crushed
2 tbsp tamarind sauce
2 tbsp dark soy sauce
2 tsp sugar
1 tsp rice or white wine vinegar

Hot mango dip
1 ripe mango
1–2 small red chillies, seeded and finely chopped
1 tbsp fish sauce
juice of 1 lime
2 tsp sugar
¼ tsp salt
2 tbsp freshly-chopped coriander leaves

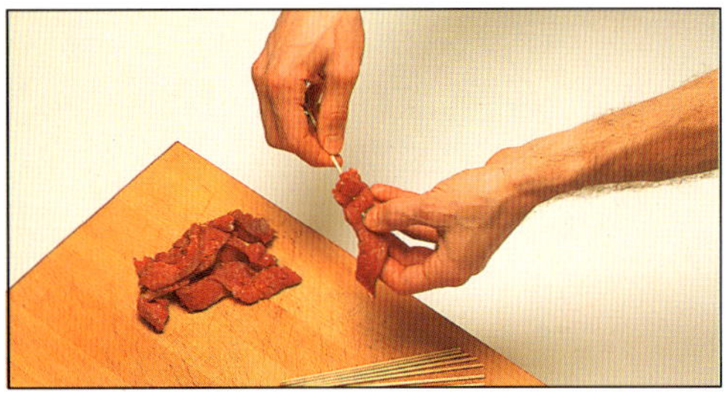

1 Slice the beef into long narrow strips and thread, zig-zag, onto 12 bamboo skewers. Lay on a flat plate and set aside.

2 For the marinade, dry-fry the seeds and nuts in a large wok until evenly brown. Place in a pestle and mortar with a rough surface and crush finely. Alternatively, blend the spices and nuts in a food processor. Add the vegetable oil, shallots or onion, ginger, garlic, tamarind and soy sauces, sugar and vinegar. Spread this mixture over the beef and leave to marinate for up to 8 hours. Cook the beef under a moderate grill (broiler) or over a barbecue for 6–8 minutes, turning to ensure an even colour. Meanwhile, make the mango dip.

3 Process the mango flesh with the chillies, fish sauce, lime juice, sugar and salt until smooth, then add the coriander.

Prawn (Shrimp) Sate with Paw Paw Sauce

Udang Sate

Fresh prawns (shrimp) are available frozen from reputable fishmongers. Chinese supermarkets also keep a good supply.

MAKES 12 SKEWERS

Ingredients
700g/1½lb whole fresh prawn (shrimp) tails or 24 king prawns (shrimp)
2 tbsp coriander seeds
2 tsp fennel seeds
2 shallots, or 1 small onion, finely chopped
1 piece fresh ginger, 12mm/½in long, peeled and finely chopped
2 cloves garlic, crushed
1 piece lemon grass, 5cm/2in long
2 tsp creamed coconut
juice of 1 lime
1 tbsp fish sauce
2 tsp chilli sauce
2 tbsp light soy sauce
4 tsp sugar
½ tsp salt
lettuce leaves, to serve

Sauce
2 ripe paw paws or papayas
juice of 1 lime
½ tsp freshly-ground black pepper
pinch of salt
2 tbsp freshly-chopped mint

1 Thread the prawns (shrimp) onto 12 bamboo skewers and lay on a flat plate.

2 Dry-fry the coriander and fennel seeds, then pound smoothly in a pestle and mortar. Add the shallots or onion, ginger, garlic and lemon grass and combine. Lastly add the coconut, lime juice, fish, chilli and soy sauces, sugar and salt. Spread the sauce over the prawns (shrimp) and leave in a cool place for up to 8 hours. Cook the prawns (shrimp) under a moderate grill (broiler) or over a barbecue for 6–8 minutes, turning once.

3 Blend the paw paw, lime juice, pepper and salt. Stir in the mint and serve.

Prawn (Shrimp) Curry with Quails' Eggs

Gulai Udang

Quails' eggs are available from speciality food shops and delicatessens. Hens' eggs may be substituted if quails' eggs are hard to come by. Use 1 hen's egg to every 4 quails' eggs.

SERVES 4

Ingredients

900g/2lb fresh prawn (shrimp) tails, peeled and de-veined
12 quails' eggs
2 tbsp vegetable oil
4 shallots or 1 medium onion, finely chopped
1 piece galingal or fresh ginger, 2.5cm/1in long, peeled and chopped
2 cloves garlic, crushed
1 piece lemon grass, 5cm/2in long, finely shredded
1–2 small red chillies, seeded and finely chopped
½ tsp turmeric
1 piece shrimp paste, 12mm/½in square, or 1 tbsp fish sauce
400g/14fl oz canned coconut milk
300ml/½ pint/1¼ cups chicken stock
115g/4oz Chinese leaves, roughly shredded
2 tsp sugar
½ tsp salt
2 spring onions (scallions), green part only, shredded, to garnish
2 tbsp shredded coconut, to garnish

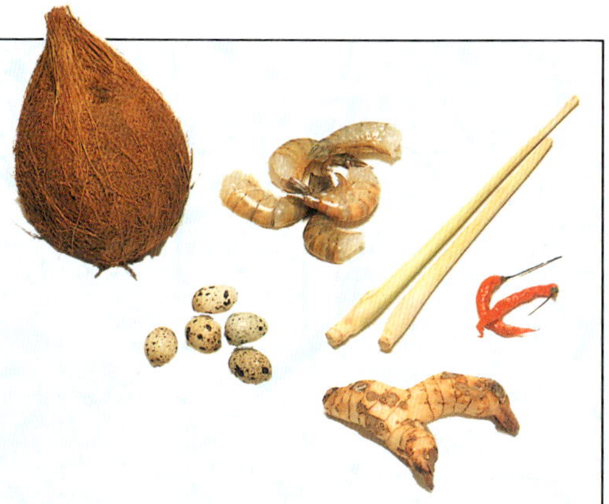

1 Boil the quails' eggs for 8 minutes. Refresh in cold water, peel by dipping in cold water to release the shells and set aside.

2 Heat the vegetable oil in a large wok, add the shallots or onion, galingal or ginger and garlic and soften without colouring. Add the lemon grass, chillies, turmeric and shrimp paste or fish sauce and fry briefly to bring out their flavours.

3 Add the prawns (shrimp) and fry briefly. Pour the coconut milk in a strainer over a bowl, then add the thin part of the milk with the chicken stock. Add the Chinese leaves, sugar and salt and bring to the boil. Simmer for 6–8 minutes.

4 Turn out onto a serving dish, halve the quails' eggs and toss in the sauce. Scatter with the spring onions (scallions) and the shredded coconut.

Grilled (Broiled) Cashew Nut Chicken

Ayam Bali

This dish comes from the beautiful island of Bali where nuts are widely used as a base for sauces and marinades. Serve with a green salad and a hot chilli dipping sauce such as Hot Chilli and Garlic Dipping Sauce.

SERVES 4–6

Ingredients
4 chicken legs

Marinade
50g/2oz raw cashew or macadamia nuts
2 shallots, or 1 small onion, finely chopped
2 cloves garlic, crushed
2 small red chillies, chopped
1 piece lemon grass, 5cm/2in long
1 tbsp tamarind sauce
2 tbsp dark soy sauce
1 tbsp fish sauce (optional)
2 tsp sugar
½ tsp salt
1 tbsp rice or white wine vinegar
Chinese leaves, to serve
radishes, sliced, to garnish
½ cucumber, sliced, to garnish

1 Using a sharp knife, slash the chicken legs several times through to the bone, chop off the knuckle end and set aside.

2 To make the marinade, place the cashew or macadamia nuts in a food processor or coarse pestle and mortar and grind.

3 Add the shallots or onion, garlic, chillies and lemon grass and blend. Add the remaining marinade ingredients.

4 Spread the marinade over the chicken and leave in a cool place for up to 8 hours. Grill (broil) the chicken under a moderate heat or over a barbecue for 15 minutes on each side. Place on a dish lined with Chinese leaves and garnish with the sliced radishes and cucumber.

Indonesian Pork and Prawn (Shrimp) Rice

Nasi Goreng

Nasi Goreng is an attractive way of using up leftovers and appears in many variations throughout Indonesia. Rice is the main ingredient, although almost anything can be added for colour and flavour.

SERVES 4–6

Ingredients
3 eggs
pinch of salt
4 tbsp vegetable oil
6 shallots, or 1 large onion, chopped
2 cloves garlic, crushed
1 piece fresh ginger, 2.5cm/1in long, peeled and chopped
2–3 small red chillies, seeded and finely chopped
1 tbsp tamarind sauce
1 piece shrimp paste, 12mm/½in square, or 1 tbsp fish sauce
½ tsp turmeric
6 tsp creamed coconut
juice of 2 limes
2 tsp sugar
½ tsp salt
350g/12oz lean pork or chicken breast fillets, skinned and sliced
350g/12oz fresh or cooked prawn (shrimp) tails, peeled
175g/6oz bean sprouts
175g/6oz Chinese leaves, shredded
175g/6oz frozen peas, thawed
250g/9oz long grain rice, cooked to make 700g/1½lb
1 small bunch coriander or basil, roughly chopped, to garnish

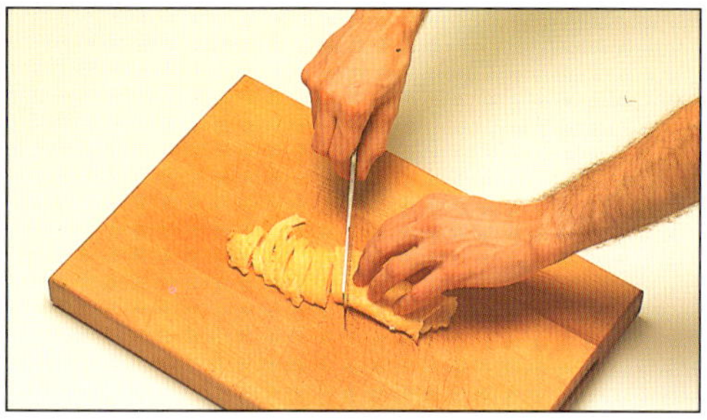

1 In a bowl, beat the eggs with a pinch of salt. Heat a non-stick frying pan over a moderate heat. Pour in the eggs and move the pan around until they begin to set. When set, roll up, slice thinly, cover and set aside.

2 Heat 1 tbsp of the oil in a wok and fry the shallots or onion until evenly brown. Remove from pan, set aside and keep warm.

3 Heat the remaining 3 tbsp of oil in the wok, add the garlic, ginger and chillies and soften without colouring. Stir in the tamarind and shrimp paste or fish sauce, turmeric, coconut, lime juice, sugar and salt. Combine briefly over a moderate heat. Add the pork or chicken and prawns (shrimp) and fry for 3–4 minutes.

4 Toss the bean sprouts, Chinese leaves and peas in the spices and cook briefly. Add the rice and stir-fry for 6–8 minutes, stirring to prevent it from burning. Turn out onto a large serving plate, decorate with shredded egg pancake, the fried shallots or onion and chopped coriander or basil.

Hot Tomato Sambal

Sambal Tomat

Sambals are placed on the table as a condiment and are used mainly for dipping meat and fish. They are quite strong and should be used sparingly.

MAKES 120ML/4 FL OZ/½ CUP

Ingredients
3 ripe tomatoes
½ tsp salt
1 tsp chilli sauce
4 tbsp fish sauce, or soy sauce
1 tbsp chopped coriander leaves

1 Cover the tomatoes with boiling water to loosen the skins. Remove the skins, halve, discard the seeds and chop finely.

2 Place the chopped tomatoes in a bowl, add the salt, chilli sauce, fish sauce or soy sauce, and coriander.

Hot Chilli and Garlic Dipping Sauce

Sambal Kecap

This sambal is particularly strong, so warn guests who are unaccustomed to spicy foods.

MAKES 120ML/4FL OZ/½ CUP

Ingredients
1 clove garlic, crushed
2 small red chillies, seeded and finely chopped
2 tsp sugar
1 tsp tamarind sauce
4 tbsp soy sauce
juice of ½ lime

1 Pound the garlic, chillies and sugar until smooth using a pestle and mortar, or grind in a food processor.

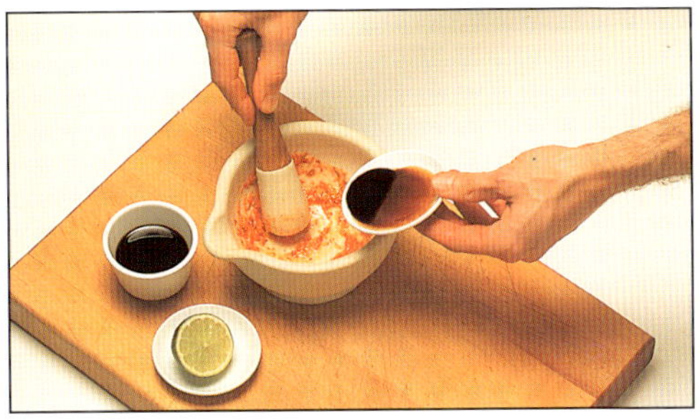

2 Add the tamarind sauce, soy sauce and lime juice.

Cucumber Sambal

Sambal Selamat

This sambal has a piquant flavour without the hotness of chillies found in other recipes.

MAKES 150ML/5FL OZ/⅔ CUP

Ingredients
1 clove garlic, crushed
1 tsp fennel seeds
2 tsp sugar
½ tsp salt
2 shallots, or 1 small onion, finely sliced
100ml/4fl oz/½ cup rice or white wine vinegar
¼ cucumber, finely diced

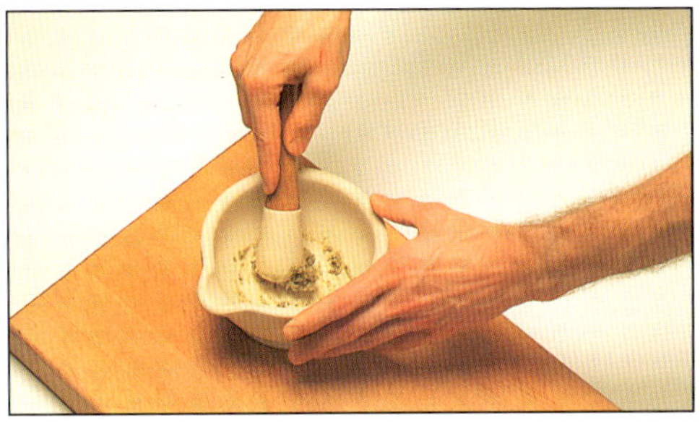

1 Place the garlic, fennel seeds, sugar and salt in a pestle and mortar and pound finely. Alternatively, grind the ingredients thoroughly in a food processor.

2 Stir in the shallots or onion, vinegar and cucumber and allow to stand for at least 6 hours to allow the flavours to combine.

Spicy Peanut Rice Cakes

Rempeyek

Serve these spicy rice cakes with a crisp green salad and a dipping sauce such as Hot Tomato Sambal.

MAKES 16 PIECES

Ingredients

- 1 clove garlic, crushed
- 1 piece fresh ginger, 12mm/½in long, peeled and finely chopped
- ¼ tsp turmeric
- 1 tsp sugar
- ½ tsp salt
- 1 tsp chilli sauce
- 2 tsp fish or soy sauce
- 2 tbsp chopped coriander leaves
- juice of ½ lime
- 115g/4oz long grain rice, cooked
- raw peanuts, chopped
- 150ml/¼ pint vegetable oil, for deep-frying

1 Pound together the garlic, ginger and turmeric using a pestle and mortar. Add the sugar, salt, chilli and fish or soy sauce, coriander and lime juice.

2 Add 85g/3oz of the cooked rice and pound until smooth and sticky. Stir in the remainder of the rice. Wet your hands and shape into thumb-size balls.

3 Roll the balls in chopped peanuts to coat evenly. Set aside until ready to cook and serve.

4 Heat the vegetable oil in a deep frying pan. Prepare a tray lined with kitchen paper to drain the rice cakes. Deep-fry 3 cakes at a time until crisp and golden, remove with a slotted spoon then drain on kitchen paper.

Vegetable Salad with a Hot Peanut Sauce

Gado Gado

Serve this vegetable salad with Indonesian Pork and Prawn (Shrimp) Rice and Prawn Crackers. The peanut sauce is served separately from the salad, and everyone helps themselves.

SERVES 4–6

Ingredients
2 medium potatoes, peeled
175g/6oz French beans, topped and tailed

Peanut sauce
150g/5oz raw peanuts
1 tbsp vegetable oil
2 shallots, or 1 small onion, finely chopped
1 clove garlic, crushed
1–2 small chillies, seeded and finely chopped
1 piece shrimp paste, 12mm/½in square, or 1 tbsp fish sauce (optional)
2 tbsp tamarind sauce
100ml/4fl oz/½ cup canned coconut milk
1 tbsp clear honey

Salad ingredients
175g/6oz Chinese leaves, shredded
1 iceberg or bib lettuce
175g/6oz bean sprouts
½ cucumber, cut into fingers
150g/5oz giant white radish, shredded
3 spring onions (scallions)
225g/8oz bean curd (tofu), cut into large dice
3 hard-boiled eggs, quartered
1 small bunch coriander

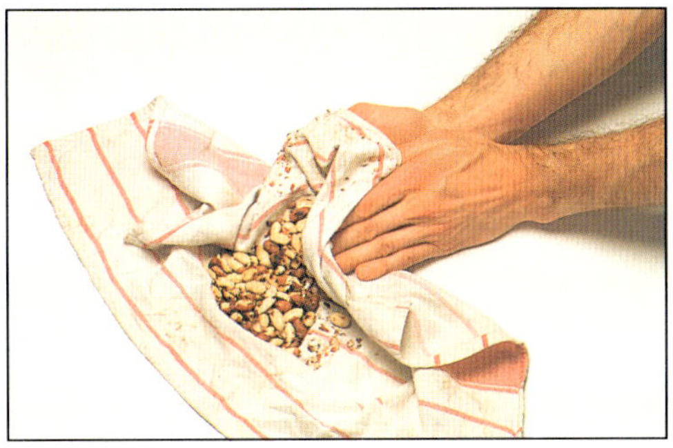

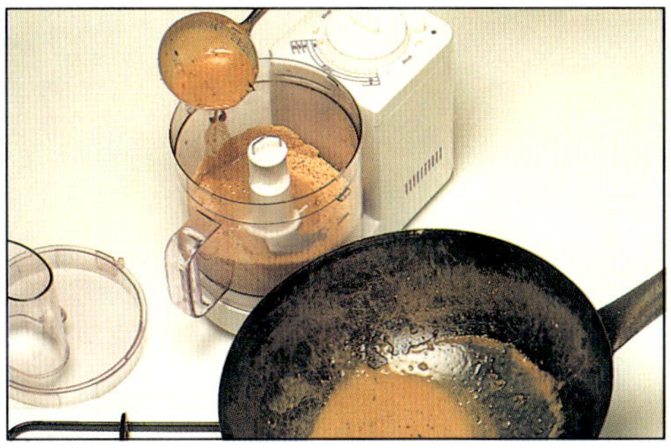

1 Bring the potatoes to the boil in salted water and simmer for 20 minutes. Cook the beans for 3–4 minutes. Drain the potatoes and beans and refresh under cold running water.

2 For the peanut sauce, dry-fry the peanuts in a wok, or place under a moderate grill, tossing them all the time to prevent burning. Turn the peanuts onto a clean cloth and rub vigorously with your hands to remove the papery skins. Place the peanuts in a food processor and blend for 2 minutes.

3 Heat the vegetable oil in a wok, and soften the shallots or onion, garlic and chillies without letting them colour. Add the shrimp paste or fish sauce if using, together with the tamarind sauce, coconut milk and honey. Simmer briefly, add to the peanuts and process to form a thick sauce.

4 Arrange the salad ingredients, potatoes and beans on a large platter and serve with a bowl of the peanut sauce.

Table-top Simmer Pot

Ta Pin Lo

This meal is well-known in many Eastern countries and serves to unite all members of the family. The idea is to cook or reheat a range of ingredients displayed around a pot of simmering chicken stock. The meal is a great social occasion, and each person chooses their own selection of food. Dipping sauces are provided to season the dishes according to taste.

SERVES 4–6

Ingredients

175g/6oz lean pork
175g/6oz fillet steak
1 chicken breast fillet, skinned
225g/8oz white fish fillets (monkfish, halibut or hokey)
225g/8oz bean curd (tofu)
16 fresh prawn (shrimp) tails, peeled and de-veined
1.75 litres/3 pints/7½ cups chicken stock
1 small red chilli, split
1 piece fresh ginger, 2.5cm/1in long, peeled and sliced
175g/6oz Chinese egg noodles, uncooked
225g/8oz Chinese leaves, roughly shredded
1 iceberg, bib or cos lettuce, shredded
6 spring onions (scallions)
½ cucumber, sliced
chilli sauce
soy sauce
juice of 3 lemons

1 Place the pork, steak and chicken in the freezer for 30 minutes to firm but not freeze. Slice the meat thinly and arrange on small side dishes.

2 Skin the fish and cut into thick chunks. Cut the bean curd (tofu) into large cubes and place it with the fish and prawns (shrimp) on a small plate.

3 Bring the chicken stock to the boil with the chilli and ginger in a saucepan or casserole that can be served at the table. A flame-lit fondue pot is ideal.

4 Simmer the noodles in a large pan of salted water according to the instructions on the packet. Refresh under cold running water, drain and place in an attractive bowl.

5 Wash all the salad ingredients in water, drain and arrange on separate plates.

6 Place the chilli sauce, soy sauce and lemon juice in three separate small dishes suitable for dipping and serve at the table. Fondue forks are ideal for dipping the meat and noodles, bean curd (tofu) and fish into the stock, although in Singapore little wire baskets are used.

Chicken Wonton Soup with Prawns (Shrimp)

Ji Wun Tun Tang

This soup is a more luxurious version of basic Wonton Soup, and is almost a meal in itself.

SERVES 4

Ingredients
325g/11oz chicken breast fillet, skin removed
200g/7oz prawn (shrimp) tails, fresh or cooked
1 tsp finely-chopped fresh ginger
2 spring onions (scallions), finely chopped
1 egg
2 tsp oyster sauce (optional)
salt and pepper
1 packet wonton skins
1 tbsp cornflour (cornstarch) paste
850ml/1½ pints/3¾ cups chicken stock
¼ cucumber, peeled and diced
1 spring onion (scallion), roughly shredded, to garnish
4 sprigs coriander leaves, to garnish
1 tomato, skinned, seeded and diced, to garnish

1 Place the chicken breast, 150g/5oz prawn (shrimp) tails, ginger and spring onions (scallions) in a food processor and mix for 2–3 minutes. Add the egg, oyster sauce and seasoning and process briefly. Set aside.

2 Place 8 wonton skins at a time on a surface, moisten the edges with flour paste and place ½ tsp of the filling in the centre of each. Fold in half and pinch to seal. Simmer in salted water for 4 minutes.

3 Bring the chicken stock to the boil, add the remaining prawn (shrimp) tails and the cucumber and simmer for 3–4 minutes. Add the wontons and simmer to warm through. Garnish and serve hot.

Malacca Fried Rice

Chow Fan

There are many versions of this dish throughout the East, all of which make use of left-over rice. Ingredients vary according to what is available, but prawns (shrimp) are a popular addition.

SERVES 4–6

Ingredients
2 eggs
salt and pepper
3 tbsp vegetable oil
4 shallots or 1 medium onion, finely chopped
1 tsp finely-chopped fresh ginger
1 clove garlic, crushed
225g/8oz prawn (shrimp) tails, fresh or cooked
1–2 tsp chilli sauce (optional)
3 spring onions (scallions), green part only, roughly chopped
225g/8oz frozen peas
225g/8oz thickly sliced roast pork, diced
3 tbsp light soy sauce
350g/12oz long grain rice, cooked

1 In a bowl, beat the eggs well, and season. Heat 1 tbsp of the oil in a large non-stick frying pan, pour in the eggs and allow to set without stirring for less than a minute. Roll up the pancake, cut into thin strips and set aside.

2 Heat the remaining vegetable oil in a large wok, add the shallots, ginger, garlic and prawn (shrimp) tails and cook for 1–2 minutes, ensuring that the garlic doesn't burn.

3 Add the chilli sauce, spring onions (scallions), peas, pork and soy sauce. Stir to heat through, then add the rice. Fry the rice over a moderate heat for 6–8 minutes. Turn into a dish and decorate with the pancake.

Pork and Peanut Wontons with Plum Sauce

Wanton Goreng

These crispy filled wontons are delicious served with Egg Pancake Salad Wrappers, a popular salad dish of Indonesia. The wontons can be filled and set aside for 8 hours before cooking.

MAKES 40–50 WONTONS

Ingredients

175g/6oz minced (ground) pork, or the contents of 175g/6oz fresh pork sausages
2 spring onions (scallions), finely chopped
2 tbsp peanut butter
2 tsp oyster sauce (optional)
salt and pepper
1 packet wonton skins
2 tbsp flour paste
vegetable oil, for deep-frying

Plum sauce

225g/8oz dark plum jam (jelly)
1 tbsp rice or white wine vinegar
1 tbsp dark soy sauce
½ tsp chilli sauce

1 Combine the minced (ground) pork, spring onions (scallions), peanut butter, oyster sauce and seasoning and set aside.

2 For the plum sauce, combine the plum jam (jelly), vinegar, soy and chilli sauces in a serving bowl and set aside.

3 To fill the wonton skins, place 8 wrappers at a time on a work surface, moisten the edges with the flour paste and place ½ tsp of the pork mixture on each one. Fold in half, corner to corner, and twist.

4 Fill a wok or deep frying pan one-third with vegetable oil and heat to 196°C/385°F. Have ready a wire strainer or frying basket and a tray lined with kitchen paper. Drop the wontons, 8 at a time, in the hot fat and fry until golden, for about 1–2 minutes. Lift out onto the paper-lined tray and sprinkle with fine salt. Place the plum sauce on a serving plate and surround with the crispy wontons.

HOT CHILLI PRAWNS (SHRIMP)

Udang

Hot Chilli Prawns can be prepared about 8 hours in advance and are best grilled (broiled) or barbecued.

SERVES 4–6

Ingredients
- 1 clove garlic, crushed
- 1 piece fresh ginger, 12mm/½in long, peeled and chopped
- 1 small red chilli, seeded and chopped
- 2 tsp sugar
- 1 tbsp light soy sauce
- 1 tbsp vegetable oil
- 1 tsp sesame oil
- juice of 1 lime
- salt, to taste
- 700g/1½lb whole raw prawns (shrimp)
- 175g/6oz cherry tomatoes
- ½ cucumber, cut into chunks
- 1 small bunch coriander, roughly chopped

1 Pound the garlic, ginger, chilli and sugar to a paste using a pestle and mortar. Add the soy sauce, vegetable and sesame oils, lime juice and salt. Cover the prawns (shrimp) with the marinade and allow to marinate for as long as possible, preferably 8 hours.

2 Thread the prawns (shrimp), tomatoes and cucumber onto bamboo skewers. Grill (broil) the prawns (shrimp) for 3–4 minutes, scatter with the coriander and serve.

PRAWN (SHRIMP) CRACKERS

Krupuk

Prawn (Shrimp) Crackers are a popular addition to many Far Eastern dishes and are often served before guests come to the table. Some supermarkets and food stores sell crackers ready for cooking.

SERVES 4–6

Ingredients
- 300ml/½ pint/1¼ cups vegetable oil
- 50g/2oz uncooked prawn (shrimp) crackers
- fine table salt, to taste

1 Line a tray with kitchen paper. Heat the oil in a large wok until it begins to smoke. Lower the heat to maintain a steady temperature.

2 Drop 3–4 prawn crackers into the oil. Remove from the oil before they begin to colour and transfer to the paper-lined tray. Serve sprinkled with salt.

SWEET AND SOUR GINGER SAMBAL

Sambal Jahe

Sambals are a common sight at Indonesian and Malaysian tables. Their purpose is to perk up or cool down hot chilli flavours. Sambals can also include simple components such as onion and cucumber.

MAKES 90ML/6 TBSP

Ingredients
- 4–5 small red chillies, seeded and chopped
- 2 shallots, or 1 small onion, chopped
- 2 cloves garlic
- 1 piece fresh ginger, 2cm/¾in long, peeled
- 2 tbsp sugar
- ¼ tsp salt
- 3 tbsp rice or white wine vinegar

1 Finely pound or grind the chillies and shallots or onion together using a pestle and mortar or food processor.

2 Add the garlic, ginger, sugar and salt and continue to grind until smooth. Lastly add the vinegar, combine and pour into a screw-top jar.

Spicy Pork with Lemon Grass and Coconut

Semur Daging

Serve this dish with plain boiled rice and Hot Tomato Sambal.

SERVES 4–6

Ingredients
700g/1½lb lean pork, loin or fillet
2 tbsp vegetable oil
4 shallots, or 1 medium onion, chopped
1 piece lemon grass, 5cm/2in long, finely shredded
1–2 small red chillies, seeded and finely chopped
1 piece shrimp paste, 12mm/½in square
400g/14oz canned coconut milk
300ml/½ pint/1¼ cups chicken stock
1 tsp sugar
juice of 1 lemon
zest of 1 satsuma, finely shredded
1 small bunch coriander, chopped

1 Place the pork in the freezer for 30 minutes. Slice the meat thinly.

2 Heat the vegetable oil in a large wok, add the shallots or onion, lemon grass, chillies and shrimp paste. Add the pork and seal.

3 Add the coconut milk, chicken stock, sugar and lemon juice, return to the boil and simmer for 15–20 minutes. Turn the pork out into a serving dish and sprinkle with the zest of the satsuma and the coriander.

Egg Pancake Salad Wrappers

Nonya Popiah

One of Indonesia's favourite snack foods, pancakes are assembled according to taste and dipped in various sauces.

MAKES 12

Ingredients
2 eggs
½ tsp salt
1 tsp vegetable oil, plus a little for frying
115g/4oz plain (all-purpose) flour
300ml/½ pint/1¼ cups water
1 iceberg or bib lettuce
115g/4oz bean sprouts

Filling
3 tbsp vegetable oil
1 piece fresh ginger, 12mm/½in long, peeled and chopped
1 clove garlic, crushed
1 small red chilli, seeded and finely chopped
1 tbsp rice or white wine vinegar
2 tsp sugar
115g/4oz giant white radish, peeled and grated
1 medium carrot, grated
115g/4oz Chinese leaf or white cabbage, shredded
2 shallots, or 1 small red onion, thinly sliced

1 Break the eggs into a bowl, add the salt, vegetable oil and flour and stir until smooth. Do not over-mix. Add the water a little at a time and strain into a jug. Allow the batter to stand for 15–20 minutes.

2 Moisten a small non-stick frying pan with vegetable oil and heat. Cover the base of the pan with batter and cook for 30 seconds. Turn over and cook briefly. Stack the pancakes on a plate, cover and keep warm.

3 Heat the oil in a large wok, add the ginger, garlic and chilli and fry gently. Add the vinegar, sugar, white radish, carrot, Chinese leaf and shallots. Cook for 3–4 minutes. Serve with the pancakes and salad.

Filipino Chicken Pot

Puchero

This nourishing main course soup is one of many brought to the Philippines by the Spanish in the sixteenth century. The recipe and method are based on Potajes, a special stew still enjoyed throughout much of Spain. In the Philippines, ingredients vary according to what is available, but the dish still retains much of its original character.

SERVES 4–6

Ingredients

175g/6oz dried haricot beans
3 chicken legs
1 tbsp vegetable oil
350g/12oz lean pork, diced
1 chorizo (optional)
1 small carrot, peeled and roughly chopped
1 medium onion, roughly chopped
1.7 litres/3 pints/7½ cups water
1 clove garlic, crushed
2 tbsp tomato purée (paste)
1 bay leaf
2 chicken stock cubes
350g/12oz sweet potatoes or new potatoes, peeled
2 tsp chilli sauce
2 tbsp white wine vinegar
3 firm tomatoes, skinned, seeded and chopped
225g/8oz Chinese leaves
salt and freshly-ground black pepper
3 spring onions (scallions), shredded
boiled rice, to serve

1 Soak the beans in plenty of cold water for 8 hours. Drain.

2 Divide the chicken drumsticks from the thighs. Chop off the narrow end of each drumstick and discard.

3 Heat the vegetable oil in a wok or large saucepan, add the chicken, pork, sliced chorizo if using, carrot and onion, then brown evenly.

4 Drain the haricot beans, and add with the water, garlic, tomato purée (paste) and bay leaf. Bring to the boil and simmer for 2 hours until the beans are almost tender.

5 Crumble in the chicken stock cubes, add the sweet or new potatoes and the chilli sauce, then simmer for 15–20 minutes until the potatoes are cooked.

6 Add the vinegar, tomatoes and Chinese leaves, then simmer for 1–2 minutes. Season to taste with salt and pepper. The Puchero is intended to provide enough liquid to be served as a first course broth. This is followed by a main course of the meat and vegetables scattered with the shredded spring onions (scallions). Serve with rice as an accompaniment.

Sweet and Sour Pork with Coconut Sauce

Adobo

Adobo is a popular dish of the Philippines. Typically the meat is tenderized in a marinade before being cooked in coconut milk, shallow-fried and returned to the sauce. Beef, chicken and fish Adobos are also popular.

SERVES 4–6

Ingredients
700g/1½lb lean pork, diced
1 clove garlic, crushed
1 tsp paprika
1 tsp cracked black pepper
1 tbsp sugar
175ml/6fl oz/⅔ cup palm or cider vinegar
2 small bay leaves
425ml/15fl oz/1¼ cups chicken stock
50g/2oz creamed coconut
150ml/¼ pint/⅔ cup vegetable oil or lard (shortening), for frying
1 under-ripe papaya or paw paw, peeled, deseeded and roughly chopped
salt
½ cucumber, peeled and cut into sticks
2 firm tomatoes, skinned, seeded and chopped
1 small bunch chives, chopped

1 Marinate the pork, garlic, paprika, black pepper, sugar, vinegar and bay leaves for 2 hours. Add the stock and coconut.

2 Simmer gently for 30–35 minutes, remove pork, and drain. Heat the oil and brown the pork evenly. Remove and drain.

3 Return the pork to the sauce with the papaya or paw paw, season and simmer for 15–20 minutes. Add garnishes and serve.

Noodles with Chicken, Prawns (Shrimp) and Ham

Pansit Guisado

Egg noodles can be cooked up to 24 hours in advance and kept in a bowl of cold water.

SERVES 4–6

Ingredients
285g/10oz dried egg noodles
1 tbsp vegetable oil
1 medium onion, chopped
1 clove garlic, crushed
1 piece fresh ginger, peeled and chopped
50g/2oz canned water chestnuts, sliced
1 tbsp light soy sauce
2 tbsp fish sauce, or strong chicken stock
175g/6oz cooked chicken breast, sliced
150g/5oz cooked ham, thickly sliced, cut into short fingers
225g/8oz prawn (shrimp) tails, cooked and peeled
175g/6oz bean sprouts
200g/7oz canned baby corn-cobs, drained
2 limes, cut into wedges, to garnish
1 small bunch coriander, shredded, to garnish

1 Cook the noodles according to the packet. Drain and set aside.

2 Fry the onion, garlic and ginger until soft. Add the chestnuts, sauces and meat.

3 Add the noodles, bean sprouts and corn-cobs. Stir-fry for 6–8 minutes.

Braised Beef in a Rich Peanut Sauce

Kari Kari

Like many dishes brought to the Philippines by the Spanish, this slow-cooking Estofado, renamed Kari Kari, retains much of its original charm. Rice and peanuts are used to thicken the juices, yielding a rich glossy sauce.

SERVES 4–6

Ingredients
900g/2lb stewing (braising) chuck, shin or blade steak
2 tbsp vegetable oil
1 tbsp annatto seeds, or 1 tsp paprika and a pinch of turmeric
2 medium onions, chopped
2 cloves garlic, crushed
285g/10oz celeriac or swede (rutabaga), peeled and roughly chopped
425ml/15fl oz/1¾ cups beef stock
350g/12oz new potatoes, peeled and cut into large dice
1 tbsp fish or anchovy sauce
2 tbsp tamarind sauce
2 tsp sugar
1 bay leaf
1 sprig thyme
3 tbsp long grain rice, soaked in water
50g/2oz peanuts or 2 tbsp peanut butter
1 tbsp white wine vinegar
salt and freshly-ground black pepper, to taste

1 Cut the beef into 2.5cm/1in cubes and set aside. Heat the vegetable oil in a flameproof casserole, add the annatto seeds if using, and stir to colour the oil dark red. Remove the seeds with a slotted spoon and discard. If you are not using annatto seeds, paprika and turmeric can be added later.

2 Soften the onions, garlic and the celeriac or swede (rutabaga) in the oil without letting them colour. Add the beef and seal to keep in the flavour. If you are not using annatto seeds to redden the sauce, stir the paprika and turmeric in with the beef. Add the beef stock, potatoes, fish or anchovy and tamarind sauces, sugar, bay leaf and thyme. Bring to a simmer and allow to cook on top of the stove for 2 hours.

3 Cover the rice with cold water and leave to stand for 30 minutes. Roast the peanuts under a hot grill (broiler), if using, then rub the skins off in a clean cloth. Drain the rice and grind with the peanuts or peanut butter using a pestle and mortar, or food processor.

4 When the beef is tender, add 4 tbsp of the cooking liquid to the ground rice and nuts. Blend smoothly and stir into the casserole. Simmer gently on the stove to thicken, for about 15–20 minutes. To finish, stir in the wine vinegar and season well with the salt and freshly-ground pepper.

Sugar Bread Rolls

Ensaimadas

In the Philippines, pots of coffee and hot milky chocolate are brought out for a special custom called the merienda. Meriendas occur morning and afternoon and call for a lavish display of cakes and breads. Many are flavoured with sweet coconut although these delicious rolls of Spanish origin are enriched with butter, eggs and cheese.

MAKES 10 ROLLS

Ingredients
350g/12oz strong white bread flour
1 tsp salt
1 tbsp caster (superfine) sugar
150ml/¼ pint/⅔ cup hand-hot water
1 tsp dried yeast
3 egg yolks
50g/2oz unsalted (sweet) butter, softened
85g/3oz Cheddar cheese, grated
6 tsp unsalted (sweet) butter, melted
50g/2oz sugar

1 Sift the flour, salt and caster (superfine) sugar into a food processor fitted with a dough blade or an electric mixer fitted with a dough hook, then make a well in the centre. Dissolve the yeast into the hand-hot water and pour into the well. Add the egg yolks and leave for a few minutes until bubbles appear on the surface of the liquid.

2 Combine the ingredients for less than a minute into a firm dough. Add the 50g/2oz of butter and knead until smooth, for about 2–3 minutes, or 4–5 minutes if using an electric mixer. Turn the dough out into a floured bowl, cover and leave to rise in a warm place until it doubles in volume.

3 Preheat the oven to 190°C/375°F Gas Mark 5. Turn the dough out onto a lightly-floured work surface and divide into 10 pieces. Spread the grated cheese over the surface and roll each of the pieces into 12.5cm/5in lengths. Coil into snail shapes and place on a lightly-greased, high-sided tray or pan measuring 30 × 20cm/12 × 8in.

4 Cover the tray with a loose-fitting plastic bag and leave to rise for a second time until the dough doubles in volume, for about 45 minutes, or up to 2 hours if conditions are not warm. Bake for 20–25 minutes. Brush with the melted butter, sprinkle with the sugar and allow to cool. Break up the rolls and serve in a lined basket.

Sweet and Sour Pork and Prawn (Shrimp) Soup

Sinegang

This main course soup has a sour, rich flavour. Under-ripe fruits and vegetables provide a special tartness.

SERVES 4–6

Ingredients
350g/12oz lean pork, diced
225g/8oz raw or cooked prawn (shrimp) tails, peeled
2 tbsp tamarind sauce
juice of 2 limes
1 small green guava, peeled, halved and seeded
1 small, under-ripe mango, peeled, flesh removed and chopped
1.4 litres/2½ pints/6¼ cups chicken stock
1 tbsp fish or soy sauce
285g/10oz sweet potato, peeled and cut into even pieces
225g/8oz unripe tomatoes, quartered
115g/4oz green beans, topped, tailed and halved
1 star fruit, thickly sliced
85g/3oz green cabbage, shredded
salt
1 tsp crushed black pepper
2 spring onions (scallions), shredded, to garnish
2 limes, quartered, to garnish

1 Trim the pork, peel the prawns (shrimp) and set aside. Measure the tamarind sauce and lime juice into a saucepan.

2 Add the pork, guava and mango. Pour in the stock. Add the fish or soy sauce and simmer, uncovered, for 30 minutes.

3 Add the remaining fruit, vegetables and prawns (shrimp). Simmer for 10–15 minutes. Adjust seasoning, garnish and serve.

Savoury Pork Pies

Empanadas

These are native to Galicia in Spain and were brought to the Philippines in the sixteenth century.

MAKES 12 PASTRIES

Ingredients
350g/12oz frozen pastry, thawed

Filling
1 tbsp vegetable oil
1 medium onion, chopped
1 clove garlic, crushed
1 tsp thyme
115g/4oz minced (ground) pork
1 tsp paprika
salt and freshly-ground black pepper
1 hard-boiled egg, chopped
1 medium gherkin (pickle), chopped
2 tbsp freshly-chopped parsley
vegetable oil, for deep-frying

1 To make the filling, heat the vegetable oil in a frying pan or wok and soften the onions, garlic and thyme without browning, for about 3–4 minutes. Add the pork and paprika then brown evenly for 6–8 minutes. Season well, turn out into a bowl and cool. When the mixture is cool, add the hard-boiled egg, gherkin (pickle) and parsley.

2 Turn the pastry out onto a floured work surface and roll out to a 37.5cm/15in square. Cut out 12 circles 12.5cm/5in diameter. Place 1 tbsp of the filling on each circle, moisten the edges with a little water, fold over and seal. Heat the vegetable oil in a deep-fryer fitted with a basket, to 196°C/385°F. Place 3 Empanadas at a time in the basket and deep-fry until golden brown. Frying should take at least 1 minute or the inside filling will not be heated through. Serve warm in a basket covered with a napkin.

Sweet Potato and Pumpkin Shrimp Cakes

Ukoy

These delicious fried cakes should be served warm with a fish sauce or a dark soy sauce.

SERVES 4–6

Ingredients
200g/7oz fresh prawn (shrimp) tails, peeled and roughly chopped
200g/7oz strong white bread flour
½ tsp salt
½ tsp dried yeast
175ml/6fl oz/¾ cup hand-hot water
1 egg, beaten
150g/5oz sweet potato, peeled and grated
225g/8oz pumpkin, peeled, seeded and grated
2 spring onions (scallions), chopped
50g/2oz water chestnuts, sliced and chopped
½ tsp chilli sauce
1 clove garlic, crushed
juice of ½ lime
vegetable oil, for deep-frying

1 Sift the flour and salt into a mixing bowl and make a well in the centre. Dissolve the yeast in the water then pour into the well. Pour in the egg and leave for a few minutes until bubbles appear. Mix to a batter.

2 Place the peeled prawns (shrimp) in a saucepan and cover with water. Bring to the boil and simmer for 10–12 minutes. Drain and refresh in cold water. Roughly chop and set aside. Add the sweet potato and pumpkin.

3 Then add the spring onions (scallions), water chestnuts, chilli sauce, garlic, lime juice and prawns (shrimp). Heat a little oil in a large frying pan. Spoon in the batter in small heaps and fry until golden. Drain and serve

Filipino Hot Chocolate

Napalet a Chocolate

This luxurious hot chocolate is served for merienda with Sugar Bread Rolls or Coconut Rice Fritters.

SERVES 2

Ingredients
2 tbsp sugar
100ml/4fl oz/½ cup water
115g/4oz best-quality plain (semi-sweet) chocolate
200ml/7fl oz/scant 1 cup evaporated milk

1 Measure the sugar and water into a non-stick saucepan. Simmer to make a basic syrup.

2 Break the chocolate into even pieces, add to the syrup and stir until melted.

3 Add the evaporated milk, return to a simmer and whisk to a froth. Divide between 2 tall mugs and serve.

Coconut Rice Fritters

Puto

These delicious fritters can be served any time, with a mug of steaming coffee or chocolate.

MAKES 28 FRITTERS

Ingredients
150g/5oz long grain rice, cooked
2 tbsp coconut milk powder
3 tbsp sugar
2 egg yolks
juice of ½ lemon
85g/3oz desiccated (shredded) coconut
oil, for deep-frying
icing (confectioners') sugar, for dusting

1 Place 85g/3oz of the cooked rice in a pestle and mortar and pound until smooth and sticky. Alternatively, use a food processor. Turn out into a large bowl, combine with the remainder of the rice, the coconut milk powder, sugar, egg yolks and lemon juice. Spread the desiccated (shredded) coconut onto a tray, divide the mixture into thumb-size pieces with wet hands and roll in the coconut into neat balls.

2 Heat a wok or deep-fat fryer fitted with a wire basket to 180°C/350°F. Fry the coconut rice balls, 3–4 at a time, for 1–2 minutes until the coconut is evenly brown. Turn out onto a plate, and dust with icing (confectioners') sugar. Place a wooden skewer in each fritter and serve with milky coffee or hot chocolate at merienda time.

Beef and Vegetables in a Table-top Broth

Shabu Shabu

Shabu Shabu is the perfect introduction to Japanese cooking and is well suited to party gatherings. The name refers to the swishing sound made as wafer-thin slices of beef, bean curd (tofu), and vegetables cook in a special broth.

SERVES 4–6

Ingredients

450g/1lb sirloin beef, trimmed
1.7 litres/3 pints/7½ cups water
½ sachet of instant Dashi powder, or ½ vegetable stock cube
150g/5oz carrots
6 spring onions (scallions), trimmed and sliced
150g/5oz Chinese leaves, roughly shredded
225g/8oz giant white radish, peeled and shredded
285g/10oz Udon, or fine wheat noodles, cooked
115g/4oz canned bamboo shoots, sliced
175g/6oz bean curd (tofu), cut into large dice
10 shiitake mushrooms, fresh or dried

Sesame dipping sauce

50g/2oz sesame seeds, or 2 tbsp tahini paste
100ml/4fl oz/½ cup instant Dashi stock, or vegetable stock
4 tbsp dark soy sauce
2 tsp sugar
2 tbsp sake (optional)
2 tsp Wasabi powder (optional)

Ponzu dipping sauce

75ml/3 tbsp/⅓ cup lemon juice
1 tbsp rice or white wine vinegar
75ml/3 tbsp/⅓ cup dark soy sauce
1 tbsp Tamari sauce
1 tbsp Mirin, or 1 tsp sugar
¼ tsp instant Dashi powder, or ¼ vegetable stock cube

1 Place the meat in the freezer for 30 minutes until firm but not frozen. Slice the meat with a large knife or cleaver. Arrange neatly on a plate, cover and set aside. Bring the water to the boil in a Japanese donabe, or any other covered flame-proof casserole that is unglazed on the outside. Stir in the Dashi powder or stock cube, cover and simmer for 8–10 minutes. Serve at the table standing on its own heat source.

2 To prepare the vegetables, bring a saucepan of salted water to the boil. Peel the carrots and with a canelle knife cut a series of grooves along their length. Slice the carrots thinly and blanch for 2–3 minutes. Blanch the spring onions (scallions), Chinese leaves and giant white radish for the same time. Arrange the vegetables with the noodles, bamboo shoots and bean curd (tofu). Slice the mushrooms (soak dried mushrooms in boiling water for 3–4 minutes).

3 To make the sesame dipping sauce, dry-fry the sesame seeds, if using, in a heavy frying pan, taking care not to burn them. Grind the seeds smoothly using a pestle and mortar with a rough surface. Alternatively, you can use tahini paste.

4 Add the remaining ingredients, combine well then pour into a shallow dish. Sesame dipping sauce will keep in the refrigerator for 3–4 days.

5 To make the Ponzu dipping sauce, put the ingredients into a screw-top jar and shake well. Provide your guests with chopsticks and individual bowls, so they can help themselves to what they want. Towards the end of the meal, each guest takes a portion of noodles and ladles the well-flavoured stock over them.

Cook's tip

Dashi is the name given to Japan's most common stock. The flavour derives from a special seaweed known as kelp. This light-tasting stock is available in powder form from oriental food stores. Diluted vegetable stock cube is a good substitute for Dashi.

Tahini paste is a purée of toasted sesame seeds that is used mainly in Greek and Turkish cooking. It is available in large supermarkets and specialist food shops.

Miso Breakfast Soup

Miso-shiru

Miso is a fermented bean paste that adds richness and flavour to many of Japan's favourite soups. This soup provides a nourishing start to the day. Miso paste is widely available in health food stores.

MAKES 1.1 LITRES/2 PINTS/5 CUPS

Ingredients
3 shiitake mushrooms, fresh or dried
1.1 litres/2 pints/5 cups Dashi, or light stock
4 tbsp Miso
115g/4oz bean curd (tofu), cut into large dice
1 spring onion (scallion), green part only, sliced

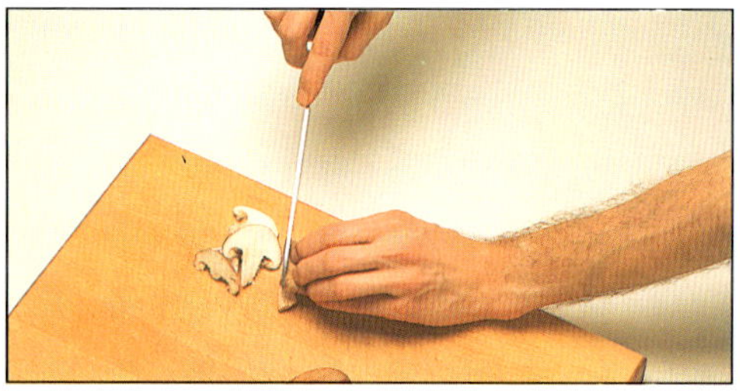

1 Slice the mushrooms thinly. If they are dried, soak them first in boiling water for 3–4 minutes. Set aside.

2 Bring the Dashi or light vegetable stock to the boil. Stir in the Miso, add the mushrooms and simmer for 5 minutes.

3 Ladle the broth into 4 soup bowls and place the bean curd (tofu) in each. Add the spring onion (scallion) and serve.

Crab and Bean Curd (Tofu) Dumplings

Kami-dofu Iridashi

These little crab and ginger dumplings are served as a delicious side accompaniment.

MAKES 30

Ingredients
115g/4oz frozen white crab meat, thawed
115g/4oz bean curd (tofu), drained
1 egg yolk
2 tbsp rice flour, or wheat flour
¼ tsp salt
2 tsp light soy sauce
2 tbsp spring onion (scallion), green part only, finely chopped
1 piece fresh ginger, 2cm/¾in long, peeled and grated
vegetable oil, for deep-frying
50g/2oz giant white radish, finely grated

Dipping sauce
100ml/4fl oz/½ cup Dashi, or light vegetable stock
3 tbsp Mirin, or 1 tbsp sugar
3 tbsp dark soy sauce

1 Squeeze as much moisture out of the crab meat as you can before using. Press the bean curd (tofu) through a fine strainer with the back of a tablespoon and combine with the crab meat in a bowl.

2 Add the egg yolk, rice flour, salt, spring onion (scallion), ginger and soy sauce to the bean curd (tofu) and crab meat and stir to form a light paste. Set aside. To make the dipping sauce, combine the Dashi or stock with the Mirin or sugar and soy sauce.

3 Line a tray with kitchen paper. Heat the vegetable oil to 196°C/385°F. Shape the mixture to make thumb-size pieces. Fry 6 at a time for 1–2 minutes. Drain on the paper. Serve with the sauce and radish.

Barbecue-glazed Chicken Skewers

Yakitori

Yakitori is popular throughout Japan and is often served as an appetizer with drinks.

MAKES 12 SKEWERS AND 8 WING PIECES

Ingredients
4 chicken thighs, skinned
4 spring onions (scallions), blanched and cut into short lengths
8 chicken wings

Basting sauce
4 tbsp sake
75ml/5 tbsp/⅓ cup dark soy sauce
2 tbsp Tamari sauce
3 tbsp Mirin, or sweet sherry
4 tbsp sugar

1 Bone the chicken thighs and cut the meat into large dice. Thread the spring onions (scallions) and chicken onto 12 skewers.

2 To prepare the chicken wings, remove the wing tip at the first joint. Chop through the second joint, revealing the two narrow bones. Take hold of the bones with a clean cloth and pull, turning the meat around the bones inside out. Remove the smaller bone and set aside.

3 Measure the basting sauce ingredients into a stainless steel or enamel saucepan and simmer until reduced by two-thirds. Cool. Heat the grill (broiler) to a moderately high temperature. Grill (broil) the skewers without applying any oil. When juices begin to emerge from the chicken baste liberally with the basting sauce. Allow a further 3 minutes for the chicken on skewers and not more than 5 minutes for the wings.

Raw Fish and Rice Parcels

Sushi

Sushi is something of an art form in Japan, but with a little practice it is possible to make sushi at home.

MAKES 8–10

Ingredients

Tuna sushi
3 sheets nori (paper-thin seaweed)
150g/5oz freshest tuna fillet, cut into fingers
1 tsp Wasabi, made into a thin paste with a little water
6 young carrots, blanched
450g/1lb cooked sushi rice

Salmon sushi
2 eggs
½ tsp salt
2 tsp sugar
5 sheets nori
450g/1lb cooked sushi rice
150g/5oz freshest salmon fillet, cut into fingers
1 tsp Wasabi, made into a thin paste with a little water
½ small cucumber, cut into strips

1 To make the tuna sushi, spread half a sheet of nori onto a bamboo mat, lay strips of tuna across the full length and season with the thinned Wasabi. Place a line of blanched carrot next to the tuna and roll tightly. Moisten the edge with water and seal. Place a square of wet greaseproof paper (non-stick baking paper) onto the bamboo mat, then spread evenly with sushi rice. Place the seaweed-wrapped tuna along the centre and wrap tightly, enclosing the seaweed completely. Remove the paper and cut into neat rounds with a wet knife.

2 To make the salmon sushi, make a simple flat omelette by beating together the eggs, salt and sugar. Heat a large non-stick pan, pour in the egg mixture, stir briefly and allow to set. Turn out onto a clean cloth and cool. Place the nori onto a bamboo mat, cover with the omelette and trim to size. Spread a layer of rice over the omelette then lay strips of salmon across the width. Season the salmon with the thinned Wasabi, then place a strip of cucumber next to the salmon. Fold the bamboo mat in half, forming a tear shape inside. Cut into neat sections with a wet knife.

Salt-grilled (Broiled) Mackerel

Shio-yaki

Shio-yaki means salt-grilled. In Japan, salt is applied to oily fish before cooking to draw out the flavours. Mackerel, garfish and snapper are the most popular choices, all of which develop a unique flavour and texture when treated with salt. The salt is washed away before cooking.

SERVES 2

Ingredients
2 small or 1 large mackerel, snapper or garfish, gutted and cleaned, with head on
2 tbsp fine sea salt

Soy ginger dip
4 tbsp dark soy sauce
2 tbsp sugar
1 piece fresh ginger, 2.5cm/1in long, peeled and finely grated

Japanese horseradish
3 tsp Wasabi powder
2 tsp water
1 medium carrot, peeled and shredded

1 Rinse the fish under cold running water and dry well with kitchen paper. Slash the fish several times on each side, cutting down as far as the bone. This will ensure that the fish will cook evenly. Salt the fish inside and out, rubbing well into the skin. Place the fish on a plate and leave to stand for 40 minutes.

2 To make the soy ginger dip, place the soy sauce, sugar and ginger in a stainless steel saucepan. Simmer for 2–3 minutes, strain and cool. To make the Japanese horseradish, measure the Wasabi powder into a small cup, add the water and stir to make a stiff paste. Shape into a neat ball and place on a heap of shredded carrot.

3 Wash the fish in plenty of cold water to remove the salt. Secure each fish in a curved position before grilling. To do this, pass two bamboo skewers through the length of the fish, one above the eye and one below.

4 Preheat a grill (broiler) or barbecue to a moderate temperature and cook the fish for 10–12 minutes, turning once. It is customary to cook the fish plainly, but you may like to baste the skin with a little of the soy ginger dip part way through cooking.

Aubergine (Egg Plant) with Sesame Chicken

Nasu Hasami-age

Young vegetables are prized in Japan for their sweet, delicate flavour. Here, small aubergines (egg plant) are stuffed with seasoned chicken.

SERVES 4

Ingredients
- 175g/6oz chicken, breast or thigh, skinned
- 1 spring onion (scallion), green part only, finely chopped
- 1 tbsp dark soy sauce
- 1 tbsp Mirin, or sweet sherry
- ½ tsp sesame oil
- ¼ tsp salt
- 4 small aubergines (egg plant), about 10cm/4in long
- 1 tbsp sesame seeds
- plain (all-purpose) flour for dusting

Dipping sauce
- vegetable oil, for deep-frying
- 4 tbsp dark soy sauce
- 4 tbsp Dashi, or vegetable stock
- 3 tbsp Mirin, or sweet sherry

1 To make the stuffing, remove the chicken meat from the bone and mince it finely in a food processor, for about 1–2 minutes. Add the spring onion (scallion), soy sauce, Mirin or sherry, sesame oil and salt.

2 Make 4 slits in the aubergines (egg plant) so they remain joined at the stem. Spoon the minced chicken into the aubergines (egg plant), opening them slightly to accommodate the mixture. Dip the fat end of the stuffed aubergine (egg plant) in the sesame seeds, then dust in flour. Set aside.

3 For the dipping sauce, combine the soy sauce, Dashi or stock and Mirin or sherry. Pour into a shallow bowl and set aside.

4 Heat the vegetable oil in a deep-fryer to 196°C/385°F. Fry the aubergines (egg plant), 2 at a time, for 3–4 minutes. Lift out with a slotted spoon onto kitchen paper.

Japanese Rice and Sushi Rice

Sushi-meshi

The Japanese prefer their rice slightly sticky so that it can be shaped and eaten with chopsticks. Authentic Japanese rice can be difficult to obtain in the West, but may be replaced by Thai or long grain rice, washed only once to retain a degree of stickiness.

YIELDS 900G/2LB COOKED RICE

Ingredients
350g/12oz Japanese, Thai or long grain rice
1.1 litres/2 pints/5 cups boiling water
1 piece giant kelp, 5cm/2in square (optional)

Dressing
3 tbsp rice vinegar or distilled white vinegar
3 tbsp sugar
2 tsp sea salt

1 If using Japanese rice, wash several times until the water runs clear. Wash Thai or long grain rice only once and drain well. Place the rice in a large heavy saucepan, cover with the measured amount of water and the kelp, if using. Stir once and simmer, uncovered, for 15 minutes. Turn off the heat, cover and stand for a further 5 minutes to allow the rice to finish cooking in its own steam. Before serving, the rice should be fluffed with a rice paddle or spoon. This rice is a Japanese staple.

2 To prepare sushi rice, make the dressing, by heating the vinegar in a small saucepan, with a lid to keep in the strong vapours. Add the sugar and salt and dissolve. Allow to cool. Spread the cooked rice onto a mat or tray and allow to cool.

3 Pour on the dressing and fluff with a rice paddle or spoon. Keep covered until ready to use.

Battered Fish, Prawns (Shrimp) and Vegetables

Tempura

Tempura is one of the few dishes brought to Japan from the West. The idea came via Spanish and Portuguese missionaries who settled in southern Japan in the late sixteenth century.

SERVES 4–6

Ingredients
- 1 sheet nori
- 8 large raw prawn (shrimp) tails
- 175g/6oz whiting or monkfish fillet, cut into fingers
- 1 small aubergine (egg plant)
- 4 spring onions (scallions), trimmed
- 6 shiitake mushrooms, fresh or dried
- plain (all-purpose) flour, for dusting
- vegetable oil, for deep-frying
- fine salt, to sprinkle
- 5 tbsp soy, or Tamari sauce, to serve

Batter
- 2 egg yolks
- 300ml/½ pint/1 ¼ cups iced water
- 225g/8oz plain (all-purpose) flour
- ½ tsp salt

De-veining prawns (shrimp)

All raw prawns (shrimp) have an intestinal tract that runs just beneath the outside curve of the tail. The tract is not poisonous but can taste unpleasant. It is therefore best to remove it.

1 Peel the prawn (shrimp) tails leaving the tail part attached.

2 Score each prawn (shrimp) lightly along its length, exposing the tract. Remove the tract with a small knife.

1 Cut the nori into 12mm/½in strips, 5cm/2in long. Moisten one end of the nori with water, and wrap around the tail end of each prawn (shrimp). Skewer the prawns (shrimp) through their length to straighten them. Skewer the fillets of white fish and set aside.

2 Slice the aubergine (egg plant) into neat sections, sprinkle with salt, layer on a plate and press lightly with your hand to expel the bitter juices. Leave for 20–30 minutes, then rinse under cold water. Dry well and place on bamboo skewers. Prepare the other vegetables on skewers and set aside.

3 The batter should be made just before it is used. Beat the egg yolks and half the iced water together in a bowl, sift in the flour and salt and stir loosely with chopsticks without mixing into a dry paste. Add the remainder of the water and stir to make a smooth batter. Avoid over-mixing.

4 Heat the vegetable oil in a deep-fryer or wok, fitted with a wire draining rack, to 180°C/350°F. Dust the fish and vegetables in flour, not more than 3 at a time. Dip into the batter, coating well, then fry in the hot oil until crisp and golden, for about 1–2 minutes. Drain well, sprinkle with fine salt and drain on kitchen paper before serving with a soy or Tamari dipping sauce.

STRAW NOODLE PRAWNS (SHRIMP) IN A SWEET GINGER DIP

Age-mono

Prawns (shrimp) are a popular feature in Japanese cooking. Rarely are they more delicious than when wrapped in crispy noodles and seaweed.

SERVES 4–6

Ingredients
85g/3oz Somen noodles, or vermicelli
2 sheets nori
12 large fresh prawn (shrimp) tails, peeled and de-veined
vegetable oil, for deep-frying

Dipping sauce
6 tbsp soy sauce
2 tbsp sugar
1 piece fresh ginger, 2cm/¾in long, grated

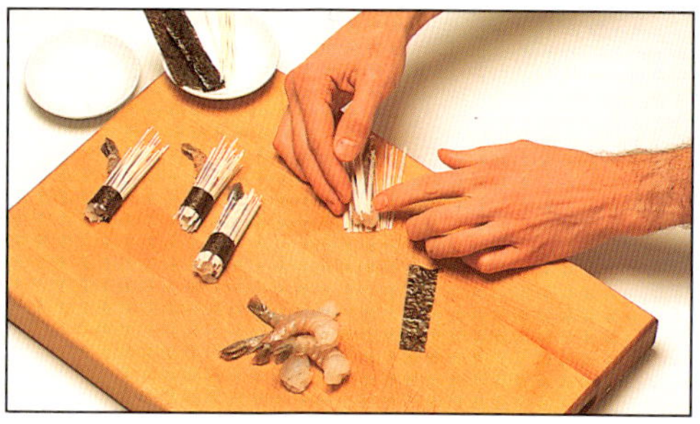

1 Cover the Somen noodles, if using, with boiling water and soak for 1–2 minutes. Drain and dry thoroughly with kitchen paper. Cut the noodles into 7.5cm/3in lengths. If using vermicelli, cover with boiling water for 1–2 minutes to soften. Cut the nori into 12mm/½in strips, 5cm/2in long, and set aside. To make the dipping sauce, bring the soy sauce to the boil with the sugar and ginger. Simmer for 2–3 minutes, strain and cool.

2 Line up the noodles or vermicelli on a wooden board. Straighten each prawn (shrimp) by pushing a bamboo skewer through its length. Roll the prawns (shrimp) in the noodles so that they adhere in neat strands. Moisten one end of the nori and secure the noodles at the fat end of the prawn (shrimp). Set aside.

3 Heat the vegetable oil in a deep-frying pan, or wok fitted with a wire draining rack, to 180°C/350°F. Fry the prawns (shrimp) in the oil, 2 at a time, until the noodles or vermicelli are crisp and golden.

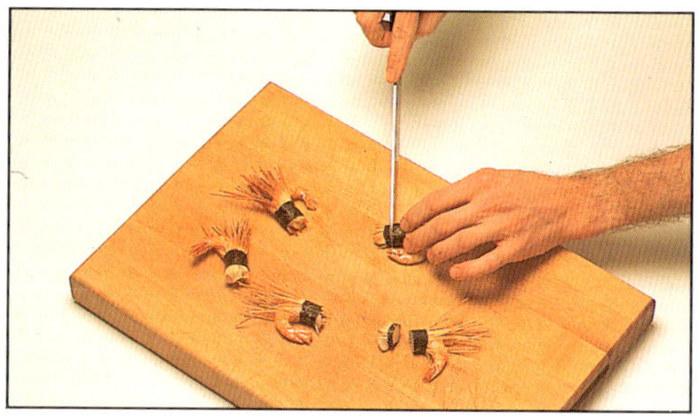

4 To finish, cut through the band of nori with a sharp knife exposing a clean section of prawn (shrimp). Drain on kitchen paper and serve with the dipping sauce in a small dish.

Sweet Potato and Chestnut Candies

Okashi

It is customary in Japan to offer special bean paste candies with tea. The candies tend to be very sweet by themselves, but contrast well with Japanese green teas; in particular, large-leaf Sencha and Banch.

MAKES 18

Ingredients

450g/1lb sweet potato, peeled and roughly chopped
¼ tsp salt
2 egg yolks
200g/7oz sugar
4 tbsp water
75g/5 tbsp rice flour or plain wheat flour
1 tsp orange flower or rose water (optional)
200g/7oz canned chestnuts in heavy syrup, drained
caster (superfine) sugar, for dusting
2 strips candied angelica
2 tsp plum or apricot preserve
3–4 drops red food colouring

1 Place the sweet potatoes in a heavy saucepan, cover with cold water and add the salt. Bring to the boil and simmer until the sweet potatoes are tender, for about 20–25 minutes. Drain well and return to the pan. Mash the sweet potatoes well, or rub through a fine strainer. Place the egg yolks, sugar and water in a small bowl, then combine the flour and orange flower or rose water if using. Add to the purée and stir over a gentle heat to thicken for about 3–4 minutes. Turn the paste out onto a tray and cool.

2 To shape the sweet potato paste, place 2 tsp of the mixture into the centre of a wet cotton napkin or handkerchief. Enclose the paste in the cotton and twist into a nut shape. If the mixture sticks, ensure the fabric is properly wet.

3 To prepare the chestnuts, rinse away the thick syrup and dry well. Roll the chestnuts in caster (superfine) sugar and decorate with strips of angelica. To finish the sweet potato candies, colour the plum or apricot preserve with red colouring and decorate each one with a spot of colour. Serve in a Japanese lacquer box or on an open plate.

Cook's tip

Sugar-coated chestnuts will keep for up to 5 days at room temperature, stored in a sealed box. Sweet potato candies will also keep, sealed and refrigerated.

TASTE OF INDIA

RAFI FERNANDEZ

The vast sub-continent of India offers a range of culinary delights as rich and diverse as its people and history. Each region has its own unique cooking style: cream, yoghurt, ghee and nuts feature in dishes in the north, while the south favours chillies, coconut and coconut oil. Fish and mustard oil predominate in the east while the west has incorporated the greatest number of foreign ingredients. One element unites these diverse styles – the use of spices to create the flavours and aromas distinctive of Indian cuisine.

THE PRINCIPLES OF INDIAN COOKING

The Indian diet is the product of many influences – economic, religious and environmental – but Indian meals will combine nutrition with a harmonious blend of textures and flavours. For this reason, care must be taken to provide the correct accompaniment to any dish. Cooling elements such as raithas and salads should be served with hot curries, with pickles and chutneys providing the perfect foil to heavily spiced dishes. There is no myth to Indian cooking. Each of the dishes in this book can be easily prepared in the Western kitchen, and the majority of ingredients are readily available in supermarkets.

EQUIPMENT AND UTENSILS

Chappati griddle (tava) (1) These are made from heavy wrought iron and allow chappatis and other breads to be cooked without burning.
Chappati rolling board (roti takta) (2) This board consists of a round wooden surface on stubby legs and helps in shaping different sizes of breads. The extra height helps disperse excess dry flour.
Chappati rolling pin (velan) (3) These are thinner in shape than Western pins and come in a variety of sizes. Use whichever best suits your hand.
Chappati spoon (roti chamcha) (4) The square-shaped flat head assists in roasting breads on the hot griddle.
Colander (channi) (5) Use a sturdy, stainless steel colander as it will not discolour.
Food processor (6) This is an essential piece of equipment. Small quantities of ingredients can be ground using a pestle and mortar or a coffee grinder.
Heat diffuser (7) Many curries are simmered gently over a low heat, and a heat diffuser helps prevent burning on the base.
Indian frying pan (karai) (8) A karai is similar to a wok but is more rounded in shape and made of heavier metal.
Knives (churrie) (9) Keep knives very sharp. It will be easier to chop ingredients and will ensure neat edges.
Oblong grinding stone and pin (sil padi) (10) This is a traditional Indian 'food processor'. The ingredients are placed on a stone made of heavy slate marked with notches. The rolling pin is used to pulverize the ingredients against the stone.
Rice spoon (chawal ke chamchi) (11) This helps prevent the rice grains from being damaged while serving.
Sizzler (garam thali) (12) This enables food to be served at the table still cooking.
Slotted spoon (channi chamchi) (13) This enables items to be removed safely from deep hot oil or other liquids.
Stainless steel pestle and mortar (hamam dasta) (14) This is ideal for grinding small amounts of wet ingredients such as ginger and garlic. The steel is everlasting and will not retain the strong flavours of the spices.
Stone pestle and mortar (pathar hamam dasta) (15) This is suitable for mixing small amounts of ingredients, both wet and dry.

SPICES

Aniseed (1) This has a delicate liquorice flavour and sweet seeds. It is a good aid to digestion.
Bay leaves (2) Bay leaves feature in a lot of dishes from the north of India. They are also used in aromatic rice.
Black cardamom (3) These large black pods are used whole. They have a menthol aroma and are mainly used in cooking from the north of India.
Black cumin (4) These aromatic seeds are mainly used whole sprinkled on breads and in rice dishes. Do not substitute with ordinary cumin seeds.
Chilli powder (5) Many brands are now available and each vary in spiciness. Add small quantities at a time and adjust accordingly.
Cinnamon bark (6) This is also available in quill form. It can be removed from the dish before serving.
Cloves (7) Cloves are used in both savoury and sweet dishes.
Coriander powder (8) Coriander powder not only adds flavour but is also used to thicken curries.
Coriander seeds (9) Coriander seeds are very rarely used whole. Dry-roast the seeds before grinding. Coriander is essential to a good curry.
Cumin powder (10) Highly aromatic cumin powder is one of the essential ingredients in curries.
Cumin seeds (11) Whole cumin seeds are mainly used in vegetarian dishes. Dry-roast the seeds before grinding.
Fennel seeds (12) The seeds of the fennel are aromatic and sweet. They may be used whole or in powdered form. They are also dry-roasted, cooled and served after meals to aid digestion and freshen the mouth.
Fenugreek powder (13) This slightly bitter-tasting ingredient must be used sparingly.
Fenugreek seeds (14) These are used whole in vegetarian dishes. When planted the seed produces a spinach.
Five-spice powder (15) This is a combination of star anise, fennel, cinnamon, clove and Sichuan pepper.
Garam masala (16) This combination of spices provides heat to the body and enhances curries. Several combinations are available.
Green cardamom (17) Green cardamom is sweet and aromatic in flavour and is used in both savoury and sweet dishes.

Mustard seeds (18) Mustard seeds are odourless but become very pungent when pounded or moistened. When planted they produce mustard spinach.
Nigella (19) Nigella is an aromatic spice with a sharp and tingling taste. It is mainly used in vegetarian dishes.
Onion seeds (20) These black teardrop-shaped seeds have an earthy aroma. They are sprinkled on breads and used in vegetarian dishes.
Peppercorns (21) Peppercorns were introduced to India by the Portuguese and are now an indispensable ingredient in much Indian cooking.
Red chillies (22) Red chillies were introduced to India by the Portuguese. The larger the chilli the less hot it is. Remove the seeds for a milder chilli taste.
Round red chillies (23) These are hot, with a pimento flavour and are delicious in pickles.
Saffron (24) Saffron is the world's most expensive spice, produced from the stigma of a particular variety of crocus. Over 100,000 crocus blossoms picked by hand are needed to produce 450g (1lb) of saffron.
Star anise (25) Star anise is a star-shaped, liquorice-flavoured pod.
Turmeric (26) Turmeric is yellow in colour with an earthy but pungent taste. It should be used with caution.

INGREDIENTS

Almond flakes (1) Almond flakes are extremely rich in vitamin B1. They are prohibitively expensive in India.
Apricots (2) Apricots are mainly used for festive occasions and celebrations. Stewed apricots are served with custard as a favourite dessert.
Asafoetida (3) This is a resin with an acrid and bitter taste and a strong odour. Store in a jar with a strong air-tight seal to prevent the smell dispersing into other ingredients.
Aubergine (egg plant) (4) Immerse aubergines (egg plant) in water immediately after cutting to prevent discoloration.
Basmati rice (5) Basmati rice is the staple grain of India. Many brands are now available in the West.
Bengal gram (6) Bengal gram is used whole in lentil curries. The flour (besan) is used to prepare bhajias and may be used to flavour and thicken certain curries.
Black-eyed beans (7) These are oval-shaped beige beans with a distinctive dark 'eye'. They are very popular in the north of India.
Black gram (8) Black gram may be used whole or split. The flour is used to make papadums.
Bottle gourd (9) The fruit of the bottle gourd is whitish-green. Remove peel and pith before using.
Chick peas (garbanzo beans) (10) These are beige heart-shaped peas, sold dry or cooked soaked in brine. Pre-cooked, soaked chick peas (garbanzo beans) save a lot of preparation time.
Coriander leaves (11) Coriander is India's most popular herb, and is well-loved for its refreshing and unique taste and aroma.
Curry leaves (12) Curry leaves are most popular in the south of India. The leaves freeze well without any special preparation.
Gentleman's toes (tindla) (13) These tender fruits look like mini cucumbers when cut. If over-ripe they will be red inside.
Ginger (14) Fresh ginger is essential to Indian cuisine and is used in a wide variety of sweet and savoury dishes.
Green chillies (15) Green chillies are not indigenous to India but have become indispensable to Indian cuisine. They are very rich in vitamins A and C.
Gypsy beans (16) These have a slightly bitter taste but are delicious when cooked. Top and tail like any other bean before using.
Indian cheese (paneer) (17) Paneer is extremely popular in the north of India and is used in many vegetarian dishes for added nutrition. Long-life vacuum-packed paneer is available from Indian supermarkets and many health food shops.
Lemon (18) Lemons and limes are used to sour curries and make pickles and chutneys.
Mace (19) Mace is the dried covering of the nutmeg. It has a slightly bitter taste.
Mango (ripe) (20) Several varieties of mango are available but the best, 'alfonso', can only be found between May and July.
Mango (green) (21) Green mangoes are mainly used to make pickles and chutneys. They are sometimes added to south Indian curries.
Melon (22) Melon is often served in India for its cooling qualities.
Mint (23) Indian mint has a stronger aroma than the varieties available in the West.
Nutmeg (24) This aromatic and sweet spice is essential to many Indian dishes.
Okra (25) Okra is a very popular vegetable in India. It must be prepared and cooked with care to prevent the sticky insides from spreading among other ingredients in a dish.
Oranges (26) Oranges are refreshing served in wedges after a meal.
Pistachios (27) Pistachios are not indigenous to India and are therefore an expensive ingredient.
Purple beans (28) These beans have a broad, greenish purple pod with dark purple seeds. Top and tail before using.
Red chillies (29) Fresh red chillies vary in strength. The hottest are the smallest, known as 'bird's eyes'.
Red gram (30) Red gram is available dry or lightly oiled.
Red onion (31) Red onions are in fact a deep purple colour. They are more pungent than ordinary onions.
Santra (32) Santra is very refreshing after a curry meal. Serve wedges sprinkled with salt and pepper.
Spinach (33) India has over 15 varieties of spinach and it features in many vegetarian dishes.
Tamarind (34) Tamarind is a sour crescent-shaped fruit.
Tomato (35) The tomato is another ingredient introduced to India by the Portuguese, which now features in many dishes.
Vermicelli (36) These hair-like strands are made from wheat and are used in savoury and sweet dishes. Indian is much finer than Italian vermicelli.
Walnuts (37) Walnuts are used in sweetmeats, salads and raitha.

Onion Fritters

Bhajias

Bhajias are a classic snack of India. The same batter may be used with a variety of vegetables.

MAKES 20–25

Ingredients

225g/8oz gram flour (besan), or channa atta
½ tsp chilli powder
1 tsp turmeric powder
1 tsp baking powder
¼ tsp asafoetida
salt, to taste
½ tsp each, nigella, fennel, cumin and onion seeds, coarsely crushed
2 large onions, finely sliced
2 green chillies, finely chopped
50g/2oz coriander leaves, chopped
cold water, to mix
vegetable oil, for deep-frying

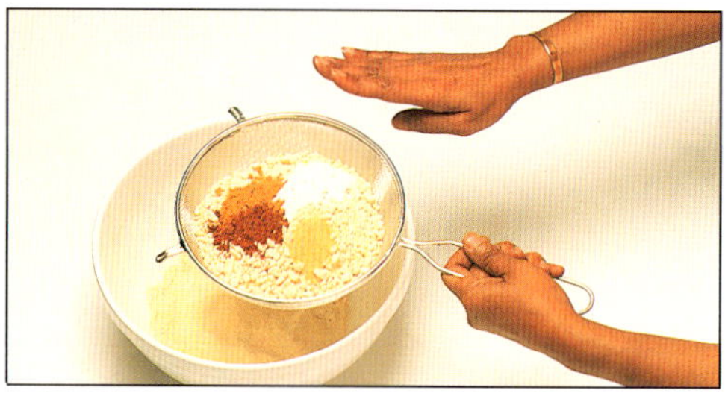

1 In a bowl, mix together the flour, chilli, turmeric, baking powder, asafoetida and salt to taste. Pass through a sieve into a large mixing bowl.

2 Add the coarsely-crushed seeds, onion, green chillies and coriander leaves and toss together well. Very gradually mix in enough cold water to make a thick batter surrounding all the ingredients.

3 Heat enough oil in a karai or wok for deep-frying. Drop spoonfuls of the mixture into the hot oil and fry until they are golden brown. Leave enough space to turn the fritters. Drain well and serve hot.

Yoghurt Soup

Karhi

Some communities in India add sugar to this soup. When Bhajias are added, it is served as a main dish.

SERVES 4–6

Ingredients

450ml/¾ pint/1½ cups natural (plain) yoghurt, beaten
4 tbsp gram flour (besan)
½ tsp chilli powder
½ tsp turmeric
salt, to taste
2–3 green chillies, finely chopped
4 tbsp vegetable oil
4 whole dried red chillies
1 tsp cumin seeds
3 cloves garlic, crushed
1 piece fresh ginger, 5cm/2in long, crushed
3–4 curry leaves
fresh coriander leaves, chopped, to garnish

1 Mix together the first 5 ingredients and pass through a strainer into a saucepan. Add the green chillies and cook gently for about 10 minutes, stirring occasionally. Be careful not to let the soup boil over.

2 Heat the oil in a frying pan and fry the remaining spices, garlic and ginger until the dried chillies turn black.

3 Pour the oil and the spices over the yoghurt soup, cover the pan and leave to rest for 5 minutes off the heat. Mix well and gently reheat for a further 5 minutes. Serve hot, garnished with the coriander leaves.

Lentil Soup

Dhal Sherva

This is a simple, mildly spiced lentil soup, which is a good accompaniment to heavily spiced meat dishes.

SERVES 4–6

Ingredients
1 tbsp ghee
1 large onion, finely chopped
2 cloves garlic, crushed
1 green chilli, chopped
½ tsp turmeric
85g/3oz red lentils (masoor dhal)
250ml/8fl oz/1 cup water
salt, to taste
400g/14oz canned tomatoes, chopped
½ tsp sugar
lemon juice, to taste
200g/7oz/1 cup plain boiled rice or 2 potatoes, boiled (optional)
coriander leaves, chopped, to garnish

1 Heat the ghee in a large saucepan and fry the onion, garlic, chilli and turmeric until the onion is translucent.

2 Add the lentils and water and bring to the boil. Reduce the heat, cover and cook until all the water is absorbed.

3 Mash the lentils with the back of a wooden spoon until you have a smooth paste. Add salt to taste and mix well.

4 Add the remaining ingredients. Reheat the soup and serve hot. To provide extra texture, fold in the plain boiled rice or potatoes cut into small cubes.

Cook's tip

When using lentils, first rinse in cold water and remove any floating items.

Potato Cakes with Stuffing

Petis

Only a few communities in India make these unusual starters. Petis can also be served as a main meal with Tomato Salad.

MAKES 7–10

Ingredients
1 tbsp vegetable oil
1 large onion, finely chopped
2 cloves garlic, finely crushed
1 piece fresh ginger, 5cm/2in long, finely crushed
1 tsp coriander powder
1 tsp cumin powder
2 green chillies, finely chopped
2 tbsp each, chopped coriander and mint leaves
225g/8oz lean minced (ground) beef or lamb
50g/2oz frozen peas, thawed
salt, to taste
juice of 1 lemon
900g/2lb potatoes, boiled and mashed
2 eggs, beaten
breadcrumbs, for coating
vegetable oil, for shallow-frying
lemon wedges, to serve

1 Heat the tbsp of oil and fry the first 7 ingredients until the onion is translucent. Add the meat and peas and fry well until the meat is cooked, then season with salt and lemon juice. The mixture should be very dry.

2 Divide the mashed potato into 8–10 portions, take a portion and flatten into a pancake in the palm of your hand. Place a spoonful of the meat in the centre and gather the sides together to enclose the meat. Flatten it slightly to make a round shape.

3 Dip each petis in beaten egg and then coat in breadcrumbs. Allow to chill in the refrigerator for about 1 hour.

4 Heat the oil in a frying pan and shallow-fry the cakes until all the sides are brown and crisp. Serve hot with lemon wedges.

South Indian Pepper Water

Tamatar Rasam

This is a highly soothing broth for winter evenings, also known as Mulla-ga-tani. Serve with the whole spices or strain and reheat if you so wish. The lemon juice may be adjusted to taste, but this dish should be distinctly sour.

SERVES 4–6

Ingredients
2 tbsp vegetable oil
½ tsp freshly-ground black pepper
1 tsp cumin seeds
½ tsp mustard seeds
¼ tsp asafoetida
2 whole dried red chillies
4–6 curry leaves
½ tsp turmeric
2 cloves garlic, crushed
300ml/½ pint/1¼ cups tomato juice
juice of 2 lemons
100ml/4fl oz/½ cup water
salt, to taste
coriander leaves, chopped, to garnish

1 In a large frying pan, heat the oil and fry the next 8 ingredients until the chillies are nearly black and the garlic golden brown.

2 Lower the heat and add the tomato juice, lemon juice, water and salt. Bring to the boil then simmer for 10 minutes. Garnish with the chopped coriander and serve.

Chicken Mulligatawny

Kozhi Mulla-ga-tani

Using the original Pepper Water – Mulla-ga-tani – this dish was created by the non-vegetarian chefs during the British Raj. The recipe was imported to the United Kingdom and today ranks highly on several restaurant menus as Mulligatawny soup.

SERVES 4–6

Ingredients
900g/2lb chicken, boned, skinned and cubed
575ml/1 pint/2½ cups water
6 green cardamom pods
1 piece cinnamon stick, 5cm/2in long
4–6 curry leaves
1 tbsp coriander powder
1 tsp cumin powder
½ tsp turmeric
3 cloves garlic, crushed
12 whole peppercorns
4 cloves
1 onion, finely chopped
115g/4oz coconut cream block
salt, to taste
juice of 2 lemons
deep-fried onions, to garnish
coriander leaves, chopped, to garnish

1 Place the chicken in a large pan with the water and cook until the chicken is tender. Skim the surface, then strain, reserving the stock and keeping the chicken warm.

2 Return the stock to the pan and reheat. Add all the remaining ingredients, except the chicken, deep-fried onions and coriander. Simmer for 10–15 minutes, then strain and return the chicken to the soup. Reheat, garnish with deep-fried onions and chopped coriander and serve.

Pastry Triangles with Spicy Filling

Samosas

Traditional samosa pastry requires a lot of time and hard work but spring roll pastry makes an excellent substitute and is readily available. One packet will make 30 samosas. They can be frozen before or after frying.

MAKES 30

Ingredients
1 packet spring roll pastry, thawed and wrapped in a damp towel
vegetable oil, for deep-frying

Filling
3 large potatoes, boiled and coarsely mashed
85g/3oz frozen peas, boiled and drained
50g/2oz canned sweetcorn, drained
1 tsp coriander powder
1 tsp cumin powder
1 tsp amchur (dry mango powder)
1 small onion (red if available), finely chopped
salt, to taste
2 green chillies, finely chopped
2 tbsp each, coriander and mint leaves, chopped
juice of 1 lemon

1 Toss all the filling ingredients together in a large mixing bowl until well blended. Adjust seasoning of salt and lemon juice, if necessary.

2 Using one strip of pastry at a time, place 1 tbsp of the filling mixture at one end of the strip and diagonally fold the pastry to form a triangle.

3 Heat enough oil for deep-frying and fry the samosas in small batches until they are golden brown. Serve hot with Fresh Coriander Relish or a chilli sauce.

Spicy Omelette

Poro

Eggs are packed with nutritional value and make wholesome and delicious dishes. This omelette, cooked with potato, onion and a touch of spices, can be put together quickly for an emergency meal.

SERVES 4–6

Ingredients
2 tbsp vegetable oil
1 medium onion, finely chopped
½ tsp cumin powder
1 clove garlic, finely crushed
1 or 2 green chillies, finely chopped
a few sprigs fresh coriander, chopped
1 firm tomato, chopped
1 small potato, cubed and boiled
25g/1oz cooked peas
25g/1oz cooked sweetcorn
salt and pepper, to taste
2 eggs, beaten
25g/1oz grated cheese

1 Heat the oil in a saucepan and fry the next 9 ingredients until well blended but the potato and tomato are firm. Season to taste.

2 Increase the heat and pour in the beaten eggs. Reduce the heat, cover and cook until the bottom layer is brown. Turn the omelette over and sprinkle with the grated cheese. Place under a hot grill and cook until the egg sets and the cheese has melted.

Rice Layered with Chicken and Potatoes

Murgh Biryani

This dish is mainly prepared for important occasions, and is truly fit for royalty. Every cook in India has a subtle variation which is kept a closely-guarded secret.

SERVES 4–6

Ingredients

- 1.3kg/3lb chicken breast fillet, skinned and cut into large pieces
- 4 tbsp biryani masala paste
- 2 green chillies, chopped
- 1 tbsp crushed fresh ginger
- 1 tbsp crushed garlic
- 50g/2oz coriander leaves, chopped
- 6–8 mint leaves, chopped, or 1 tsp mint sauce
- 150ml/½ pint/⅔ cup natural (plain) yoghurt, beaten
- 2 tbsp tomato purée (paste)
- 4 onions, finely sliced, deep-fried and crushed
- salt, to taste
- 450g/1lb basmati rice, washed and drained
- 1 tsp black cumin seeds
- 1 piece cinnamon stick, 5cm/2in long
- 4 green cardamoms
- 2 black cardamoms
- vegetable oil, for shallow-frying
- 4 large potatoes, peeled and quartered
- 175ml/6fl oz/¾ cup milk, mixed with 85ml/3fl oz/⅓ cup water
- 1 sachet saffron powder, mixed with 6 tbsp milk
- 2 tbsp ghee or unsalted (sweet) butter

Garnish

- ghee or unsalted (sweet) butter, for shallow-frying
- 50g/2oz cashew nuts
- 50g/2oz sultanas (white raisins)
- 2 hard-boiled eggs, quartered
- deep-fried onion slices

1 Mix the chicken with the next 10 ingredients in a large bowl and allow to marinate for about 2 hours. Place in a large heavy pan and cook gently for about 10 minutes. Set aside.

2 Boil a large pan of water and soak the rice with the cumin seeds, cinnamon stick and green and black cardamoms for about 5 minutes. Drain well. Some of the whole spices may be removed at this stage.

3 Heat the oil for shallow-frying and fry the potatoes until they are evenly browned on all sides. Drain and set aside.

4 Place half the rice on top of the chicken in the pan in an even layer. Then make an even layer with the potatoes. Put the remaining rice on top of the potatoes and spread to make an even layer.

5 Sprinkle the water mixed with milk all over the rice. Make random holes through the rice with the handle of a spoon and pour into each a little saffron milk. Place a few knobs of ghee or butter on the surface, cover and cook over a low heat for 35–45 minutes.

6 While the biryani is cooking, make the garnish. Heat a little ghee or butter and fry the cashew nuts and sultanas (white raisins) until they swell. Drain and set aside. When the biryani is ready, gently toss the rice, chicken and potatoes together, garnish with the nut mixture, hard-boiled eggs and onion slices and serve hot.

Rice Layered with Prawns (Shrimp)

Jingha Gucci Biryani

This dish makes a meal in itself, requiring only pickles or raitha as an accompaniment. If serving for a party, complete your table with Boiled Egg Curry and Potatoes in a Hot Red Sauce.

SERVES 4–6

Ingredients
2 large onions, finely sliced and deep fried
300ml/½ pint/1¼ cups natural yoghurt
2 tbsp tomato purée (paste)
4 tbsp green masala paste
2 tbsp lemon juice
salt, to taste
1 tsp black cumin seeds
1 piece cinnamon stick, 5cm/2in long, or ¼ tsp cinnamon
4 green cardamoms
450g/1lb fresh king prawns (shrimp), peeled and de-veined
225g/8oz small whole button mushrooms
225g/8oz frozen peas, thawed and drained
450g/1lb basmati rice soaked for 5 minutes in boiled water and drained
300ml/½ pint/1¼ cups water
1 sachet saffron powder mixed in 6 tbsp milk
2 tbsp ghee or unsalted (sweet) butter

1 Mix the first 9 ingredients together in a large bowl. Fold the prawns (shrimp), mushrooms and peas into the marinade and leave for about 2 hours.

2 Grease the base of a heavy pan and add the prawns (shrimp), vegetables and any marinade juices. Cover with the drained rice and smooth the surface gently until you have an even layer.

3 Pour the water all over the surface of the rice. Make random holes through the rice with the handle of a spoon and pour into each a little saffron milk.

4 Place a few knobs of ghee or butter on the surface and place a circular piece of foil directly on top of the rice. Cover and cook over a low heat for 45–50 minutes. Gently toss the rice, prawns (shrimp) and vegetables together and serve hot.

Unleavened Bread Roasted with Ghee

Paratha

A richer, softer and flakier variation on chappatis, parathas require longer preparation time so plan your menu well ahead. Like chappatis, parathas can be kept warm wrapped in foil.

MAKES 12–15

Ingredients
350g/12oz atta (wholemeal flour)
50g/2oz plain (all-purpose) flour
salt, to taste
6 tsp ghee
2 tsp ghee, melted
water, to mix
50g/2oz atta (wholemeal flour), for dusting

1 Sift the flours and salt into a large mixing bowl. Make a well in the centre and add 2 tsp of the ghee and fold into the flour to make a crumbly texture. Very gradually add enough water to make a soft but pliable dough. Cover and leave to rest for 1 hour.

2 Divide the dough into 12–15 equal portions and keep covered. Take one portion at a time and roll out on a lightly-floured surface to about 10cm/4in in diameter. Brush with a little of the melted ghee and sprinkle with atta. With a sharp knife, make a straight cut from the centre to the edge.

3 Lift a cut edge and roll the dough into a cone shape. Lift it and flatten it again into a ball. Roll the dough again on a floured surface until it is 17.5cm/7in wide.

4 Heat a griddle and cook one paratha at a time, placing a little of the remaining ghee along the edges. Cook on each side until golden brown. Serve hot.

ROASTED UNLEAVENED BREAD

Chappati

Chappatis are prepared daily in most Indian homes. They are best eaten as soon as they are cooked although they can be kept warm, wrapped in foil and placed in a warm oven.

MAKES 10–12

Ingredients
350g/12oz atta (wholemeal flour)
1 tsp salt
water, to mix
a few drops of vegetable oil, for brushing
50g/2oz atta (wholemeal flour), for dusting
ghee or unsalted (sweet) butter, for spreading

1 Sift the flour and salt into a large bowl. Make a well in the centre and slowly add small quantities of water until you have a smooth but pliable dough. Grease the palms of your hands and knead the dough well. Keep covered until you are ready to use.

2 Divide the dough into 10–12 equal portions, using one portion at a time and keeping the rest covered. Knead each portion into a ball, then flatten with your hands and place on a floured surface. Roll out until you have a circle about 17.5cm/7in in diameter.

3 Heat a heavy griddle and, when hot, roast the chappatis on each side, pressing the edges down gently. When both sides are ready, brush the first side lightly with ghee or butter.

LEAVENED BREAD

Naan

Traditionally, naans are baked in a tandoor or clay oven, though grilled naans look just as authentic.

MAKES 6–8

Ingredients
2 tsp dry active yeast
4 tbsp warm milk
2 tsp sugar
450g/1lb plain (all-purpose) flour
1 tsp baking powder
½ tsp salt
150ml/¼ pint/⅔ cup milk
150ml/¼ pint/⅔ cup natural (plain) yoghurt, beaten
1 egg, beaten
25g/1oz melted ghee
flour, for dusting
ghee, for greasing
chopped coriander leaves and onion seeds, to sprinkle

1 Mix the yeast, warm milk and sugar and leave to become frothy. Sift the flour, baking powder and salt. Make a well in the centre and add the yeast mixture, milk, yoghurt, egg and ghee. Fold in all the ingredients.

2 Knead the dough well. Tightly cover the bowl and keep in a warm place until the dough doubles. To test, push a finger into the dough – it should spring back. Roll out the dough on a floured surface.

3 Make each naan slipper-shaped, about 25cm/10in long and about 15cm/6in wide, tapering to 5cm/2in. Sprinkle with the coriander and onion seeds. Place on greased trays and bake at 200°C/400°F/Gas Mark 6.

Plain Boiled Rice

Chawal

In India, rice is consumed in great quantities by all members of society. There are numerous ways in which it can be prepared, but plain boiled rice is the most common.

SERVES 4–6

Ingredients

1 tbsp ghee, unsalted (sweet) butter or olive oil
350g/12oz basmati rice, washed and drained
500ml/¾ pint/2 cups water
salt, to taste

1 Heat the ghee, butter or oil in a saucepan and sauté the drained rice thoroughly for about 2–3 minutes.

2 Add the water and salt and bring to the boil. Reduce the heat to low, cover and cook gently for 15–20 minutes. To serve, fluff the grains gently with a fork.

Cook's tip

To make Kesar Chawal or fragrant rice, sauté 4–6 green cardamoms, 4 cloves, 5cm/2in piece cinnamon stick, ½ tsp black cumin seeds and 2 bay leaves. Add 350g/12oz drained basmati rice and proceed as for plain boiled rice. For an even more luxurious rice, add 6–8 strands of saffron and sauté with the spices.

Fragrant Rice with Meat

Yakhni Pilau

This rice dish acquires its delicious taste from not only the spices but the richly flavoured meat stock.

SERVES 4–6

Ingredients

900g/2lb chicken pieces, or lean lamb, cubed
575ml/1 pint/2½ cups water
4 green cardamoms
2 black cardamoms
10 whole peppercorns
4 cloves
1 medium onion, sliced
salt, to taste
450g/1lb basmati rice, washed and drained
8–10 saffron strands
2 cloves garlic, crushed
1 piece fresh ginger, 5cm/2in long, crushed
1 piece cinnamon stick, 5cm/2in long
175g/6oz sultanas (white raisins) and peeled almonds, sautéed, to garnish

1 In a large saucepan, cook the chicken or lamb in the water with the cardamoms, peppercorns, cloves, onion and salt until the meat is cooked. Remove the meat and keep warm. Strain the stock if you wish, and return to the saucepan.

2 Add the rice, saffron, garlic, ginger and cinnamon to the stock and bring the contents to the boil.

3 Quickly add the meat and stir well. Bring back to the boil, reduce the heat and cover. Cook covered for about 15–20 minutes. Remove from the heat for 5 minutes. Add the contents of the saucepan. Garnish with sultanas (white raisins) and almonds and serve.

Rice Layered with Lentils and Gourd Curry

Dhal Chawal Palida

Bhori Muslims in India have their own special style of cooking and have adapted many of the traditional dishes from other Indian communities. Palida is prominently flavoured with fenugreek and soured with kokum (dried mangosteen). Lemon juice will provide the same effect.

SERVES 4–6

Ingredients

175g/6oz bengal gram
575ml/1 pint/2½ cups water
½ tsp turmeric powder
50g/2oz deep-fried onions, crushed
3 tbsp green masala paste
a few mint and coriander leaves, chopped
salt, to taste
350g/12oz basmati rice, cooked
2 tbsp ghee
a little water
4 tbsp vegetable oil
¼ tsp fenugreek seeds
15g/½oz dried fenugreek leaves
2 cloves garlic, crushed
1 tsp coriander powder
1 tsp cumin seeds
1 tsp chilli powder
4 tbsp gram flour mixed with 4 tbsp water
450g/1lb bottle gourd peeled, pith and seeds removed and cut into bite-size pieces or marrow (squash) or firm courgettes (zucchini)
175ml/6fl oz/¾ cup tomato juice
6 kokum (dried mangosteen), or juice of 3 lemons
salt, to taste
coriander leaves, to garnish

1 For the rice, boil the bengal gram in the water with the turmeric until the grains are soft but not mushy. Drain and reserve the water for the curry.

2 Toss the bengal gram gently with the deep-fried onions, green masala paste, chopped mint and coriander leaves, and salt.

3 Grease a heavy pan and place a layer of rice in the bottom. Add the bengal gram mixture and another layer of the remaining rice. Place small knobs of ghee on top, sprinkle with a little water and gently heat until steam gathers in the pan.

4 To make the curry, heat the oil in a pan and fry the fenugreek seeds and leaves and garlic until the garlic turns golden brown.

5 Mix the spice powders to a paste with a little water. Add to the pan and simmer until all the water evaporates.

6 Add the remaining ingredients, and cook until the gourd is soft and transparent. Garnish with the coriander leaves and serve hot with Dhal Chawal.

Moghul-style Roast Lamb

Shahi Raan

This superb dish is just one of many fine examples of fabulous rich food once enjoyed by Moghul Emperors. Try it as a variation to roast beef.

SERVES 4–6

Ingredients
4 large onions, chopped
4 cloves garlic
1 piece fresh ginger, 5cm/2in long chopped
3 tbsp ground almonds
2 tsp cumin powder
2 tsp coriander powder
2 tsp turmeric
2 tsp garam masala
4–6 green chillies
juice of 1 lemon
salt, to taste
300ml/½ pint/1¼ cups natural (plain) yoghurt, beaten
1.8kg/4lb leg of lamb
8–10 cloves
4 firm tomatoes, halved and grilled, to serve
1 tbsp blanched almond flakes, to garnish

1 Place the first 11 ingredients in a food processor and blend to a smooth paste. Gradually add the yoghurt and blend. Grease a large, deep baking tray and preheat the oven to 190°C/375°F/Gas Mark 5.

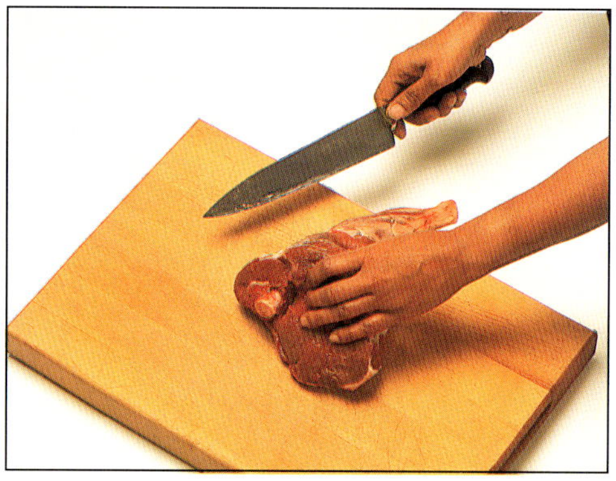

2 Remove most of the fat and skin from the lamb. Using a sharp knife, make deep pockets above the bone at each side of the thick end. Make deep diagonal gashes on both sides.

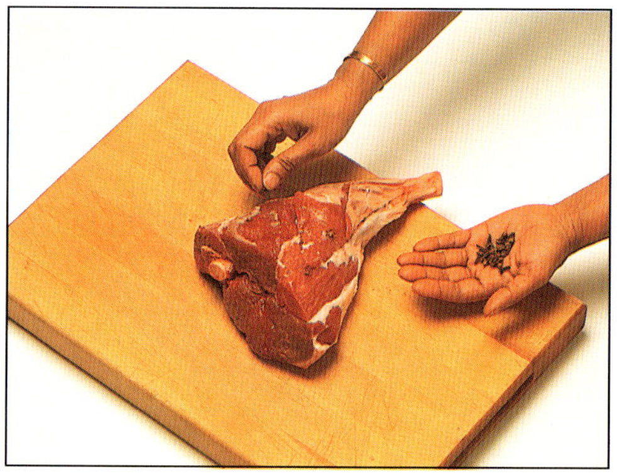

3 Push the cloves into the meat at random.

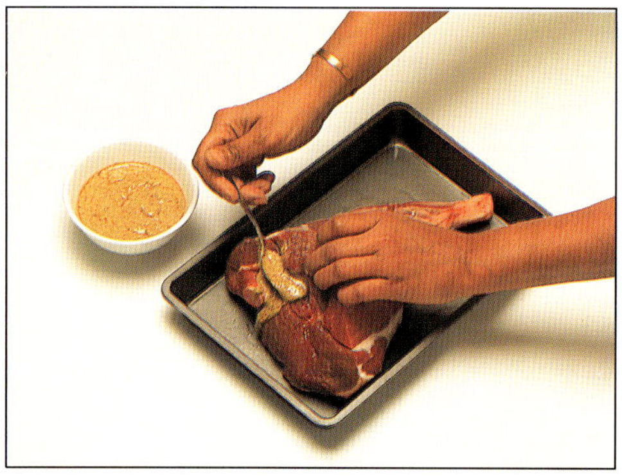

4 Push some of the spice mixture into the pockets and gashes and spread the remainder evenly all over the meat.

5 Place the meat on the baking tray and loosely cover the whole tray with foil. Roast for 2–2½ hours or until the meat is cooked, removing the foil for the last 10 minutes of cooking time.

6 Remove from the oven and allow to rest for 10 minutes before carving. Serve with grilled tomatoes and garnish the joint with almond flakes.

Kashmiri-style Lamb

Rogan Josh

This curry originated in Kashmir, and derives its name from the large quantities of red chillies used in the dish. They may be reduced for a milder flavour, with paprika and 2 tsp tomato purée (paste) added to retain the colour.

SERVES 4–6

Ingredients
4 tbsp vegetable oil
¼ tsp asafoetida
900g/2lb lean lamb, cubed
1 piece fresh ginger, 5cm/2in long, crushed
2 cloves garlic, crushed
4 tbsp rogan josh masala paste
1 tsp chilli powder or 2 tsp sweet paprika
8–10 strands saffron (optional)
salt, to taste
150ml/¼ pint/⅔ cup natural (plain) yoghurt, beaten
blanched almond flakes, to garnish

1 Heat the oil in a frying pan and fry the asafoetida and lamb, stirring well to seal the meat. Reduce the heat, cover and cook for about 10 minutes.

2 Add the remaining ingredients except the yoghurt and almonds and mix well. If the meat is too dry, add a very small quantity of boiling water. Cover and cook on a low heat for a further 10 minutes.

3 Remove the pan from the heat and leave to cool a little. Add the yoghurt, 1 tbsp at a time, stirring constantly to avoid curdling. Cook uncovered on low until the gravy becomes thick. Garnish and serve hot.

Hot Dry Meat Curry

Sookha Gosht

This dish is nearly as hot as phaal (India's hottest curry), but the spices can still be distinguished above the chilli.

SERVES 4–6

Ingredients
2 tbsp vegetable oil
1 large onion, finely sliced
1 piece fresh ginger, 5cm/2in long, crushed
4 cloves garlic, crushed
6–8 curry leaves
3 tbsp extra hot curry paste, or 4 tbsp hot curry powder
3 tsp chilli powder
1 tsp five-spice powder
1 tsp turmeric
salt, to taste
900g/2lb lean lamb, beef or pork, cubed
175ml/6fl oz/¾ cup thick coconut milk
2 large tomatoes, finely chopped, to garnish

1 Heat the oil and fry the onion, ginger, garlic and curry leaves until the onion is soft. Add the curry paste, chilli and five-spice powder, turmeric and salt.

2 Add the meat and stir well over a medium heat to seal and evenly brown the meat pieces. Keep stirring until the oil separates. Cover and cook for about 20 minutes.

3 Add the coconut milk, mix well and simmer until the meat is cooked. Towards the end of cooking, uncover the pan to reduce the excess liquid. Garnish and serve hot.

Spicy Meat Loaf

Lagan Ki Seekh

This mixture is baked in the oven and provides a hearty breakfast on cold winter mornings.

SERVES 4–6

Ingredients
5 eggs
450g/1lb lean minced (ground) beef
2 tbsp finely-ground ginger
2 tbsp finely-ground garlic
6 green chillies, chopped
2 small onions, finely chopped
½ tsp turmeric
50g/2oz coriander leaves, chopped
175g/6oz potato, grated
salt, to taste

1 Preheat the oven to 180°C/350°F/Gas Mark 4. Beat 2 eggs until fluffy and pour into a greased baking tray.

2 Knead the meat, ginger and garlic, 4 green chillies, 1 chopped onion, 1 beaten egg, the turmeric, coriander leaves, potato and salt. Pack into the baking tray and smooth the surface. Cook for 45 minutes.

3 Beat the remaining eggs and fold in the remaining green chillies and onion. Remove the baking tray from the oven and pour the mixture all over the meat. Return to the oven and cook until the eggs have set.

Spicy Kebabs

Kofta

Serve these tasty kebabs piping hot with Leavened Bread, Raitha and Tomato Salad. Leftover kebabs can be coarsely chopped and packed into pitta bread spread with Fresh Coriander Relish.

MAKES 20–25

Ingredients
450g/1lb lean minced (ground) beef or lamb
2 tbsp finely-ground ginger
2 tbsp finely-ground garlic
4 green chillies, finely chopped
1 small onion, finely chopped
1 egg
½ tsp turmeric
1 tsp garam masala
50g/2oz coriander leaves, chopped
4–6 mint leaves, chopped, or ½ tsp mint sauce
175g/6oz raw potato
salt, to taste
vegetable oil, for deep-frying

1 Place the first 10 ingredients in a large bowl. Grate the potato into the bowl, and season with salt. Knead together to blend well and form a soft dough.

2 Shape the mixture into portions the size of golf balls. Leave to rest for about 25 minutes.

3 In a wok or frying pan, heat the oil to medium-hot and fry the koftas in small batches until they are golden brown in colour. Drain well and serve hot.

Mince Kebabs

Shammi Kebab

Serve this Indian hamburger in a bun with chilli sauce and salad or unaccompanied as a starter.

SERVES 4–6

Ingredients
2 onions, finely chopped
250g/9oz lean lamb, cut into small cubes
50g/2oz bengal gram
1 tsp cumin seeds
1 tsp garam masala
4–6 green chillies
1 piece fresh ginger, 5cm/2in long, crushed
salt, to taste
175ml/6fl oz/¾ cup water
a few coriander and mint leaves, chopped
juice of 1 lemon
1 tbsp gram flour
2 eggs, beaten
vegetable oil, for shallow-frying

1 Put the first 8 ingredients and the water into a pan and bring to the boil. Simmer, covered, until the meat and dhal are cooked. Cook uncovered to reduce the excess liquid. Cool, and grind to a paste.

2 Place the mixture in a mixing bowl and add the coriander and mint leaves, lemon juice and gram flour. Knead well. Divide into 10–12 portions and roll each into a ball, then flatten slightly. Chill for 1 hour. Dip the kebabs in the beaten egg and shallow-fry each side until golden brown. Serve hot.

Curried Mince

Kheema

This can be served as a main dish or mixed with fried or scrambled eggs for a brunch. It also makes a good pizza topping.

SERVES 4–6

Ingredients
1 tsp vegetable oil
1 large onion, finely chopped
2 cloves garlic, crushed
1 piece fresh ginger, 5cm/2in long, crushed
4 green chillies, chopped
2 tbsp curry powder
450g/1lb lean minced (ground) beef, or lamb
225g/8oz frozen peas, thawed
salt, to taste
juice of 1 lemon
a few coriander leaves, chopped

1 Fry the onion, garlic, ginger and chillies until the onion is translucent. Lower the heat, add the curry powder and mix well.

2 Add the meat and stir well, pressing the meat down with the back of a spoon. Add the peas, salt and lemon juice, mix well, cover and simmer. Fold in the coriander. Serve hot.

Portuguese Pork

Soovar Vindaloo

This dish displays the influence of Portuguese cooking on Indian cuisine.

SERVES 4–6

Ingredients
115g/4oz deep-fried onions, crushed
4 red chillies, or 1 tsp chilli powder
4 tbsp vindaloo masala paste
6 tbsp white wine vinegar
6 tbsp tomato purée (paste)
½ tsp fenugreek seeds
1 tsp turmeric
1 tsp crushed mustard seeds, or ½ tsp mustard powder
salt, to taste
1½ tsp sugar
900g/2lb boneless pork spareribs, cubed
1 cup water
plain boiled rice, to serve

1 Place all the ingredients except the water and rice in a heavy steel pan or mixing bowl and mix well. Marinate for about 2 hours

2 Add the water and mix well. Simmer gently for about 2 hours. Adjust the seasoning. Serve hot with the plain boiled rice.

Steak and Kidney with Spinach

Sag Gosht

When this dish is cooked in India, the spinach is often pulverized. Here, it is coarsely chopped and added in the last stages of cooking, which retains the nutritional value of the spinach and gives the dish a lovely appearance.

SERVES 4–6

Ingredients
2 tbsp vegetable oil
1 large onion, finely chopped
1 piece fresh ginger, 5cm/2in long, crushed
4 cloves garlic, crushed
4 tbsp mild curry paste, or 4 tbsp mild curry powder
¼ tsp turmeric
salt, to taste
900g/2lb steak and kidney, cubed
450g/1lb fresh spinach, trimmed, washed and chopped or 450g/1lb frozen spinach, thawed and drained
4 tbsp tomato purée (paste)
2 large tomatoes, finely chopped

1 Heat the oil in a frying pan and fry the onion, ginger and garlic until the onion is soft and the ginger and garlic turn golden brown.

2 Lower the heat and add the curry paste or powder, turmeric, salt and meat and mix well. Cover and cook until the meat is nearly tender.

3 Add the spinach and tomato purée (paste) and mix well. Cook uncovered until the spinach is softened and most of the liquid evaporated.

4 Fold in the chopped tomatoes. Increase the heat and cook for about 5 minutes.

Madras

Madras Attu Erachi

This popular South Indian curry is mainly prepared by Muslims and is traditionally made with beef.

SERVES 4–6

Ingredients
4 tbsp vegetable oil
1 large onion, finely sliced
3–4 cloves
4 green cardamoms
2 whole star anise
4 green chillies, chopped
2 red chillies, chopped (fresh or dried)
3 tbsp madras masala paste
1 tsp turmeric
450g/1lb lean beef, cubed
4 tbsp tamarind juice
salt, to taste
sugar, to taste
a few coriander leaves, chopped, to garnish

1 Heat the oil in a frying pan and fry the onion until it is golden brown. Lower the heat and add all the spice ingredients and fry for a further 2–3 minutes.

2 Add the beef and mix well. Cover and cook on low heat until the beef is tender. Cook uncovered on a higher heat for the last few minutes to reduce any excess liquid.

3 Fold in the tamarind juice, salt and sugar. Reheat the dish and serve hot, garnished with the chopped coriander leaves.

Lamb in a Creamy Sauce

Korma

This is a creamy, aromatic dish with no 'hot' taste. It comes from the kitchens of the Nizam of Hyderabad.

SERVES 4–6

Ingredients
1 tbsp white sesame seeds
1 tbsp white poppy seeds
50g/2oz almonds, blanched
2 green chillies, seeded
6 cloves garlic, sliced
1 piece fresh ginger, 5cm/2in long, sliced
1 onion, finely chopped
3 tbsp ghee or vegetable oil
6 green cardamoms
1 piece cinnamon stick, 5cm/2in long
4 cloves
900g/2lb lean lamb, cubed
1 tsp cumin powder
1 tsp coriander powder
salt, to taste
300ml/½ pint/1¼ cups double (heavy) cream mixed with ½ tsp cornflour (cornstarch)
roasted sesame seeds, to garnish

1 Heat a frying pan without any liquid and dry-roast the first 7 ingredients. Cool the mixture and grind to a fine paste using a pestle and mortar or food processor. Heat the ghee or oil in a frying pan.

2 Fry the cardamoms, cinnamon and cloves until the cloves swell. Add the lamb, cumin and coriander powders and the prepared paste, and season. Cover and cook until the lamb is almost done.

3 Remove from the heat, cool a little and gradually fold in the cream, reserving 1 tsp to garnish. To serve, gently reheat the lamb uncovered and serve hot, garnished with the sesame seeds and the remaining cream.

Tandoori Chicken

Tandoori Murgh

This is probably the most famous of Indian dishes. Marinate the chicken well and cook in an extremely hot oven for a clay-oven-baked taste. If you wish authentic 'burnt' spots on the chicken, place the dish under a hot grill for a few minutes after cooking.

SERVES 4–6

Ingredients
1.3kg/3lb ready-to-roast chicken
225ml/8oz/1 cup natural (plain) yoghurt, beaten
4 tbsp tandoori masala paste
salt, to taste
85g/3oz ghee
lettuce, to serve
lemon wedges and onion rings, to garnish

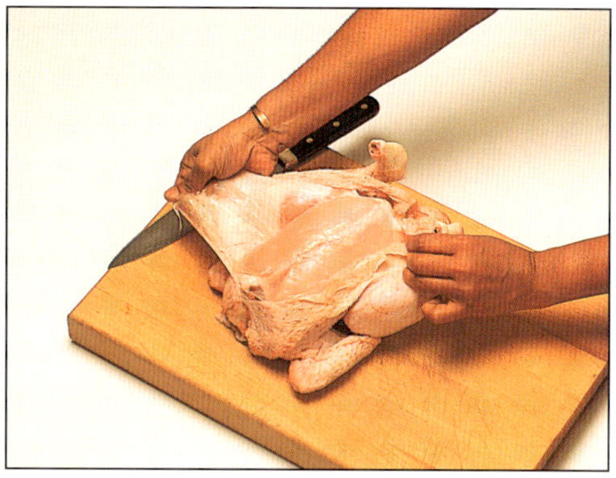

1 Using a sharp knife or scissors, remove the skin from the chicken and trim off any excess fat. Using a fork, beat the flesh at random.

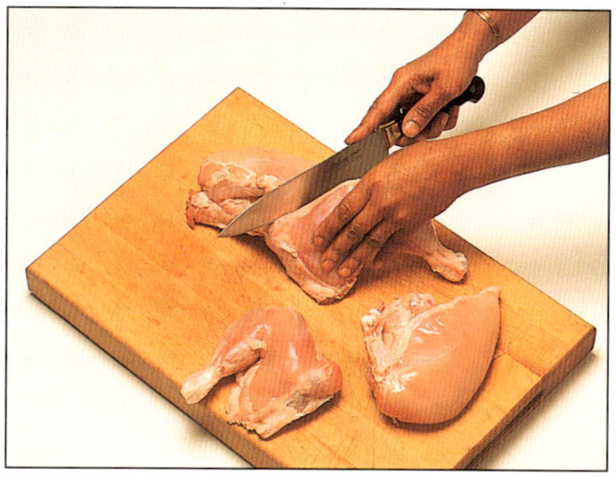

2 Cut the chicken in half down the centre and through the breast. Cut each piece in half again. Make a few deep gashes diagonally into the flesh. Mix the yoghurt with the masala paste and salt. Spread the chicken evenly with the yoghurt mixture, spreading some into the gashes. Leave for at least 2 hours, but preferably overnight.

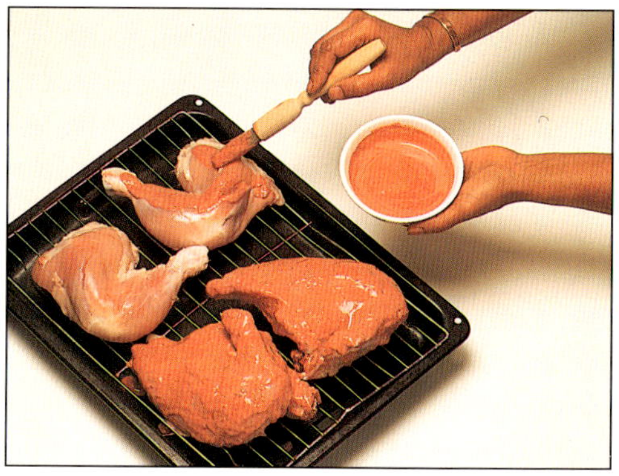

3 Place the chicken quarters on a wire rack in a deep baking tray. Spread the chicken with any excess marinade, reserve a little for basting halfway through cooking time.

4 Melt the ghee and pour over the chicken to seal the surface. This helps to keep the centre moist during the roasting period. Cook in the oven for 10 minutes at maximum heat, then remove, leaving the oven on.

5 Baste the chicken pieces with the remaining marinade. Return to the oven and switch off the heat. Leave the chicken in the oven for about 15–20 minutes without opening the door. Serve on a bed of lettuce and garnish with the lemon and onion rings.

Stuffed Roast Chicken

Murgh Mussallam

At one time, this dish was only cooked in royal palaces and ingredients varied according to individual chefs. The saffron and rich stuffing make it a truly royal dish.

SERVES 4–6

Ingredients
1 sachet saffron powder
½ tsp ground nutmeg
1 tbsp warm milk
1.3kg/3lb whole chicken
6 tbsp ghee
75ml/5 tbsp/⅓ cup hot water

Stuffing
3 medium onions, finely chopped
2 green chillies, chopped
50g/2oz sultanas (white raisins)
50g/2oz ground almonds
50g/2oz dried apricots, soaked until soft
3 hard-boiled eggs, coarsely chopped
salt, to taste

Masala
4 spring onions (scallions), chopped
2 cloves garlic, crushed
1 tsp five-spice powder
4–6 green cardamoms
½ tsp turmeric
1 tsp freshly-ground black pepper
2 tbsp natural (plain) yoghurt
50g/2oz desiccated (shredded) coconut

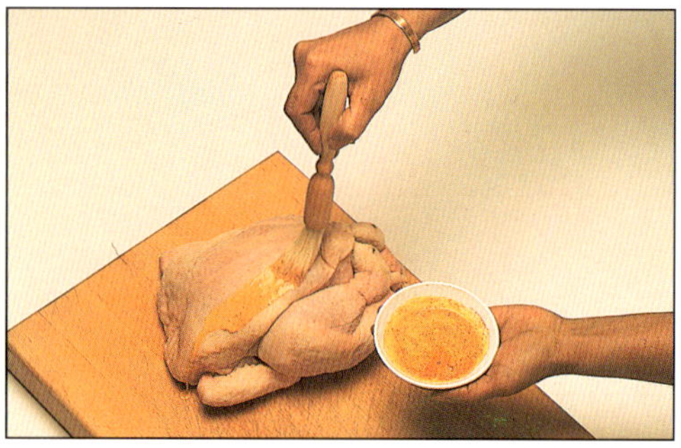

1 Mix together the saffron, nutmeg and milk. Brush the inside of the chicken with the mixture and carefully spread some under the skin. Heat 4 tbsp of the ghee in a large frying pan or wok and fry the chicken on all sides to seal it. Remove and keep warm.

2 To make the stuffing, in the same ghee, fry the onions, chillies, and sultanas (white raisins) for 2–3 minutes. Remove from the heat, allow to cool and add the ground almonds, apricots, chopped eggs and salt. Toss the mixture well, then stuff the chicken.

3 Heat the remaining ghee in a large heavy pan and gently fry all the masala ingredients except the coconut for 2–3 minutes. Add the water. Place the chicken on the bed of masala, cover the pan and cook until the chicken is tender. Set aside keeping warm.

4 Return the pan to the heat and cook to reduce excess fluids in the masala. When the mixture thickens, pour over the chicken. Sprinkle with toasted coconut and serve hot.

Chicken Curry

Murgh Ka Salan

Chicken curry is always popular when served at a family dinner or banquet. This version is cooked covered, giving a thin consistency. If you would prefer it thick, cook uncovered for the last 15 minutes.

SERVES 4–6

Ingredients

4 tbsp vegetable oil
4 cloves
4–6 green cardamoms
1 piece cinnamon stick, 5cm/2in long
3 whole star anise
6–8 curry leaves
1 large onion, finely chopped
1 piece fresh ginger, 5cm/2in long, crushed
4 cloves garlic, crushed
4 tbsp mild curry paste
1 tsp turmeric
1 tsp five-spice powder
1.3kg/3lb chicken, skinned and jointed
400g/14oz canned tomatoes, chopped
115g/4oz creamed coconut
½ tsp sugar
salt, to taste
50g/2oz coriander leaves, chopped

1 Heat the oil in a frying pan and fry the cloves, cardamoms, cinnamon stick, star anise and curry leaves until the cloves swell and the curry leaves are slightly burnt.

2 Add the onion, ginger and garlic and fry until the onion turns brown. Add the curry paste, turmeric and five-spice powder and fry until the oil separates.

3 Add the chicken pieces and mix well. When all the pieces are evenly sealed, cover and cook until the meat is nearly done.

4 Add the chopped tomatoes and the creamed coconut. Simmer gently until the coconut dissolves. Mix well and add the sugar and salt. Fold in the coriander leaves, reheat and serve hot.

Boiled Egg Curry

Andoan Ka Salan

This dish is usually served with biryani or pilau but it is equally good with Fried Whole Fish.

SERVES 4–6

Ingredients
2 tsp white poppy seeds
2 tsp white sesame seeds
2 tsp whole coriander seeds
2 tbsp desiccated (shredded) coconut
350ml/12fl oz/1½ cups tomato juice
2 tsp gram flour (besan)
1 tsp finely-crushed fresh ginger
1 tsp chilli powder
¼ tsp asafoetida
salt, to taste
1 tsp sugar
6 hard-boiled eggs, halved
2 tbsp sesame oil
1 tsp cumin seeds
4 whole dried red chillies
6–8 curry leaves
4 cloves garlic, finely sliced

1 Heat a frying pan and dry-fry the poppy, sesame and coriander seeds for 3–4 minutes. Add the desiccated (shredded) coconut and dry-fry until it browns. Cool and grind the ingredients together using a pestle and mortar or a food processor.

2 Take a little of the tomato juice and mix with the gram flour (besan) to a smooth paste. Add the ginger, chilli powder, asafoetida, salt and sugar and the ground spices. Add the remaining tomato juice, place in a saucepan and simmer gently for 10 minutes.

3 Add the hard-boiled eggs and cover with the gravy. Heat the oil in a frying pan and fry the remaining ingredients until the chillies turn dark brown. Pour the spices and oil over the egg curry, fold the ingredients together and reheat. Serve hot.

Eggs Baked on Chipsticks

Sali Pur Eeda

Parsis love eggs, and have developed a variety of unique egg-based dishes such as this one.

SERVES 4–6

Ingredients
225g/8oz ready-salted chipsticks
2 green chillies, finely chopped
a few coriander leaves, finely chopped
¼ tsp turmeric
4 tbsp vegetable oil
75ml/5 tbsp/⅓ cup water
6 eggs
salt and freshly-ground black pepper, to taste
3 sprigs spring onions (scallions), finely chopped

1 In a bowl, mix the chipsticks, chillies, coriander and turmeric. Heat 2 tbsp of the oil in a frying pan. Add the chipstick mixture and water. Cook until the chipsticks have softened, then fry until crisp.

2 Place a plate over the frying pan, turn the pan over and remove the chipstick pancake onto it. Reheat the remaining oil in the pan and slide the pancake back to the frying pan to brown the other side.

3 Gently break the eggs over the pancake, cover the frying pan and allow the eggs to set over a low heat. Season and sprinkle with the spring onions (scallions). Cook until the base is crisp. Serve hot.

Moghul-style Chicken

Moghlai Murgh

This delicate curry can be served as a starter followed by stronger curries and rice. Saffron is crucial to the dish, but as it is very expensive prepare it for special occasions.

SERVES 4–6

Ingredients

- 2 eggs, beaten with salt and pepper
- 4 chicken breasts, rubbed with a little garam masala
- 6 tbsp ghee
- 1 large onion, finely chopped
- 1 piece fresh ginger, 5cm/2in long, finely crushed
- 4 cloves garlic, finely crushed
- 4 cloves
- 4 green cardamoms
- 1 piece cinnamon stick, 5cm/2in long
- 2 bay leaves
- 15–20 strands of saffron
- 150ml/¼ pint/⅔ cup natural (plain) yoghurt, beaten with 1 tsp cornflour (cornstarch)
- salt, to taste
- 75ml/5 tbsp/⅓ cup double (heavy) cream
- 50g/2oz ground almonds

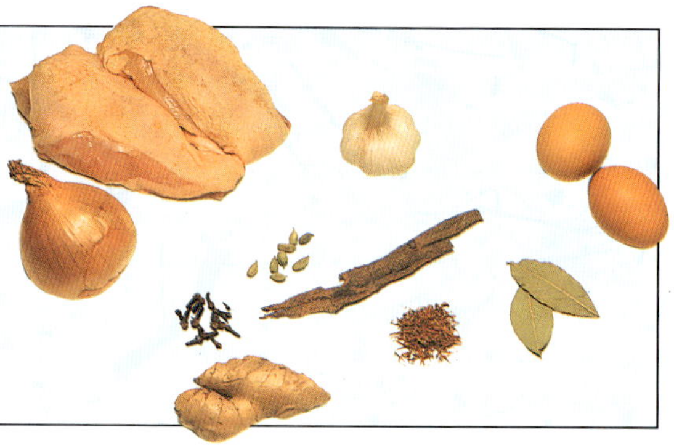

1 Brush the chicken breasts with the beaten eggs. In a frying pan, heat the ghee and fry the chicken. Remove and keep warm.

2 In the same ghee, fry the onion, ginger, garlic, cloves, cardamoms, cinnamon and bay leaves. When the onion turns golden, remove the pan from the heat, allow to cool a little and add the saffron and yoghurt. Mix well to prevent the yoghurt from curdling.

3 Return the chicken mixture to the pan with any juices and gently cook until the chicken is tender. Adjust the seasoning if necessary.

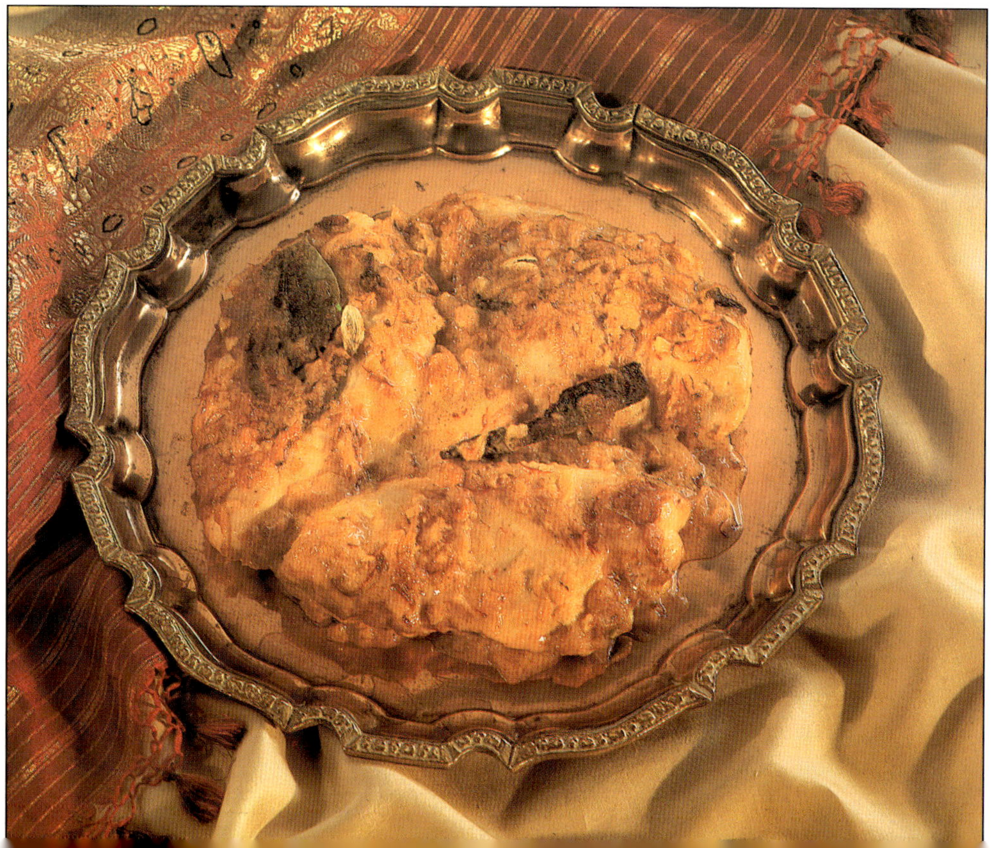

4 Just before serving, fold in the cream and ground almonds. Serve hot.

Chicken in a Hot Red Sauce

Kashmiri Murgh

In India, small chickens are used for this dish and served as an individual starter with Unleavened Bread. If you wish to serve it as a starter, use 4 poussins instead of chicken joints. Skin them first and make small gashes with a sharp knife to enable the spices to seep in.

SERVES 4–6

Ingredients

4 tsp kashmiri masala paste
4 tbsp tomato sauce (ketchup)
1 tsp Worcestershire sauce
1 tsp five-spice powder
salt, to taste
1 tsp sugar
8 chicken joints, skinned but not boned
3 tbsp vegetable oil
1 fresh piece ginger, 5cm/2in long, finely shredded
4 cloves garlic, finely crushed
juice of 1 lemon
a few coriander leaves, finely chopped

1 To make the marinade, mix together the kashmiri masala, tomato sauce (ketchup), Worcestershire sauce, five-spice powder, salt and sugar. Allow to rest in a warm place until the sugar has dissolved.

2 Rub the chicken pieces with the marinade and allow to rest for a further 2 hours, or overnight if possible.

3 Heat the oil in a frying pan and fry half the ginger and all the garlic until golden brown. Add the chicken pieces, and fry without overlapping until both sides are sealed. Cover and cook until the chicken is nearly tender and the gravy clings with the oil separating.

4 Sprinkle the chicken with the lemon juice, remaining ginger and coriander leaves. Mix well, reheat and serve hot.

Chicken in Spicy Onions

Murgh Do Piyaza

This is one of the few dishes of India in which onions appear prominently. Chunky onion slices infused with toasted cumin seeds and shredded ginger add a delicious contrast to the flavour of the chicken.

SERVES 4–6

Ingredients

1.3kg/3lb chicken, jointed and skinned
½ tsp turmeric
½ tsp chilli powder
salt, to taste
4 tbsp oil
4 small onions, finely chopped
175g/6oz coriander leaves, coarsely chopped
1 piece fresh ginger, 5cm/2in long, finely shredded
2 green chillies, finely chopped
2 tsp cumin seeds, dry-roasted
75ml/5 tbsp/⅓ cup natural (plain) yoghurt
75ml/5 tbsp/⅓ cup double (heavy) cream
½ tsp cornflour (cornstarch)

1 Rub the chicken joints with the turmeric, chilli powder and salt. Heat the oil in a frying pan and fry the chicken pieces without overlapping until both sides are sealed. Remove and keep warm.

2 Reheat the oil and fry 3 of the chopped onions, 150g/5oz of the coriander leaves, half the ginger, the green chillies and the cumin seeds until the onions are translucent. Return the chicken to the pan with any juices and mix well. Cover and cook gently for 15 minutes.

3 Remove the pan from the heat and allow to cool a little. Mix together the yoghurt, cream and cornflour (cornstarch) and gradually fold into the chicken, mixing well.

4 Return the pan to the heat and gently cook until the chicken is tender. Just before serving, stir in the reserved onion, coriander and ginger. Serve hot.

Hot Sweet and Sour Duck Casserole

Dekchi Badak

This recipe can be made with any game bird, or even rabbit. It is a distinctively sweet, sour and hot dish best eaten with rice as an accompaniment.

SERVES 4–6

Ingredients
1.3kg/3lb duck, jointed and skinned
4 bay leaves
3 tbsp salt
75ml/5 tbsp/⅓ cup vegetable oil
juice of 5 lemons
8 medium-sized onions, finely chopped
50g/2oz garlic, crushed
50g/2oz chilli powder
300ml/½ pint/1¼ cups pickling vinegar
115g/4oz fresh ginger, finely sliced or shredded
115g/4oz/½ cup sugar
50g/2oz garam masala

1 Place the duck, bay leaves and salt in a large pan and cover with cold water. Bring to the boil then simmer until the duck is fully cooked. Remove the pieces of duck and keep warm. Reserve the liquid as a base for stock or soups.

2 In a large pan, heat the oil and lemon juice until it reaches smoking point. Add the onions, garlic and chilli powder and fry the onions until they are golden brown.

3 Add the vinegar, ginger and sugar and simmer until the sugar dissolves and the oil has separated from the masala.

4 Return the duck to the pan and add the garam masala. Mix well, then reheat until the masala clings to the pieces of duck and the gravy is thick. Adjust the seasoning if necessary. If you prefer a thinner gravy, add a little of the reserved stock.

Bombay Duck Pickle

Bomil Achar

This unusual fish is found off the west coast of India during the monsoon season. It is salted and dried in the sun and is characterized by a strong smell and distinctive piquancy. How this fish acquired the name Bombay Duck in the Western world still remains a mystery!

SERVES 4–6

Ingredients
6–8 pieces bomil (Bombay duck), soaked in water for 5 minutes
4 tbsp vegetable oil
2 fresh red chillies, crushed
1 tbsp sugar
450g/1lb cherry tomatoes, halved
115g/4oz deep-fried onions

1 Pat the soaked fish dry with kitchen paper. Heat the oil in a frying pan and fry the Bombay duck pieces for about 30–45 seconds on both sides until crisp. Be careful not to burn them as they will taste bitter. Drain well on kitchen paper. When cool, break the fish into small pieces.

2 In the same oil, cook the remaining ingredients until the tomatoes become pulpy and the onions are blended into a gravy. Fold in the Bombay duck pieces and serve hot or cold.

Fish Cakes

Macchli Kebabs

Kebabs are usually thought to be made with meat or chicken. These tasty fish kebabs can be made slightly larger and served as fish burgers, or made into small balls served as cocktail snacks.

MAKES 20

Ingredients
450g/1lb skinned haddock, coley or cod
2 medium potatoes, peeled, boiled and mashed
4 spring onions (scallions), finely chopped
4 green chillies, finely chopped
1 piece fresh ginger, 5cm/2in long, finely crushed
a few coriander and mint leaves, chopped
salt and freshly-ground black pepper, to taste
2 eggs
breadcrumbs, for coating
vegetable oil, for shallow-frying
chilli sauce or sweet chutney, to serve

1 Place the fish in a lightly greased steamer and steam until cooked. Remove but leave on the steaming tray to cool.

2 When the fish is cool, crumble it coarsely into a large bowl and mix in the potatoes, spring onions (scallions), spices, coriander and mint, seasonings and 1 egg.

3 Shape into cakes. Beat the remaining egg and dip the cakes in it, then coat with the breadcrumbs. Heat the oil and fry the rissoles until brown on all sides.

Prawns (Shrimp) and Fish in Herb Sauce

Haré Masalé Me Jingha Aur Macchi

Bengalis are famous for their seafood dishes and always use mustard oil in recipes because it imparts a unique taste, flavour and aroma. No feast in Bengal is complete without one of these celebrated fish dishes.

SERVES 4–6

Ingredients

3 cloves garlic
1 piece fresh ginger, 5cm/2in long
1 large leek, roughly chopped
4 green chillies
1 tsp vegetable oil (optional)
4 tbsp mustard oil, or vegetable oil
1 tbsp coriander powder
½ tsp fennel seeds
1 tbsp crushed yellow mustard seeds, or 1 tsp mustard powder
175ml/6fl oz/¾ cup thick coconut milk
225g/8oz huss, skate blobs or monkfish
225g/8oz fresh king prawns (shrimp), peeled and de-veined with tails intact
salt, to taste
115g/4oz fresh coriander leaves, chopped

1 In a food processor, grind the garlic, ginger, leek and chillies to a coarse paste. Add vegetable oil if the mixture is too dry.

2 In a frying pan, heat the mustard or vegetable oil with the paste until it is well blended. Keep the window open and take care not to overheat the mixture as any smoke from the mustard oil will sting the eyes.

3 Add the coriander powder, fennel seeds, mustard and coconut milk. Gently bring to the boil and then simmer, uncovered, for about 5 minutes.

4 Add the fish and simmer for 2 minutes then fold in the prawns (shrimp) and cook until the prawns (shrimp) turn a bright orange/pink colour. Season with salt, fold in the coriander leaves and serve hot.

Pickled Fish Steaks

Macchi Achar

This dish is served cold and makes a lovely starter. It makes an ideal main course on a hot summer day served with a crisp salad. Make a day or two in advance to allow the flavours to blend.

SERVES 4–6

Ingredients

juice of 4 lemons
1 piece fresh ginger, 2.5cm/1in long, finely sliced
2 cloves garlic, finely minced
2 fresh red chillies, finely chopped
3 green chillies, finely chopped
4 thick fish steaks (any firm fish)
4 tbsp vegetable oil
4–6 curry leaves
1 onion, finely chopped
½ tsp turmeric
1 tbsp coriander powder
150ml/¼ pint/½ cup pickling vinegar
3 tsp sugar
salt, to taste

1 In a bowl, mix the lemon juice with the ginger, garlic and chillies. Pat the fish dry with kitchen paper and rub the mixture on all sides of the fish. Allow to marinate for 3–4 hours in the refrigerator.

2 Heat the oil in a frying pan and fry the curry leaves, onion, turmeric and coriander until the onion is translucent.

3 Place the fish steaks in the frying pan with the marinade and cover with the onion mixture. After 5 minutes, turn the fish over gently to prevent damaging the steaks.

4 Pour in the vinegar and add the sugar and salt. Bring to the boil and then lower the heat and simmer until the fish is cooked. Delicately transfer the steaks to a large platter or individual serving dishes and pour over the vinegar mixture. Chill for 24 hours before serving.

Prawns (Shrimp) Cooked with Okra

Jingha Aur Bhendi

This dish has a sweet taste with a strong chilli flavour. It should be cooked fast to prevent the okra from breaking up and releasing its distinctive, sticky interior.

SERVES 4–6

Ingredients
4–6 tbsp oil
225g/8oz okra, washed, dried and left whole
4 cloves garlic, crushed
1 piece fresh ginger, 5cm/2in long, crushed
4–6 green chillies, cut diagonally
½ tsp turmeric
4–6 curry leaves
1 tsp cumin seeds
450g/1lb fresh king prawns (shrimp), peeled and de-veined
salt, to taste
2 tsp brown sugar
juice of 2 lemons

1 Heat the oil in a frying pan and fry the okra on a fairly high heat until they are slightly crisp and browned on all sides. Remove from the oil and keep aside on a piece of kitchen paper.

2 In the same oil, gently fry the garlic, ginger, chillies, turmeric, curry leaves and cumin seeds for 2–3 minutes. Add the prawns (shrimp) and mix well. Cook until the prawns (shrimp) are tender.

3 Add the salt, sugar, lemon juice and fried okra. Increase the heat and quickly fry for a further 5 minutes, stirring gently to prevent the okra from breaking. Adjust the seasoning, if necessary. Serve hot.

Fried Whole Fish

Tali Huvey Macchi

In southern India, fish is prepared daily in some form or other but most often it is just fried and served with a lentil curry and a nice hot pickle.

SERVES 4–6

Ingredients
1 small onion, coarsely chopped
4 cloves garlic, peeled
1 piece fresh ginger, 5cm/2in long, peeled
1 tsp turmeric
2 tsp chilli powder
salt, to taste
4 red mullets
vegetable oil, for shallow-frying
1 tsp cumin seeds
3 green chillies, finely sliced
lemon wedges, to serve

1 Using a food processor, grind the first 6 ingredients to a smooth paste. Make gashes on both sides of the fish and rub them with the paste. Leave to rest for 1 hour. Lightly pat the fish dry with kitchen paper without removing the paste. Excess fluid will be released as the salt dissolves.

2 Heat the oil in a large frying pan and fry the cumin seeds and chillies for about 1 minute. Add the fish and fry on one side without overlapping. When the first side is sealed, turn the fish over very gently to ensure they do not break. Fry until they are golden brown on both sides, drain well and serve hot with lemon or lime wedges.

Stuffed Fish

Bharey Huvey Macchi

Every community in India prepares stuffed fish but the Parsi version must rank top of the list. The most popular fish in India is the pomfret. These are available from Indian and Chinese grocers or large supermarkets.

SERVES 4

Ingredients

2 large pomfrets, or Dover or lemon sole
2 tsp salt
juice of 1 lemon

Masala

8 tbsp desiccated (shredded) coconut
115g/4oz fresh coriander, including the tender stalks
8 green chillies (or to taste)
1 tsp cumin seeds
6 cloves garlic
2 tsp sugar
2 tsp lemon juice

Cook's tip

In India, this fish dish is always steamed wrapped in banana leaves. Banana leaves are generally available from Indian or Chinese grocers but vine leaves from Greek food shops could be used instead.

1 Scale the fish and cut off the fins. Gut the fish and remove the heads, if desired. Using a sharp knife, make 2 diagonal gashes on each side, then pat dry with kitchen paper.

2 Rub the fish inside and out with salt and lemon juice and allow to stand for 1 hour. Pat dry thoroughly.

3 For the masala, grind all the ingredients together using a pestle and mortar or food processor, stuff the fish with the masala mixture and rub any remaining into the gashes and all over the fish on both sides.

4 Place each fish on a separate piece of greased foil. Tightly wrap the foil over each fish. Place in a steamer and steam for 20 minutes or bake for 30 minutes at 200°C/400°F/Gas Mark 6 or until cooked. Remove from the foil and serve hot.

Parsi Prawn (Shrimp) Curry

Kalmino Patio

This dish comes from the west coast of India, where fresh seafood is eaten in abundance. Fresh king prawns (shrimp) or 'tiger' prawns (shrimp) are ideal for Patio.

SERVES 4–6

Ingredients
4 tbsp vegetable oil
1 medium onion, finely sliced
6 cloves garlic, finely crushed
1 tsp chilli powder
1½ tsp turmeric
2 medium onions, finely chopped
50ml/2fl oz/¼ cup tamarind juice
1 tsp mint sauce
1 tbsp demerara sugar
salt, to taste
450g/1lb fresh king prawns (shrimp), peeled and de-veined
85g/3oz coriander leaves, chopped

1 Heat the oil in a frying pan and fry the sliced onion until golden brown. In a bowl, mix the garlic, chilli powder and turmeric with a little water to form a paste. Add to the browned onion and simmer for 3 minutes.

2 Add the chopped onions and fry until they become translucent, then fold in the tamarind juice, mint sauce, sugar and salt. Simmer for a further 3 minutes.

3 Pat the prawns (shrimp) dry with kitchen paper. Add to the spice mixture with a small amount of water and stir-fry until the prawns (shrimp) turn a bright orange/pink colour.

4 When the prawns (shrimp) are cooked, add the coriander leaves and stir-fry on a high heat for a few minutes to thicken the gravy. Serve hot.

Hot and Sour Meat and Lentil Curry

Dhansak

This is one of the best-known Parsi dishes and is a favourite for Sunday lunch. This dish has a hot, sweet and sour flavour, through which should rise the slightly bitter flavour of fenugreek.

SERVES 4–6

Ingredients
- 6 tbsp vegetable oil
- 5 green chillies, chopped
- 1 piece fresh ginger, 2.5cm/1in long, crushed
- 3 cloves garlic, crushed
- 1 clove garlic, sliced
- 2 bay leaves
- 1 piece cinnamon stick, 5cm/2in long
- 900g/2lb lean lamb, cut in large pieces
- 575ml/1 pint/2½ cups water
- 175g/6oz red gram
- 50g/2oz each bengal gram, husked moong and red lentils
- 2 potatoes, cut and soaked in water
- 1 aubergine (egg plant), cut and soaked in water
- 4 onions, finely sliced, deep-fried and drained
- 50g/2oz fresh spinach, trimmed, washed and chopped or 50g/2oz frozen spinach, thawed and drained
- 25g/1oz fenugreek leaves, fresh or dried
- 115g/4oz carrots or pumpkin if in season
- 115g/4oz fresh coriander leaves, chopped
- 50g/2oz fresh mint leaves, chopped, or 1 tbsp mint sauce
- 2 tbsp dhansak masala
- 2 tbsp sambhar masala
- salt, to taste
- 2 tsp brown sugar
- 4 tbsp tamarind juice

Cook's tip

Chicken or prawns (shrimp) can be used instead of the lamb. If using chicken, reduce the cooking time so that the meat does not become shredded or stringy; if you are using prawns (shrimp), cook only until the tails turn bright orange/pink in colour.

1 Heat 3 tbsp of the oil in a saucepan or deep frying pan and fry the green chillies, ginger and crushed garlic cloves for 2 minutes. Add the bay leaves, cinnamon, lamb and water. Bring to the boil then simmer until the lamb is half cooked.

2 Drain the water into another pan and put the lamb aside. Add the lentils to the water and cook until they are tender. Mash the lentils with the back of a spoon.

3 Drain the aubergine (egg plant) and potatoes and add to the lentils with 3 of the deep-fried onions, the spinach, fenugreek and carrot or pumpkin. Add some hot water if the mixture is too thick. Cook until the vegetables are tender, then mash again with a spoon, keeping the vegetables a little coarse.

4 Heat 1 tbsp of the oil and gently fry the coriander and mint leaves (saving a little to garnish) with the dhansak and sambhar masala, salt and sugar. Add the lamb and fry gently for about 5 minutes.

5 Return the lamb and spices to the lentil and vegetable mixture and stir well. As lentils absorb fluids, adjust the consistency if necessary. Heat gently until the lamb is fully cooked.

6 Add the tamarind juice and mix well. Heat the remaining oil and fry the sliced clove of garlic until golden brown. Pour over the dhansak. Garnish with the remaining deep-fried onion and the reserved coriander and mint leaves. Serve hot.

Lentils Seasoned with Fried Spices

Tarka Dhal

Dhal is cooked in every house in India in one form or another. This recipe is a simplified version.

SERVES 4–6

Ingredients
115g/4oz red gram, washed and picked over
50g/2oz bengal gram, washed and picked over
350ml/12fl oz/1 ½ cups water
4 whole green chillies
1 tsp turmeric
1 large onion, sliced
salt, to taste
400g/14oz canned plum tomatoes, crushed
4 tbsp vegetable oil
½ tsp mustard seeds
½ tsp cumin seeds
1 clove garlic, crushed
6 curry leaves
2 whole dried red chillies
¼ tsp asafoetida
deep-fried onions and fresh coriander leaves, to garnish

1 Place the first 6 ingredients in a heavy pan and bring to the boil. Simmer, covered, until the lentils are soft and the water has evaporated.

2 Mash the lentils with the back of a spoon. When nearly smooth, add the salt and tomatoes and mix well. If necessary, thin the mixture with hot water.

3 Fry the remaining ingredients until the garlic browns. Pour the oil and spices over the lentils and cover. After 5 minutes, mix well, garnish and serve.

South Indian Lentils and Vegetables

Sambhar

This is a favourite south Indian dish served for breakfast with dosai (Indian pancakes) or idli (rice dumplings).

SERVES 4–6

Ingredients
4 tbsp vegetable oil
½ tsp mustard seeds
½ tsp cumin seeds
2 whole dried red chillies
¼ tsp asafoetida
6–8 curry leaves
2 cloves garlic, crushed
2 tbsp desiccated (shredded) coconut
225g/8oz red lentils picked, washed and drained
2 tsp sambhar masala
½ tsp turmeric
450ml/¾ pint/1 ½ cups water
450g/1lb mixed vegetables (okra, courgettes/zucchini, cauliflower, shallots and bell peppers)
4 tbsp tamarind juice
4 firm tomatoes, quartered
4 tbsp vegetable oil
2 cloves garlic, finely sliced
a handful coriander leaves, chopped

1 Fry the next 7 ingredients until the coconut browns. Mix in the lentils, sambhar masala, turmeric and water.

2 Simmer until the lentils are mushy. Add the vegetables, tamarind juice and tomatoes. Cook so the vegetables are crunchy.

3 Fry the garlic slices and coriander leaves. Pour over the lentils and vegetables. Mix at the table before serving.

Curried Chickpeas with Potato Cakes

Ragda Petis

No other city in India is quite like Bombay. Its cuisine is typical of food you can buy right off the streets, which is the way the Bombayites like it – spicy, quick and nutritious.

MAKES 10–12

Ingredients
2 tbsp vegetable oil
2 tbsp coriander powder
2 tbsp cumin powder
½ tsp turmeric
½ tsp salt
½ tsp sugar
2 tbsp flour paste
450g/1lb boiled chickpeas (garbanzo beans), drained
2 fresh green chillies, chopped
1 piece fresh ginger, 5cm/2in long, finely crushed
85g/3oz coriander leaves, chopped
2 firm tomatoes, chopped

Petis
450g/1lb potatoes, boiled and coarsely mashed
4 green chillies, finely chopped
50g/2oz coriander leaves, finely chopped
1½ tsp cumin powder
1 tsp amchur (dry mango powder)
salt, to taste
vegetable oil, for shallow-frying

1 For the Ragda, heat the oil in a saucepan and fry the coriander, cumin, turmeric, salt, sugar and flour paste until the water has evaporated and the oil separated.

2 Add the chickpeas (garbanzo beans), chillies, ginger, coriander leaves and tomatoes. Toss well and simmer for 5 minutes. Remove to a serving dish and keep warm.

3 To make the Petis, in a large mixing bowl mix the mashed potato with the green chillies, coriander, cumin and amchur powders and salt. Mix until all the ingredients are well blended.

4 Using your hands, shape the Petis mixture into little cakes. Heat the oil in a shallow frying pan or griddle and fry the cakes on both sides until golden brown. Transfer to a serving dish and serve with the Ragda.

Black Gram in a Spicy Cream Sauce

Masala Urad

Dhabas – highway cafes – are very lively eating places serving a variety of dishes. This recipe is commonly served, and is one of the most popular.

SERVES 4–6

Ingredients

175g/6oz black gram soaked overnight
50g/2oz red gram
100g/4fl oz/½ cup double (heavy) cream
100g/4fl oz/½ cup natural (plain) yoghurt
1 tsp cornflour (cornstarch)
3 tbsp ghee
1 onion, finely chopped
1 piece fresh ginger, 5cm/2in long, crushed
4 green chillies, chopped
1 tomato, chopped
½ tsp chilli powder
½ tsp turmeric
½ tsp cumin powder
salt, to taste
2 cloves garlic, sliced

1 Drain the black gram and place in a heavy pan with the red gram. Cover with water and bring to the boil. Reduce the heat, cover the pan and simmer until the gram are tender. The black gram will remain whole but the red gram will be mushy. Gently mash with a spoon. Allow to cool.

2 In a bowl, mix together the cream, yoghurt and cornflour (cornstarch). Mix the cream mixture into the gram without damaging the whole black gram grains.

3 Heat 1tbsp of the ghee in a frying pan and fry the onion, ginger, 2 of the green chillies and the tomato until the onion is soft. Add the spices and salt and fry for a further 2 minutes. Add it all to the gram mixture and mix well. Reheat and transfer to a heatproof serving dish and keep warm.

4 Heat the remaining ghee in a frying pan and fry the garlic slices and remaining chillies until the garlic slices are golden brown. Pour over the gram and serve, folding the garlic and chilli into the gram just before serving. Place extra cream on the table for the diners to add more if they wish.

Black-eyed Beans and Potato Curry

Lobia Aloo

Lobia are beige and kidney-shaped with a distinctive dark dot. This can be served as a starter or snack.

SERVES 4–6

Ingredients

- 225g/8oz lobia (black-eyed beans), soaked overnight and drained
- ¼ tsp bicarbonate of soda
- 1 tsp five-spice powder
- ¼ tsp asafoetida
- 2 onions, finely chopped
- 1 piece fresh ginger, 2.5cm/1in long, crushed
- a few mint leaves
- 450ml/¾ pint/scant 2 cups water
- 4 tbsp vegetable oil
- ½ tsp each, turmeric, coriander, cumin and chilli powders
- 4 green chillies, chopped
- 75ml/5 tbsp/⅓ cup tamarind juice
- 2 potatoes, peeled, cubed and boiled
- 115g/4oz coriander leaves, chopped
- 2 firm tomatoes, chopped
- salt, to taste

1 Place the lobia with the next 7 ingredients in a heavy pan. Simmer until the beans are soft. Remove any excess water and reserve.

2 Gently fry the spice powders, chillies and tamarind juice, until they are well blended. Pour over the lobia and mix.

3 Add the potatoes, coriander leaves, tomatoes and salt. Mix well, and if necessary add a little reserved water. Reheat and serve.

Bengal Gram and Bottle Gourd Curry

Doodhi Channa

This is an Anglo-Indian version of dhal, which is characteristically hot, and with the dhals left whole.

SERVES 4–6

Ingredients

- 175g/6oz bengal gram, washed
- 450ml/¾ pint/scant 2 cups water
- 4 tbsp vegetable oil
- 2 green chillies, chopped
- 1 onion, chopped
- 2 cloves garlic, crushed
- 1 piece fresh ginger, 5cm/2in long, crushed
- 6–8 curry leaves
- 1 tsp chilli powder
- 1 tsp turmeric
- salt, to taste
- 450g/1lb bottle gourd or marrow, courgettes (zucchini), squash or pumpkin, peeled, pithed and sliced
- 4 tbsp tamarind juice
- 2 tomatoes, chopped
- a handful fresh coriander leaves, chopped

1 In a saucepan, cook the lentils in the water until the grains are tender but not mushy. Put aside without draining away any excess water.

2 Fry the chillies, onion, garlic, ginger, curry leaves, chilli powder and turmeric and salt. Add the gourd pieces and mix. Cover and cook until the gourd is soft.

3 Add the lentils and water and bring to the boil. Add the tamarind juice, tomatoes and coriander. Simmer until the gourd is cooked. Serve hot with a dry meat curry.

FLAVOURED GREEN GRAM AND RICE

Kitchdee

The whole spices are edible, but it is advisable to warn the diners about them.

SERVES 4–6

Ingredients
4 tbsp ghee
1 onion, finely chopped
2 cloves garlic, crushed
1 piece ginger, 2.5cm/1in long, shredded
4 green chillies, chopped
4 whole cloves
1 piece cinnamon stick, 2.5cm/1in long
4 whole green cardamoms
1 tsp turmeric
salt, to taste
350g/12oz patna rice, washed and soaked for 20 minutes
175g/6oz split green gram, washed and soaked for 20 minutes
575ml/1pint/2½ cups water

1 Gently heat the ghee in a large heavy pan with a tight-fitting cover and fry the onion, garlic, ginger, chillies, cloves, cinnamon, cardamoms, turmeric and salt until the onion is soft and translucent.

2 Drain the rice and gram, add to the spices and sauté for 2–3 minutes. Add the water and bring to the boil. Reduce the heat, cover and cook for about 20–25 minutes or until all the water is absorbed.

3 Take the pan off the heat and leave to rest for 5 minutes. Just before serving gently toss the mixture with a flat spatula.

DRY MOONG DHAL WITH COURGETTES (ZUCCHINI)

Sookhi Moong Aur Chingri

Most dhal dishes are runny but this one provides texture with the addition of the courgettes (zucchini).

SERVES 4–6

Ingredients
175g/6oz moong dhal
½ tsp turmeric
300ml/½ pint/1¼ cups water
4 tbsp vegetable oil
1 large onion, finely sliced
2 cloves garlic, crushed
2 green chillies, chopped
½ tsp mustard seeds
½ tsp cumin seeds
¼ tsp asafoetida
a few coriander and mint leaves, chopped
6–8 curry leaves
salt, to taste
½ tsp sugar
200g/7oz canned tomatoes, chopped
225g/8oz courgettes (zucchini), cut into small pieces
4 tbsp lemon juice

1 In a saucepan, boil the moong dhal and turmeric in the water and then simmer until the dhal is cooked but not mushy. Drain and reserve both the liquid and the dhal.

2 Heat the oil in a frying pan and fry the remaining ingredients except the lemon juice. Cover and cook until the courgettes (zucchini) are nearly tender but still crunchy.

3 Fold in the drained dhal and the lemon juice. If the dish is too dry, add a small amount of the reserved water. Reheat and serve.

Bombay Potato

Bumbai Aloo

This authentic dish belongs to the Gujerati, a totally vegetarian sect and the largest population in Bombay.

SERVES 4–6

Ingredients
450g/1lb whole new potatoes
salt, to taste
1 tsp turmeric
4 tbsp vegetable oil
2 whole dried red chillies
6–8 curry leaves
2 onions, finely chopped
2 green chillies, finely chopped
50g/2oz coriander leaves, coarsely chopped
¼ tsp asafoetida
½ tsp each, cumin, mustard, onion, fennel and nigella seeds
lemon juice, to taste

1 Scrub the potatoes under running water and cut them into small pieces. Boil the potatoes in water with a little salt and ½ tsp of the turmeric until tender. Drain well then coarsely mash. Put aside.

2 Heat the oil and fry the red chillies and curry leaves until the chillies are nearly burnt. Add the onions, green chillies, coriander, remaining turmeric and spice seeds and cook until the onions are soft.

3 Fold in the potatoes and add a few drops of water. Cook on low heat for about 10 minutes, mixing well to ensure the even distribution of the spices. Add lemon juice to taste, and serve.

Curried Cauliflower

Phul Gobi Salan

In this dish the creamy, spiced coconut sauce disguises the strong smell of the spiced cauliflower.

SERVES 4–6

Ingredients
1 tbsp gram flour
100ml/4fl oz/½ cup water
1 tsp chilli powder
1 tbsp coriander powder
1 tsp cumin powder
1 tsp mustard powder
1 tsp turmeric
salt, to taste
4 tbsp vegetable oil
6–8 curry leaves
1 tsp cumin seeds
1 cauliflower, broken into florets
175ml/6fl oz/¾ cup thick coconut milk
juice of 2 lemons

1 Mix the gram flour with a little of the water to make a smooth paste. Add the chilli, coriander, cumin, mustard, turmeric and salt. Add the remaining water and keep mixing to blend all the ingredients well.

2 Heat the oil in a frying pan and fry the curry leaves and cumin seeds. Add the spice paste and simmer for about 5 minutes. If the gravy has become too thick, add a little hot water.

3 Add the cauliflower and coconut milk. Bring to the boil, reduce the heat, cover and cook until the cauliflower is tender but crunchy. Cook longer if you prefer. Add the lemon juice, mix well and serve hot.

Stuffed Okra

Bharé Huvey Bhendi

A delicious accompaniment to any dish, this can also be served on a bed of strained Greek yoghurt which gives an excellent contrast in flavour.

SERVES 4–6

Ingredients
225g/8oz large okra
1 tbsp amchur (dry mango powder)
½ tsp ginger powder
½ tsp cumin powder
½ tsp chilli powder (optional)
½ tsp turmeric
salt, to taste
a few drops of vegetable oil
2 tbsp cornflour (cornstarch), placed in a plastic bag
vegetable oil, for frying

1 Wash the okra and dry on kitchen paper. Carefully trim off the tops without making a hole. Using a sharp knife, make a slit lengthways in the centre of each okra but do not cut all the way through.

2 In a bowl, mix the amchur, ginger, cumin, chilli if using, turmeric and salt with a few drops of oil. Leave the mixture to rest for 1 or 2 hours.

3 Using your fingers, part the slit of each okra carefully without opening it all the way and fill each with as much filling as possible. Put all the okra into the plastic bag with the cornflour (cornstarch) and shake the bag carefully to cover the okra evenly.

4 Fill the frying pan with enough oil to sit 2.5cm/1in deep, heat it and fry the okra in small batches for about 5–8 minutes or until they are brown and slightly crisp. Serve hot.

Mixed Vegetable Curry

Sabzi Salan

This is a very delicately spiced vegetable dish that makes an appetizing snack when served with plain yoghurt. It is also a good accompaniment to a main meal of heavily spiced curries.

SERVES 4–6

Ingredients

350g/12oz mixed vegetables (beans, peas, potatoes, cauliflower, carrots, cabbage, mange-touts/snow peas and button mushrooms)
2 tbsp vegetable oil
1 tsp cumin seeds, freshly-roasted
½ tsp mustard seeds
½ tsp onion seeds
1 tsp turmeric
2 cloves garlic, crushed
6–8 curry leaves
1 whole dried red chilli
salt, to taste
1 tsp sugar
150ml/¼ pint/⅔ cup natural (plain) yoghurt mixed with 1 tsp cornflour (cornstarch)

1 Prepare all the vegetables you have chosen: string the beans, thaw the peas, if frozen; cube the potatoes; cut the cauliflower into florets; dice the carrots; shred the cabbage; top and tail the mange-touts (snow peas); wash the mushrooms and leave whole.

2 Heat a large pan with enough water to cook all the vegetables and bring to the boil. First add the potatoes and carrots and cook until nearly tender then add all the other vegetables and cook until still firm. All the vegetables should be crunchy except the potatoes. Drain well.

3 Heat the oil in a frying pan and fry the spices gently until the garlic is golden brown and the chilli nearly burnt. Reduce the heat.

4 Fold in the drained vegetables, add the sugar and salt and gradually add the yoghurt mixed with the cornflour (cornstarch). Heat to serving temperature and serve immediately.

Curried Spinach and Potato

Palak Aloo Sag

India is blessed with over 18 varieties of spinach. If you have access to an Indian or Chinese grocer, look out for some of the more unusual varieties.

SERVES 4–6

Ingredients
4 tbsp vegetable oil
225g/8oz potato
1 piece fresh ginger, 2.5cm/1in long, crushed
4 cloves garlic, crushed
1 onion, coarsely chopped
2 green chillies, chopped
2 whole dried red chillies, coarsely broken
1 tsp cumin seeds
salt, to taste
225g/8oz fresh spinach, trimmed, washed and chopped or 225g/8oz frozen spinach, thawed and drained
2 firm tomatoes, coarsely chopped, to garnish

1 Wash the potatoes and cut into quarters. If using small new potatoes, leave them whole. Heat the oil in a frying pan and fry the potatoes until brown on all sides. Remove and put aside.

2 Remove the excess oil leaving 1 tbsp in the pan. Fry the ginger, garlic, onion, green chillies, dried chillies and cumin seeds until the onion is golden brown.

3 Add the potatoes and salt and stir well. Cook covered until the potatoes are tender when pierced with a sharp knife.

4 Add the spinach and stir well. Cook with the pan uncovered until the spinach is tender and all the excess fluids have evaporated. Garnish with the chopped tomatoes and serve hot.

Curried Mushrooms, Peas and Indian Cheese

Gucci Mattar Paneer

Paneer is a traditional cheese made from rich milk and is most popular with northern Indians. Rajasthani farmers eat this dish for lunch with thick parathas as they work in the fields.

SERVES 4–6

Ingredients

6 tbsp ghee or vegetable oil
225g/8oz paneer, cubed
1 onion, finely chopped
a few mint leaves, chopped
50g/2oz coriander leaves, chopped
3 green chillies, chopped
3 cloves garlic
1 piece fresh ginger, 2.5cm/1in long, sliced
1 tsp turmeric
1 tsp chilli powder (optional)
1 tsp garam masala
salt, to taste
225g/8oz tiny button mushrooms, washed and left whole
225g/8oz frozen peas, thawed and drained
175ml/6fl oz/¾ cup natural (plain) yoghurt, mixed with 1 tsp cornflour (cornstarch)
tomatoes and coriander leaves, to garnish

1 Heat the ghee or oil in a frying pan and fry the paneer cubes until they are golden brown on all sides. Remove and drain on kitchen paper.

2 Grind the onion, mint, coriander, chillies, garlic and ginger in a pestle and mortar or food processor to a fairly smooth paste. Remove and mix in the turmeric, chilli powder if using, garam masala and salt.

3 Remove excess ghee or oil from the pan leaving about 1 tbsp. Heat and fry the paste until the raw onion smell disappears and the oil separates.

4 Add the mushrooms, peas and paneer. Mix well. Cool the mixture and gradually fold in the yoghurt. Simmer for about 10 minutes. Garnish with tomatoes and coriander and serve hot.

Corn on the Cob Curry

Butta Salan

Corn-cobs are roasted on charcoal and rubbed with lemon juice, salt and chilli powder in India. In season, vendors fill the atmosphere with these delicious aromas. Corn is also a popular curry ingredient.

SERVES 4–6

Ingredients

4 whole corn-cobs, fresh, canned or frozen
vegetable oil, for frying
1 large onion, finely chopped
2 cloves garlic, crushed
1 piece fresh ginger, 5cm/2in long, crushed
½ tsp turmeric
½ tsp onion seeds
½ tsp cumin seeds
½ tsp five-spice powder
chilli powder, to taste
6–8 curry leaves
½ tsp sugar
200ml/7fl oz/scant 1 cup plain yoghurt

1 Cut each corn-cob in half, using a sharp, heavy knife or cleaver to make clean cuts and prevent damaging the kernels. Heat the oil in a wok and fry the corn pieces until golden brown on all sides. Remove the corn-cobs and keep aside.

2 Remove any excess oil leaving about 2 tbsp in the wok. Grind the onion, garlic and ginger to a paste using a pestle and mortar or food processor. Remove and mix in all the spices, curry leaves and sugar.

3 Heat the oil gently and fry the onion mixture until all the spices have blended well and the oil separates from the masala.

4 Cool the mixture and gradually fold in the yoghurt. Mix well until you have a smooth sauce. Add the corn to the mixture and mix well so all the pieces are evenly covered with the gravy. Gently reheat for about 10 minutes. Serve hot.

CURRIED STUFFED (BELL) PEPPERS

Bharey Huvey Mirchi Ka Salan

This is one of the most famous dishes of Deccan. Hot, spicy and extremely delicious, it is often prepared for weddings. It is made with extra oil several days in advance to allow the spices to mature.

SERVES 4–6

Ingredients
- 1 tbsp sesame seeds
- 1 tbsp white poppy seeds
- 1 tsp coriander seeds
- 4 tbsp desiccated (shredded) coconut
- ½ onion, sliced
- 1 piece fresh ginger, 2.5cm/1in long, sliced
- 4 cloves garlic, sliced
- a handful of coriander leaves
- 2 green chillies
- 4 tbsp vegetable oil
- 2 potatoes, boiled and coarsely mashed
- salt, to taste
- 2 each, green, red and yellow (bell) peppers
- 2 tbsp sesame oil
- 1 tsp cumin seeds
- 4 green chillies, slit
- 4 tbsp tamarind juice

1 In a frying pan, dry-fry the sesame, poppy and coriander seeds, then add the desiccated (shredded) coconut and continue to roast until the coconut turns golden brown. Add the onion, ginger, garlic, coriander, and chillies and roast for a further 5 minutes. Cool, and grind to a paste using a pestle and mortar or food processor. Put aside.

2 Heat 2 tbsp of the vegetable oil in a frying pan and fry the ground paste for 4–5 minutes. Add the potatoes and salt and stir well until the spices have blended evenly into the potatoes.

3 Slice the tail ends off the (bell) peppers and reserve. Remove the seeds and any white pith. Fill the (bell) peppers with even amounts of the potato mixture and replace the tail ends on the top.

4 Heat the sesame oil and remaining vegetable oil in a frying pan and fry the cumin seeds and the green chillies. When the chillies turn white, add the tamarind juice and bring to the boil. Place the (bell) peppers over the mixture, cover the pan and cook until the peppers are nearly done.

Potatoes in a Hot Red Sauce

Lal Batata

This dish should be hot and sour but, if you wish, reduce the chillies and add extra tomato purée (paste) instead.

SERVES 4–6

Ingredients
450g/1lb small new potatoes, washed and dried
25g/1oz whole dried red chillies, preferably kashmiri
1½ tsp cumin seeds
4 cloves garlic
6 tbsp vegetable oil
4 tbsp thick tamarind juice
2 tbsp tomato purée (paste)
4 curry leaves
salt, to taste
1 tsp sugar
¼ tsp asafoetida
coriander leaves and lemon wedges, to garnish

1 Boil the potatoes until they are fully cooked, ensuring they do not break. To test, insert a thin sharp knife into the potatoes. It should come out clean when the potatoes are fully cooked. Drain well.

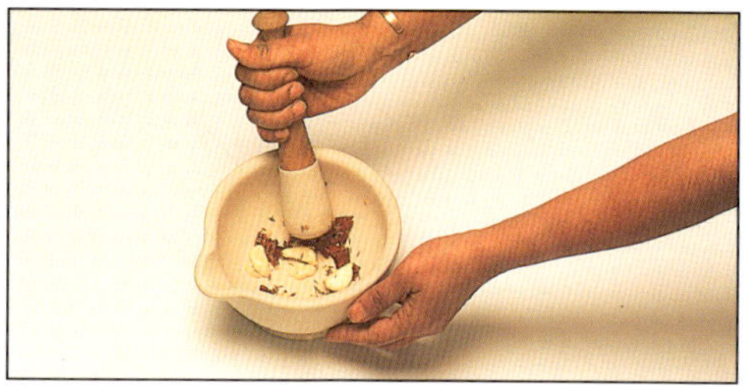

2 Soak the chillies for 5 minutes in warm water. Drain and grind with the cumin seeds and garlic to a coarse paste using a pestle and mortar or food processor.

3 Fry the paste, tamarind juice, tomato purée (paste), curry leaves, salt, sugar and asafoetida until the oil separates. Add the potatoes. Reduce the heat, cover and simmer for 5 minutes. Garnish and serve.

Cucumber Curry

Kakri Ka Salan

This makes a pleasant accompaniment to fish dishes and may be served cold with cooked meats.

SERVES 4–6

Ingredients
100ml/4fl oz/½ cup water
115g/4oz creamed coconut
½ tsp turmeric
salt, to taste
1 tsp sugar
1 large cucumber, cut into small pieces
1 large red (bell) pepper, cut into small pieces
50g/2oz salted peanuts, coarsely crushed
4 tbsp vegetable oil
2 dried red chillies
1 tsp cumin seeds
1 tsp mustard seeds
4–6 curry leaves
4 cloves garlic, crushed
a few whole salted peanuts, to garnish

1 Bring the water to the boil in a heavy pan and add the creamed coconut, turmeric, salt and sugar. Simmer until the coconut dissolves to obtain a smooth, thick sauce.

2 Add the cucumber, red (bell) pepper and crushed peanuts and simmer for about 5 minutes. Transfer to a heat-proof serving dish and keep warm.

3 Fry the chillies and cumin with the mustard seeds until they start to pop. Reduce the heat, add the curry leaves and garlic and fry. Pour over the cucumber mixture and stir well. Garnish and serve hot.

Hot Lime Pickle

Nimbu Achar

A good lime pickle is not only delicious served with any meal, but it increases the appetite and aids digestion.

MAKES 450G/1LB/2 CUPS

Ingredients
25 limes
225g/8oz salt
50g/2oz fenugreek powder
50g/2oz mustard powder
150g/5oz chilli powder
15g/½oz turmeric
575ml/1pint/2½ cups mustard oil
1 tsp asafoetida
25g/1oz yellow mustard seeds, crushed

1 Cut each lime into 8 pieces and remove the pips, if you wish. Place the limes in a large sterilized jar or glass bowl. Add the salt and toss with the limes. Cover and leave in a warm place until they become soft and dull brown in colour, for 1 to 2 weeks.

2 Mix together the fenugreek, mustard powder, chilli powder and turmeric and add to the limes. Cover and leave to rest in a warm place for a further 2 or 3 days.

3 Heat the mustard oil in a frying pan and fry the asafoetida and mustard seeds. When the oil reaches smoking point, pour it over the limes. Mix well, cover with a clean cloth and leave in a warm place for about 1 week before serving.

Green Chilli Pickle

Mirchi Ka Achar

Southern India is the source of some of the hottest curries and pickles, which are said to cool the body.

MAKES 450–550G/1–1¼ LB/2–2½ CUPS

Ingredients
50g/2oz yellow mustard seeds, crushed
50g/2oz freshly-ground cumin seeds
25g/1oz turmeric
50g/2oz garlic cloves
150ml/¼ pint/⅔ cup white vinegar
85g/3oz sugar
2 tsp salt
150ml/¼ pint/⅔ cup mustard oil
20 small garlic cloves, peeled and left whole
450g/1lb small green chillies, washed, dried and halved

1 Mix the mustard seeds, cumin, turmeric, crushed garlic, vinegar, sugar and salt together in a sterilized glass bowl. Cover with a cloth and allow to rest for 24 hours. This enables the spices to infuse and the sugar and salt to melt.

2 Heat the mustard oil and gently fry the spice mixture for about 5 minutes. (Keep a window open while cooking with mustard oil as it is pungent and the smoke may irritate the eyes.) Add the garlic cloves and fry for a further 5 minutes.

3 Add the chillies and cook gently until tender but still green in colour. This will take about 30 minutes on a low heat. Cool thoroughly and pour into sterilized bottles, ensuring the oil is evenly distributed if you are using more than one bottle. Leave to rest for a week before serving.

Spiced Yoghurt

Tarka Dahi

Yoghurt is always a welcome accompaniment to hot curries. This has been given a final fry with spices just to flavour the yoghurt slightly.

MAKES 450ML/¾ PINT/2 CUPS

Ingredients

450ml/¾ pint/scant 2 cups plain yoghurt
½ tsp freshly-ground fennel seeds
salt, to taste
½ tsp sugar
4 tbsp vegetable oil
1 whole dried red chilli
¼ tsp mustard seeds
¼ tsp cumin seeds
4–6 curry leaves
a pinch each asafoetida and turmeric

1 In a heat-proof serving dish, mix together the yoghurt, fennel seeds, salt and sugar and chill until you are nearly ready to serve.

2 Heat the oil in a frying pan and fry the chilli, mustard and cumin seeds, curry leaves, asafoetida and turmeric. When the chilli turns dark, pour the oil and spices over the yoghurt. Fold the yoghurt together with the spices at the table before serving.

Yoghurt Salad

Mava Raitha

Raithas are served to cool the effect of hot curries. Cucumber and mint raitha is most commonly served, so why not try a variation?

SERVES 4

Ingredients

350ml/12fl oz/1½ cups natural (plain) yoghurt
85g/3oz seedless grapes, washed and dried
50g/2oz shelled walnuts
2 firm bananas
1 tsp sugar
salt, to taste
1 tsp freshly-ground cumin seeds
¼ tsp freshly-roasted cumin seeds, chilli powder or paprika, to garnish

1 Place the yoghurt in a chilled bowl and add the grapes and walnuts. Slice the bananas directly into the bowl and fold in gently before the bananas turn brown.

2 Add the sugar, salt and ground cumin, and gently mix together. Chill, and just before serving, sprinkle on the cumin seeds, chilli powder or paprika.

Tomato Salad

Tamatar Kasondi

This is a simple salad served with most meals. It provides a contrast to hot curries, with its crunchy texture and refreshing ingredients.

SERVES 4–6

Ingredients

2 limes
½ tsp sugar
salt and freshly-ground black pepper, to taste
2 onions, finely chopped
4 firm tomatoes, finely chopped
½ cucumber, finely chopped
1 green chilli, finely chopped
a few coriander leaves, chopped
a few mint leaves, to garnish

1 Extract the juice of the limes into a small bowl and add the sugar, salt and pepper. Allow to rest until the sugar and salt have dissolved. Mix together well.

2 Add the onions, tomatoes, cucumber, chilli and coriander leaves, reserving a few. Chill, and garnish with coriander and mint before serving.

Fresh Coriander Relish

Hara Dhaniya Chutney

Delicious as an accompaniment to kebabs, samosas and bhajias, this relish can also be used as a spread for cucumber or tomato sandwiches.

MAKES 400G/14OZ/1¾ CUPS

Ingredients

2 tbsp vegetable oil
1 dried red chilli
¼ tsp each, cumin, fennel and onion seeds
¼ tsp asafoetida
4 curry leaves
115g/4oz desiccated (shredded) coconut
2 tsp sugar
salt, to taste
3 green chillies
175g–225g/6–8oz coriander leaves
4 tbsp mint sauce
juice of 3 lemons

1 Fry the red chilli, cumin, fennel and onion seeds, asafoetida, curry leaves, desiccated (shredded) coconut, sugar and salt until the coconut turns golden brown. Cool.

2 Grind the spice mixture with the green chillies, coriander leaves and mint sauce. Moisten with lemon juice. Remove, and chill before serving.

Tomato Chutney

Kachoomber

This delicious relish is especially suited to lentil dishes. If kept refrigerated, it can be made a week before serving.

MAKES 450–500G/16–18OZ/2–2¼ CUPS

Ingredients

6 tbsp vegetable oil
1 piece cinnamon stick, 5cm/2in long
4 cloves
1 tsp freshly-roasted cumin seeds
1 tsp nigella seeds
4 bay leaves
1 tsp mustard seeds, crushed
4 cloves garlic, crushed
1 piece fresh ginger, 5cm/2in long, crushed
1 tsp chilli powder
1 tsp turmeric
4 tbsp brown sugar
800g/1¾ lb canned, chopped tomatoes, drained (reserving juices)

1 Heat the oil on a medium heat and fry the cinnamon, cloves, cumin and nigella seeds, bay leaves and mustard seeds for about 5 minutes. Add the garlic and fry until golden.

2 Add the ginger, chilli powder, turmeric, sugar and the reserved tomato juices. Simmer until reduced, add the tomatoes and cook for 15–20 minutes. Cool and serve.

Mango Chutney

Kairi Ki Chutni

Chutneys are usually served as an accompaniment to curry but this one is particularly nice served in a cheese sandwich or as a dip with papadums.

MAKES 450G/1LB/2 CUPS

Ingredients

50ml/2fl oz/¼ cup malt vinegar
½ tsp dried chillies, crushed
6 whole cloves
6 whole peppercorns
1 tsp roasted cumin seeds
½ tsp onion seeds
salt, to taste
175g/6oz sugar
450g/1lb unripe mango, peeled and cubed
1 piece fresh ginger, 5cm/2in long, finely sliced
2 cloves garlic, crushed
thin peel of 1 orange or lemon (optional)

1 In a saucepan, heat the vinegar with the chillies, cloves, peppercorns, cumin and onion seeds, salt and sugar. Simmer until the flavours of the spices infuse into the vinegar – about 15 minutes on low heat.

2 Add the mango, ginger, garlic and peel, if using. Simmer until the mango is mushy and most of the vinegar has evaporated. When cool, pour into sterilized bottles. Leave for a few days before serving.

AVOCADO SALAD

Makhan Chaat

In India, avocados are called butter fruit, reflecting their subtle taste. This delicate dish makes a good starter.

SERVES 4

Ingredients

2 avocados
75ml/5 tbsp/⅓ cup natural (plain) yoghurt, beaten
115g/4oz cottage cheese with chives
1 clove garlic, crushed
2 green chillies, finely chopped
salt and pepper, to taste
a little lemon juice
a few lettuce leaves, shredded (a mixed variety makes a good display)
paprika and mint leaves, to garnish

1 Halve the avocados and remove the stones (pits). Gently scoop out the flesh, reserving the skins, and cut into small cubes. In a bowl, mix the yoghurt, cottage cheese, garlic, chillies and salt and pepper and fold in the avocado cubes. Chill in the refrigerator.

2 Rub the avocado skins with some lemon juice and line each cavity with some shredded lettuce. Top with the chilled mixture, garnish with the paprika and mint leaves and serve immediately.

INDIAN FRUIT SALAD

Phul Chaat

This is a very appetizing and refreshing salad, with a typically Indian combination of citrus fruits seasoned with salt and pepper. It will provide the perfect ending to a heavy meal.

SERVES 6

Ingredients

115g/4oz seedless green and black grapes
225g/8oz canned mandarin segments, drained
2 navel oranges, peeled and segmented
225g/8oz canned grapefruit segments, drained
balls from one honeydew melon
balls from ½ watermelon (when in season)
1 fresh mango, peeled and sliced
juice of 1 lemon
salt and freshly-ground black pepper, to taste
½ tsp sugar
¼ tsp freshly-ground cumin seeds

1 Place all the fruit in a large serving bowl and add the lemon juice. Gently toss to prevent damaging the fruit.

2 Mix together the remaining ingredients and sprinkle over the fruit. Gently toss, chill thoroughly and serve.

RICE PUDDING

Kheer

Both Muslim and Hindu communities prepare this sweet, which is traditionally served at mosques and temples.

SERVES 4–6

Ingredients

1 tbsp ghee
1 piece cinnamon stick, 5cm/2in long
175g/6oz soft brown sugar
115g/4oz coarsely-ground rice
1.11/2 pints/5 cups full cream (whole) milk
1 tsp ground cardamom
50g/2oz sultanas (white raisins)
25g/1oz almond flakes
½ tsp freshly-ground nutmeg, to serve

1 In a heavy pan, melt the ghee and fry the cinnamon and sugar. Keep frying until the sugar begins to caramelize. Reduce the heat immediately when this happens.

2 Add the rice and half the milk. Bring to the boil, stirring constantly to avoid the milk boiling over. Reduce the heat and simmer until the rice is cooked, stirring regularly.

3 Add the remaining milk, cardamom, sultanas (white raisins) and almonds and leave to simmer, but keep stirring to prevent the kheer from sticking to the base of the pan. When the mixture has thickened, serve hot or cold, sprinkled with the nutmeg.

VERMICELLI PUDDING

Shirkhuma

This sweet is prepared by Muslims very early in the morning of Id-ul-Fitr, the feast after the 30 days of Ramadan.

SERVES 4–6

Ingredients

6 tbsp ghee
115g/4oz vermicelli, coarsely broken
25g/1oz almond flakes
25g/1oz pistachios, slivered
25g/1oz cudapah nuts
50g/2oz sultanas (white raisins)
50g/2oz dates, stoned (pitted) and slivered
1.11/2 pints/4 cups full cream (whole) milk
4 tbsp dark brown sugar
1 sachet saffron powder

1 Heat 4 tbsp of the ghee in a frying pan and sauté the vermicelli until golden brown. (If you are using the Italian variety, sauté it a little longer.) Remove and keep aside.

2 Heat the remaining ghee and fry the nuts, sultanas (white raisins) and dates until the sultanas (white raisins) swell. Add to the vermicelli.

3 Heat the milk in a large heavy pan and add the sugar. Bring to the boil, add the vermicelli mixture and boil, stirring constantly. Reduce the heat and simmer until the vermicelli is soft and you have a fairly thick pudding. Fold in the saffron powder and serve hot or cold.

Indian Ice Cream

Kulfi

Kulfi-wallahs (ice cream vendors) have always made kulfi, and continue to this day, without using modern freezers. Kulfi is packed into metal cones sealed with dough and then churned in clay pots until set. Try this method – it works extremely well in an ordinary freezer.

SERVES 4–6

Ingredients
3 × 400ml/14fl oz cans evaporated milk
3 egg whites, whisked until peaks form
350g/12oz icing (confectioners') sugar
1 tsp cardamom powder
1 tbsp rose water
175g/6oz pistachios, chopped
85g/3oz sultanas (white raisins)
85g/3oz sliced almonds
25g/1oz glacé (candied) cherries, halved

1 Remove the labels from the cans of evaporated milk and lay the cans down into a pan with a tight-fitting cover. Fill the pan with water to reach three-quarters up the cans. Bring to the boil, cover and simmer for 20 minutes. When cool, remove and chill the cans in the refrigerator for 24 hours.

2 Open the cans and empty the milk into a large, chilled bowl. Whisk until it doubles in quantity, then fold in the whisked egg whites and icing (confectioners') sugar.

3 Gently fold in the remaining ingredients, seal the bowl with cling film (plastic wrap) and leave in the freezer for 1 hour.

4 Remove the ice cream from the freezer and mix well with a fork. Transfer to a serving container and return to the freezer for a final setting. Remove from the freezer 10 minutes before serving.

Mango Sorbet (Sherbet) with Sauce

Baraf Ke Aamb

After a heavy meal, this makes a very refreshing dessert. Mango is said to be one of the oldest fruits cultivated in India, having been brought by Lord Shiva for his beautiful wife, Parvathi.

SERVES 4–6

Ingredients
900g/2lb mango pulp
½ tsp lemon juice
peel of 1 orange and 1 lemon, grated
4 egg whites, whisked until peaks form
50g/2oz caster (superfine) sugar
100ml/4fl oz/½ cup double (heavy) cream
50g/2oz icing (confectioners') sugar

1 In a large, chilled bowl, mix 425g/15oz of the mango pulp with the lemon juice and the peel.

2 Gently fold in the egg whites and caster (superfine) sugar. Cover with cling film (plastic wrap) and place in the freezer for at least 1 hour.

3 Remove and beat again. Transfer to an ice cream container, and freeze until fully set.

4 Whip the double (heavy) cream with the icing (confectioners') sugar and the remaining mango pulp. Chill the sauce for 24 hours. Remove the sorbet (sherbet) 10 minutes before serving. Scoop out individual servings and cover with a generous helping of mango sauce. Serve immediately.

Tea and Fruit Punch

Chai Sherbet

This delicious punch may be served hot or cold. White wine or brandy may be added to taste.

MAKES 875ML/1¾ PINTS/3½ CUPS

Ingredients
575ml/1 pint/2½ cups water
1 cinnamon stick
4 cloves
2½ tsp Earl Grey tea leaves
175g/6oz sugar
450ml/¾ pint/1½ cups tropical soft drink concentrate
1 lemon, sliced
1 small orange, sliced
½ cucumber, sliced

1 Bring the water to the boil in a saucepan with the cinnamon and cloves. Remove from the heat and add the tea leaves and allow to brew for 5 minutes. Stir and strain into a large chilled bowl.

2 Add the sugar and the soft drink concentrate and allow to rest until the sugar has dissolved and the mixture cooled. Place the fruit and cucumber in a chilled punch bowl and pour over the tea mix. Chill for 24 hours before serving.

Buttermilk

Lassi

Buttermilk is prepared by churning yoghurt with water and then removing the fat. To make this refreshing drink without churning, use low-fat natural (plain) yoghurt.

SERVES 4

Ingredients
450ml/¾ pint/1½ cups natural (plain) yoghurt
300ml/½ pint/1¼ cups water
1 piece fresh ginger, 2.5cm/1in long, finely crushed
2 green chillies, finely chopped
½ tsp cumin powder
salt and freshly-ground black pepper, to taste
a few coriander leaves, chopped, to garnish

1 In a bowl, whisk the yoghurt and water until well blended. The consistency should be that of full cream (whole) milk. Adjust by adding more water if necessary.

2 Add the ginger, chillies and cumin powder, season with the salt and pepper and mix well. Divide into 4 serving glasses and chill. Garnish with coriander before serving.

Cook's tip

To make sweet lassi, mix the yoghurt and water together with 6 tbsp sugar, 1 tsp freshly-ground cumin powder, ½ tsp cardamom powder and a pinch of salt and pepper. Whisk all the ingredients together, chill and serve.

ACKNOWLEDGEMENTS

The authors and publishers would like to thank the following for generously supplying food products and equipment:

B E International Foods Limited
Grafton House
Stockingwater Lane
Enfield
Middlesex EN3

Cherry Valley Farms Ltd
Rotherwell, Lincoln

Wing Yip
395 Edgeware Road
London NW2

The authors and publishers would like to thank the following for their invaluable advice and assistance:

Mrs Duc Cung; Shobana Jeyasingh; Jane Wheeler; Yum Yum Restaurant, London N16

STOCKISTS AND SUPPLIERS

United States

Chinese food and equipment

Arizona

G&L Import-Export Corp. 4828 East 22nd Street, Tuscon, Arizona, 85706, (602) 790-9016

California

Chinese Grocer 209 Post Street, San Francisco, California, 94108, (415) 982-0125

Good Earth Seed Co. P.O. Box 5644, Redwood City, California, 94603, (415) 595-2270

Illinois

Bangkok Oriental Grocery 7430 Harlem Avenue, Bridgeview, Illinois 60455, (708) 458-1810

Chang Oriental Foods 5214 North Lincoln Avenue, Chicago, Illinois, 60646, (312) 271-5050

Massachusetts

Chung Wah Hong Co. 55 Beach Street, Boston, Massachusetts, 02111, (617) 426-3619

See Sun Co. 25 Harrison Avenue, Boston, Massachusetts, 02111 (617) 426-0954

New Jersey

Chinese Kitchen P.O. Box 218, Stirling, New Jersey, 07980 (201) 665-2234

New York

Eastern Trading Co. 2801 Broadway, New York, New York, 10025

The Oriental Country Store 12 Mott Street, New York, New York, 10013

Ohio

Crestview Market 200 Crestview Road, Columbus, Ohio, 43202 (614) 267-2723

Texas

Minika's Oriental Food Mart 2505 West Holcombe Avenue, Houston, Texas, 77003, (713) 668-9850

Washington D.C.

Da Hus Market Company 623 H Street, NW, Washington, D.C. 20005, (202) 371-8888

Indian food and equipment

Arizona

G&L Import-Export Corp. 4828 East 22nd Street, Tuscon, Arizona, 85706, (602) 790-9016

Manila Oriental Foodmart 3557 West Dunlap Avenue, Phoenix, Arizona, 85021, (602) 841-2977

California

Indian Food Mill 650 San Bruno Avenue East, San Bruno, California, 94014, (415) 583-6559

Connecticut

India Spice & Gift Shop 3295 Fairfield Avenue, Fairfield, Connecticut, 06605, (203) 384-0666

Florida

Grocery Mahat & Asian Spices 1026 South Military Trail, West Palm Beach, Florida, 33436, (407) 433-3936

Illinois

Indian Groceries & Spices 7300 St Louis Avenue, Skokie, Illinois 60076, (708) 2480

Maryland

India Supermarket 8107 Fenton Street, Silver Springs, Maryland, 20910, (301) 589-8423

Massachusetts

India Groceries Oak Square, Boston, Massachusetts, 02111, (617) 254-5540

New Jersey

Maharaja Indian Foods 130 Speedwell Avenue, Morristown, New Jersey, 07960, (210) 829-0048

New York

Indian Groceries and Spices 61 Wythe Avenue, Brooklyn, New York, 11211, (718) 963-0477

Ohio

Crestview Market 200 Crestview Road, Columbus, Ohio, 43202 (614) 267-2723

Pennsylvania

Gourmail Inc. Drawer 516, Berwyn, Pennsylvania, 19312 (215) 296-4620

Texas

MGM Indian Foods 9200 Lamar Boulevard, Austin, Texas, 78513, (512) 835-6937

South-east Asian food and equipment

Arizona

Kempo Oriental Market 5595 East 5th Street, Tuscon, Arizona, 85711, (602) 750-9009

Massachusetts

Yoshinoya 36 Prospect Street, Cambridge, Massachusetts, 02139, (617) 491-8221

Minnesota

M.F. Oriental Food 747 Franklin Avenue, Minneapolis, Minnesota, 55404, (612) 870-4002

New York

Katagiri Company 224 East 59th Street, New York, New York, 10022, (212) 755-3566

Siam Grocery 2745 Broadway, New York, New York, 10024 (212) 864 3690

Canada

Dah's Oriental Food 822 Broadview, Toronto, Ontario, M4K 2P7, (416) 463-8109

Hong Kong Emporium 364 Young Street, Toronto, Ontario, M5B 1S5, (416) 977-3386

U-Can-Buy Oriental Food 5692 Victoria Avenue, Montreal, Quebec, H3W 2P8

New Zealand

Chinese Food Centre Davis Trading Company Ltd, Te Puni Street, Petone, 568-2009

South Africa

Akhalwaya and Sons Gillies Street, Burgersdorp, Johannesburg, (11) 838-1008

Kashmiris Spice Centre 95 Church Street, Mayfair, Johannesburg, (11) 839-3883

Haribak and Sons Ltd 31 Pine Street, Durban (31) 32-662

United Kingdom

Chinese food and equipment

Chung Wah 31–32 Great George Square, Liverpool L1 5D2 (051) 709-2637

Janson Hong St Martins House, 17–18 Bull Ring, Birmingham B5 5DD, (021) 643-4681

See Woo Supermarket 18–20 Lisle Street, London WC2, (071) 734-9940

Wing Lee Hong 8 Edward Street, Leeds LS2 7NN (0532) 457203

Wing Yip 395 Edgware Road, Cricklewood, London NW2 6LN (081) 450-0422

Indian food and equipment

M. and S. Patel 372–382 Romford Road, London E7 8BS (081) 472-6201

Rafi's Spice Box c/o 31 Schoolfield, Glemsford, Suffolk, CO10 7RE (mail order)

The Spice Shop 115–117 Drummond Street, London NW1 2HL (071) 387-4526

South-east Asian food and equipment

Duc Cung 122 Upper Clapton Road, London E5, (081) 806-0241

Golden Gate Hong Kong Ltd 14 Lisle Street, London WC2 (071) 439-8325

Loon Fung Supermarket 42–44 Gerrard Street, London W1 (071) 437-7332

Matahari 102 Westbourne Grove, London W2, (071) 221-7468

Ninjin 244 Great Portland Street, London W1, (071) 388-2511

Sri Thai 56 Shepherds Bush Road, London W6, (071) 602-5760

Australia

Korean, Japanese and Oriental Food Store 14 Oxford Street, Sydney 2000

Oriental Import 406a Brighton Road, Brighton, South Australia

INDEX